"Steve Clifford's passion for Christia[...] [...]d and moving book. The autobiograph[...] [...]he theological reflections are rich and [...] [...]he UK Evangelical Alliance is infor[...] [...]e's history, and he draws illuminating [...] [...]ure priorities for a church called to be one, that the world m[...]..."

Revd Dr David Hilborn, Principal, St John's School of Mission, Nottingham

"In every age the Spirit of God calls the people of God to unite, but there seems to be a particular urgency to that call in our time. As we remember the events of the Reformation five hundred years ago, and as our post-modern, post-christendom world increasingly fragments, unity seems more necessary, more complicated and yet more possible than ever before. Steve Clifford is a natural-born reconciler. He holds his convictions humbly, speaks kindly, and practises the gift of friendship indiscriminately. Steve has been living the message of this book, privately as well as publicly, for as long as I have known him."

Pete Greig, 24-7 Prayer | Emmaus Rd

"This is an absolutely captivating reflection of one man's persistent, and at times painful, pursuit of Christ-like unity in every area of his life. Instead of telling us how rubbish we often are in the Church at living out our One-ness, Steve reminds us of who we already are; God's people called to one hope. And this revelation has the power to transform how we talk, disagree, forgive, pray and live together. I hope this book encourages you, as it has me, to ensure our world knows we belong to Jesus, not by our ability to fight, but our eagerness to really love each other."

Rachel Gardner, Relationships Lead, Youthscape

"This is a timely book, an exhortation to the Church to seek unity despite our differences, and to love one another well even when we disagree. Steve asks challenging questions and approaches his subject with honesty and integrity, reminding us that whilst unity doesn't always come easily, we must never cease pursuing it in order to bring glory to Jesus."

Mike Pilavachi, Soul Survivor

"Good family conversations have far-reaching potentials. Steve Clifford does well in inviting evangelicals to reflect on our experience and what the world looks like from our perspective. One significant conclusion is that relationships matter. Drawing on his own experience of family life and churchmanship he illustrates examples of how to engage effectively with one another and the significance of unity in our mission and witness. There is much to be gained from this contribution to Christian publications."

Bishop Donald Bolt, National Administrative Bishop, New Testament Church Of God England and Wales and Superintendent for the United Kingdom

"I have often pictured church unity as an 'elusive butterfly', something beautiful but hard to catch or get hold of. Steve Clifford has managed to catch something which is still in flight. He has thoroughly and honestly got to the heart of what Jesus passionately prayed for, 'that all of them might be one'."

Stuart Bell, Senior Pastor, Alive Church and Leader, Ground Level network

"In a dangerously divided world, we need the constant reminder of the blessings of unity and reconciliation. The real inspiration of this book is the personal commitment of the author over many years to bring divided people together. The blending of biblical insights with warts and all testimony underlines the vital importance of striving to maintain Jesus' gift of unity between Christians"

David Coffey OBE, Global Ambassador BMS World Mission and Past President of the Baptist World Alliance

"For the Chinese, fried rice is what you do with leftovers. For a familiar subject that is more often talked about than practised, Steve has given us some 'fresh' rice to enjoy and reflect. There are both personal, challenging, and authentic stories of his journey towards oneness that is both local and global. They are stories worth hearing so we understand a little of the big ideas and heart of Jesus' John 17 prayer. Read and be challenged."

S H Ong (Osh), Pastor Ambassador, Chinese Church in London

"One is a thoughtful and practical read underpinned with excellent theological reflections and personal experience. From marriage, to family, to households, through to local church, towns and cities, Steve explores the power of unity. He is not afraid to tackle the pain of disagreement or the challenges of integration across ethnic and generational divides. I hope this book provokes us all to action, to unity, to love."

Billy Kennedy, Leader, Pioneer

"Unity is not just about ideas, it is about the concrete reality of daily life and the choices that we make in specific situations. Steve Clifford's life is like a parable of what it means to build unity and find a way of standing together. As I read these pages I was reminded that unity is always a choice. We can allow ourselves to disconnect from one another or we can choose to protect the precious gift of unity by the things that we do and the attitudes we adopt. From our personal lives to our public ministries, unity is a thread that weaves its way through the fabric of our lives. Steve Clifford's commitment to unity is woven across the whole of his life. This book not only inspires me to be a better leader, it also inspires me to be a better husband, father and friend. May we hear the tone of this book and set our own lives to the pitch of God's beating heart. He has united us and we must, as much as is possible, stick together. That's what family does."

Malcom Duncan, Lead Pastor, Gold Hill Baptist Church and chair of the Spring Harvest Leadership Team

"Steve's journey of faith to date puts him in a unique position to write this book, addressing the joys and challenges of living as one in fulfilling Jesus' prayer. It is written in a beautifully warm style, so honest and so down to earth! I particularly enjoyed reading about the centrality of living in unity at home. The book is full of wonderfully practical guidelines gained from Steve's experience over many years of church leadership. There is no doubting his passion for the church of Jesus Christ; how different the church would look if every church leader committed to living by the ideals espoused in this book."

Tani Omideyi, Senior Pastor, Love & Joy Ministries UK and Chair of EA

"Steve Clifford's passionate call for unity needs to be heard in today's evangelical community. He combines thoughtful biblical reflection, analysis of the history and contribution of the Evangelical Alliance, and powerful personal testimony to build a compelling vision for unity that touches numerous areas of life. What gives this book its unique power and perspective is that it is written by someone who has (often at considerable personal cost) lived out its message with remarkable consistency."

John Risbridger, Minister and Team Leader, Above Bar Church, Southampton and Chair of Keswick Ministries

"Years ago, Steve Clifford played in goal at what is now London School of Theology. This wonderfully personal account of his life, ministry, and perspectives on a huge range of issues for evangelical Christians reveals him as an all-round 'spiritual footballer': shot-stopper, great defensive work, creative in midfield, and scoring some memorable goals for Christ. Like me, you'll be informed, challenged and encouraged to play better for Jesus. Highly recommended."

Dr Steve Brady, Moorlands College, Christchurch, UK

"*Steve's book puts flesh on the Biblical and theological bones of unity within the church. The book reads a little like a travelogue of Steve's life and experience and this is the very thing that encourages the reader to be practical and not just theoretical about the important doctrine of unity. Very few stones are left unturned. This is a helpful and challenging read.*"

Elaine Duncan, Chief Executive, Scottish Bible Society

"*This book is one of 'lived out theology'. It marries together a deep biblical conviction that a united church makes God's love visible, together with all the many and varied ways Steve has implemented the ramifications of this revelation into his life and relationships. It is, as anyone who knows Steve would expect, full of honesty, wisdom, integrity and humility. A great read!*"

Ness Wilson, Team Leader of Open Heaven Church

"*In this book, Steve tells us his own journey of how he has come to understand what it means for Christians to be one with each other – just as Jesus prayed – and confronts us with the reality of what that means. It is personal, honest, painful and challenging. It is a helpful read as the evangelical community considers what it means to be 'one body'.*"

Dave Richards, Rector, St Paul's and St George's, Edinburgh

"*This book is disarmingly dangerous! Engagingly written from Steve's personal experience, this is a deeply honest and sometimes painful look at Christian, Evangelical, Unity. Be prepared to be challenged out of our isolated 'silos' – for this book will enlarge your heart, so that we make visible the glory of Christ in our one-ness. Read it – thoughtfully!*"

Steve James, Rector, Holy Trinity Platt, Manchester

"*I know Steve to be a generous, authentic, and graciously candid leader. In his new debut book, One, he is just that! Steve gives a personal and honest account of his journey and pursuit of unity; the joy, power, and beauty of it, as well as the challenges, pain, and difficult lessons it involves. One is not only rich in story, but Steve has made it wonderfully practical. With a great scattering of church history, humour and family life.*"

Kiera Phyo, Head of Youth and Emerging Generation, Tearfund

ONE

Unity in diversity

a personal journey

STEVE CLIFFORD

MONARCH
BOOKS

Oxford, UK & Grand Rapids, USA

Published by Monarch Books
an imprint of
Lion Hudson plc
Wilkinson House, Jordan Hill Road,
Oxford OX2 8DR, England
Email: monarch@lionhudson.com
www.lionhudson.com/monarch

ISBN 978 0 85721 819 3
e-ISBN 978 0 85721 820 9

First edition 2017

Acknowledgments
Scripture quotations taken from the Holy Bible, New International Version
Anglicised. Copyright ©1979, 1984, 2011 Biblica, formerly International Bible
Society. Used by permission of Hodder & Stoughton Ltd, an Hachette UK
company. All rights reserved. "NIV" is a registered trademark of Biblica. UK
trademark number 1448790.
Scripture quotations marked ESV are from The Holy Bible, English Standard
Version® (ESV®) copyright © 2001 by Crossway, a publishing ministry of Good
News Publishers. All rights reserved.
Extracts pp. 39, 60 from *The Gospel According to John* © 1990, D. A. Carson.
Used by permission of IVP.
Extracts p. 191 from *Knowing the Times: Addresses Delivered on Various Occasions
1942 – 1977* © 1989, Martyn Lloyd Jones. Used by permission of Banner of
Truth, www. banneroftruth.org.
Extract p. 141 from *Are Women Human?* © 1971, Dorothy L. Sayers. Used by
permission of Eerdmans.
Extracts pp. 113, 204 from *All One in Christ* © 2009, David Coffey. Used by
permission of the author.
Extract p.209 from *Christianity* Magazine © 2013, Steve Chalke. Used by
permission of Premier Media.
Extract pp.60–61 from *The Mark of the Christian* © 1970, Francis Schaeffer.
Used by permission of IVP.

A catalogue record for this book is available from the British Library

Printed and bound in Great Britain by
Marston Book Services Ltd, Oxfordshire

Contents

Foreword

"How wonderful, how beautiful, when brothers and sisters get along!" Psalm 133:1 (MSG)

Unity is every leader's dream. It is the thing that so many of us strive for, but also the thing that eludes so many of us as we attempt to break down walls between people groups, denominations, and cultural backgrounds. And yet unity is the greatest asset and the glue that holds together any strong nation, organization, or family unit.

Our God is a God of unity. Time and again throughout the Bible, His people are called to be as one. God hates the strife that is brought about through division, particularly among those who profess to follow Him.

God Himself was challenged by the unity of humanity when they began as one to build the tower of Babel contrary to His plan and purpose for man. So He intervened and confused their language thereby creating diversity. So the God of unity also introduced diversity.

The very fact of diversity introduces a complexity into our efforts to be united. Unity is beautiful, but it is not easy.

I was challenged by the following verses in Ezekiel 37:16-17: "As for you, son of man, take a stick for yourself and write on it: 'For Judah and for the children of Israel, his companions.' Then take another stick and write on it, 'For Joseph, the stick of Ephraim, and for all the house of Israel, his companions.' Then join them one to another for yourself into one stick, and they will become one in your hand" (NKJV).

This was at a time a number of years ago when I was being asked why I did not join the African Caribbean Evangelical Alliance (ACEA) or the Evangelical Alliance (EA). I merely did this as a protest to express my belief that the two organizations needed to become one organization. I never doubted the importance of ACEA but I believed it had served its purpose and now it was time for the two sticks to become one.

Over those years, I wondered whose "hand" God would use to facilitate this process to be one and strengthen the growing bonds of unity within the culturally and ethnically diverse evangelical community. That hand belonged to Steve Clifford. His appointment as the general director of the Evangelical Alliance did just that – strengthening those bonds between God's wonderfully diverse church. I watched on as Steve relentlessly pursued relationships and a vision of unity amidst the diversity of the evangelical community. This was something that I wanted to be a part of. It is seeing Steve's commitment to unity despite differences that has drawn me towards the work of the Evangelical Alliance and the One People Commission once again. In the honest, personal reflections that follow in the pages to come, you will hear more about this work and the journey that has led us to this point that so many of us dreamed of and desired to see.

This book is a great testimony of Steve's personal journey with God through his networks of relationships at home, in the church, and across the nation. Steve's well-researched analysis of biblical unity challenges us all to be intentional about strengthening our relationships and not to shy away from conflict or differences of opinion. Steve didn't just write this book, he first lived it before translating it for us to read, with his trademark sign off, "Your friend, Steve."

As you read this book, be assured that its words are written by a man who practises what he preaches. For Steve Clifford, time and time again, the journey towards unity begins with a hand extended in friendship. His commitment to spending time getting to know leaders from different backgrounds to his own, to laughing together and – most importantly – eating together, is an amazing example to us all of how wonderful and how pleasant it is when brothers and sisters dwell in unity.

Pastor Nims Obunge MBE DL, Peace Alliance and Church Leader

Acknowledgments

I walk through life deeply grateful for those whom God has put alongside me in this amazing adventure of faith.

Ann, my wife, and best friend who assured me this could be done, and Jake and Jordan, our son and daughter, joined in marriage by Asha and Stuart – they supported me in facing many of the joys and tests of life. We have laughed, cried, and enjoyed our journey together.

This book is about relationships. I'm indebted to so many who have both befriended me and modelled friendship to me: my church, Bless Community Church, the Pioneer network of churches (founded by Gerald Coates), which I served for over twenty years, and more recently my friends and colleagues at the Evangelical Alliance (with particular thanks to Janis Wrobel, Jenny Fraser, Katie Nurse, and Cassie Shields, who have worked with me as PAs). In following and serving Jesus with these amazing people, I have found fresh faith, learned to hear Him better, and come to love Him more.

I write this book as an act of obedience, but I'm tremendously grateful to a small group – David Hilborn, Kim Walker, Emrys Jones, Rachel Gardner, David Coffey, Peter Lynas, and Elfed Godding, who checked and challenged large sections of the draft notes.

I'm especially indebted to the amazing commitment, encouragement, and skill of Chine McDonald, who has worked with me in refining, editing, and, at times, making sense of my stumbling words.

This book is about relationships and is the product of relationships, and I trust you will find it a celebration of relationships.

Preface

There are so many ways to approach a conversation about unity.

We could dive into a deep theological exploration of the importance of unity, using Jesus' prayer in John 17 as our starting point.

We could explore the modern ecumenical movement and the crucial role evangelicals are playing in the emerging "unity movements" that are gathering momentum across the UK and indeed the world.

We could throw ourselves into a historical thesis on church unity through the centuries and see what we could learn and how it might provide us with guidance for the future.

We could define a manifesto for the Evangelical Alliance (the organization I have the privilege of leading), and outline our contribution to the church in the past and our hopes and prayers for the future.

These would be excellent.

But my heart's desire is to humbly offer you my own personal exploration of unity, my honest reflections on the challenge of being one.

This is my story, warts and all; a journey that explores the challenge of "oneness" – in my inner life, my marriage, my family, my household, the local church, and way beyond. It's a journey that reflects on lessons learned and mistakes made within the amazing diversity of this family of God's people. It's a story that explores how we work together as men and women, young and old, across ethnic, theological, and ecclesiastical differences. We'll explore what happens when things go wrong and conflict occurs.

At the heart of this book is a conviction that the unity God has both given us and called us to maintain will not be achieved through organizational structures, events, assemblies, councils, great declarations, or large institutions. The great Christian unity movements across the UK and the rest of the world, including the

Evangelical Alliance UK and the World Evangelical Alliance, will never achieve what Jesus had in mind in His prayer in John 17. We can simply work to create a context, an environment, a culture in which relationships can be built and oneness developed.

This book is all about relationships – relationships in the family, the family that has the privilege of praying "Our Father in heaven", the family that looks around and sees brothers and sisters in Christ within all sections of His church.

Within the evangelical tradition to which I belong, and for whose members this book is primarily written, we have strong convictions. We are passionate for truth, which means we can sometimes come over as arrogant, narrow-minded, even unfriendly. As an evangelical family, we are having to learn how to respect, honour, and learn from each other. This means at times discovering how to disagree with each other well and maintain relationships, even in our disagreement. It means, for some of us, discovering the rich insights and practices outside our denominational networks, which will influence our own personal spiritual experiences and knowledge of God.

As we evangelicals find fresh confidence in our own relationships and identity, this will also help us in our relationships within the wider church. Ecumenical relationships have always provided a challenge to evangelicals, as indeed they have to other worldwide church bodies. Relationships built on mutual respect, often facilitated by ecumenical bodies, are providing opportunities for collaboration in areas of shared interest and concern. We won't be able to do everything together, but there is much that we agree on and are able to speak and act together in even if there are areas where we remain in disagreement.

This story is an adventure of relationships with an amazing array of people who have shaped, challenged, and encouraged me. But this is also a story that carries a deep conviction – that our relationships within the family are not for us alone. Our relationships carry a missionary imperative, a purpose found in the very heartbeat of God. It's to be found at the core of the great prayer in John 17. Within the

Godhead, there's a passion for the world, and we have the privilege of being included in God's mission for the world – that through the life, death, and resurrection of Jesus, people might come into a relationship with the living God. Or, in the words of the prayer and on the lips of Jesus, "So that the world might believe you sent me."

Chapter 1

One: Who got me into this?

"What gives me the most hope every day is God's grace: knowing His grace is going to give me the strength for whatever I face, knowing nothing is a surprise to God."
Rick Warren

"Faith is living in advance what we will only understand in reverse."
Wayne Cordeiro, *Leading on Empty*

God's idea, not mine

As I stood addressing the crowd at Bradford Cathedral – nearly fifty years to the day since my father had been killed in an accident with a drunken lorry driver – I was tangibly made aware of how God is able to create good from tragedy; able to draw a much larger circle around our disappointments, and use those of us who feel totally underqualified for His glory.

This was my first speaking engagement as General Director of the Evangelical Alliance. The invitation to preach at this cathedral in my home town had stood out among the piles of requests that followed the announcement of my taking on the role.

My father, Albert, grew up just a few hundred yards from Bradford Cathedral. As a young lad he attended services there, came to faith, and met my mother there. She recalls her first encounter with my father when he was taking up the collection, singing heartily, and she thought: "I could marry that man." I'm not sure whether it was the singing or the money that attracted her, but in due course they were indeed married there.

My father was sent from the cathedral to train in theology at Oak Hill College and, on his return, was ordained at the cathedral. He took up his first post as a vicar less than a mile away, and within a short period I was born, followed by my younger brother. I was just five years old when he was taken from us. How quickly life can change. We were living in a house that belonged to the church and didn't know if we would be able to keep our home. My mother had to go out to work and my brother to nursery, while I started school. Life became very different from the one we thought we had mapped out before us.

As I arrived at Bradford Cathedral on Easter Sunday evening in 2008, along with my mother, brother, wife, son, and daughter-in-law, there was a wonderful sense of endorsement. I felt it was a wonderful sign of the amazing truth that God was with us, and in a strange yet beautiful way able to bring healing following the events surrounding the death of a husband and father.

After I had spoken, the evening concluded with the Bishop of Bradford inviting the congregation to pray for me as I took up this new role. I was holding back the tears as my frail mother, who was in her eighties, came to the front and prayed a prayer of blessing.

Looking back, I am amazed by the steps that led to my standing in that pulpit that day. If someone had told me even a few months earlier that I would be invited to take the role of General Director at the Alliance, I would have laughed out loud.

My background, you see, is as a "new-church" leader. In fact, since way back in the 1980s, when they used to be called house churches, I've been involved in church leadership. That means I'm a card-carrying charismatic, who's been involved in church-planting, overseen churches, and supported leaders and leadership training for years. I was part of the Pioneer network of churches and continue to attend a Pioneer church in west London, working with the likes of founder Gerald Coates, worship leader Noel Richards, writer and preacher Jeff Lucas, church-planter Roger Ellis, Pete Greig (leader of the 24-7 movement) and Martin Smith of Delirious? fame.

In my perception, new church leaders like me would not have been seen as the best qualified to lead an alliance of evangelicals that had existed since 1846. I had, however, been involved with the Alliance for some years. Clive Calver – who was its general secretary between 1983 and 1997 – was looking to broaden the reach of the Alliance and invited me onto the Council and eventually the Board. Over the years, I had enjoyed making a contribution – during both Clive's years and those of Joel Edwards, who took on the leadership role when Clive stood down to run World Relief in the United States. I had particularly appreciated the opportunity to develop relationships with leaders from parts of the church that I would normally have little to do with, and indeed would differ from on a number of areas of biblical interpretation, and certainly on models and practices of expressing ourselves as church. Some of my friends had left churches led by people I was now hanging out with; churches were being planted by Pioneer and other new-church networks in towns and cities where some of my fellow Council members had been established for years. Indeed, on a national level, I had provided support as friends of mine launched Fusion – a student ministry on university campuses across the UK, connecting students with local churches in the cities. This had been a painful process, as it was regarded as a threat to gospel unity in reaching students for Christ.

In bringing leadership to the Evangelical Alliance, Joel Edwards had been an amazing servant, not only of evangelicals but of the whole church in the UK. He had worked with the African Caribbean Evangelical Alliance (ACEA) and the Alliance for over twenty years, eleven of which were spent as General Director. I was in the room when he indicated his intention to step down from the role. Joel was going on to head up Micah Challenge – a coalition of Christian agencies and churches mobilizing Christians around the world against global poverty and seeking to hold governments to account in order to see the Millennium Development Goals met by 2015.

As Joel told the Board of his plans, I'm not sure many of us were shocked, but, as always at times like this, there was an air of uncertainty. As the meeting came to a conclusion and I was packing my bag before setting off for home, an older highly respected leader from the more conservative wing of the church made his way over to me and took me to one side. He asked whether I would consider making myself available to take on the director's role. My response was immediate and, it turned out, ill-considered. I have to confess, I laughed.

"Why on earth would I want to do that?" I asked. I explained briefly how full my life was, how satisfying and fulfilling the work I was doing. There was, to be honest, a subtext: I had observed so many of the struggles and pains that Joel had faced during his time in the role. Why would I want to put myself through that? Following my laughter and brief explanation of the reason I couldn't consider it, my friend quietly and graciously rebuked me by reminding me that sometimes the Lord requires of us obedience – even if it might not fit into our plans.

I returned home that evening rebuked and challenged, but certainly not convinced that this was the job for me. As I relayed the events of the day to my wife Ann, particularly Joel's announcement and the subsequent conversation, she simply said: "Steve, whatever you do, don't dismiss it."

I've learned over the years that if my wife says something like this, I do need to take it seriously. However, 2008 was a very full year. It was the year of HOPE 08 and I was the chair, working with Mike Pilavachi of Soul Survivor, Andy Hawthorne from The Message Trust, and Roy Crowne from Youth for Christ in bringing leadership to what proved to be an amazing year of mission.

There have been a few occasions in my life when I've had the privilege of being caught up in something that we just know is so much bigger than any of us – and HOPE was one of them. It felt like a movement of God that had caught the imagination of

Christians all over the country. It was also seeing churches working together from across the whole ecclesiastical and theological spectrum. Building on the experience of events in Manchester in 2000 and London in 2004, this was a vision to see the church in every village, town, and city united in mission. The strapline said it all: "Do more, do it together, and do it in word and action." As I'm sure you can imagine, busy as I was as the chair of HOPE, my life was already full; not least because I also carried my own responsibilities within the Pioneer network of churches. So, while I wasn't dismissing the Evangelical Alliance, it certainly wasn't at the centre of my attention.

But God has a unique way of challenging and prompting us. Over the weeks and months that followed, people would take me aside or give me a call or send me an email, and there was a consistent message:

"Steve, have you considered…?"

"Steve, I was just wondering if…"

"Steve, I was just praying for you and…"

I find it so encouraging, the way God deals with us. He is so creative. He chooses to use people like you and me, if we are willing to be obedient.

My Aberdeen moment

The summer of 2008 came to an end, and the deadline for applications to be the new General Director of the Evangelical Alliance was looming. An exacting interview procedure had been put in place and a whole series of consultations and conversations had been initiated with evangelical leaders from across the breadth of the evangelical world.

I hadn't totally "dismissed" it. Others had reminded me, but I just knew I couldn't go down this pathway unless I had a deep conviction that God had asked me to.

So it came to what I now refer to as "my Aberdeen moment". I had been asked to participate in a large conference in Aberdeen. I was speaking at and leading some of the meetings, but the timetable wasn't packed and there was space to think, to read, to pray, and to ask God to speak to me.

So I flew off to Aberdeen with the prayer, "OK, God, if You're asking me to throw my hat into the ring, this is the right time for You to speak to me." This was perhaps not the most appropriate or even respectful of prayers, but this was where I was at. I really needed God to speak to me, to confirm whether this was a step He wanted me to take. It seems to me that, for some Christians, there's a telephone line permanently connected between them and the Almighty. God seems to speak to them all the time. I, however, have never heard an audible voice. For me, God's voice often manifests itself in a strong impression. It might be as I'm reading Scripture, or engaging in a conversation with a Christian friend; sometimes it's a little phrase that comes to mind when I'm praying or in worship. On occasions I've seen something in the world around me and it's carried a significance for me as if God were speaking to me through it. There have also been occasions when God has used people who might be described as having a prophetic gift, to speak into my life. I really didn't care how God chose to speak. All I knew was that I really wanted to hear from Him.

Over the weekend, I think I saw Aberdeen at its best: Sunday morning on the beach in glorious sunlight; and at its worst: Saturday afternoon in central Aberdeen in torrential rain. I had prayed, I had read Scripture, I had listened. But nothing. And so it came to the final meeting in the large conference centre at the heart of the city where we were meeting. I was leading the meeting, so, after worship and prayer, I introduced our speaker and sat down to listen. As the speaker introduced his talk, I was transfixed. This is what I had been praying for. In a very simple, non-dramatic way, the speaker referred us to a passage of Scripture at the beginning of Genesis 12. It has been pivotal for Ann and me in our understanding of our call to Christian ministry: God's call to Abraham to leave his own country and his own people, the place where Abraham felt safe and secure – and to go to a place he did not know and would be a stranger in. But with the call came the promise of blessing. It's a piece of Scripture we have lived with, reflected on, and prayed over many times throughout our married life. We have so often found the passage helpful as we've considered some of the big decisions of our lives. As I sat through the rest of the meeting, I did so with a sense deep down that God had spoken. When I returned home the next morning, I told Ann what had happened and indicated that I felt I would be disobedient not at the very least to make myself available to take on the role.

Over the years that have followed, I have often thought back to that Aberdeen weekend. I can't tell you how important it was and continues to be for me – particularly on the bad days when things are tough: a vote in Westminster that hasn't gone the way we had hoped and worked and prayed for; when there's an article in the press that speaks ill of the church or of the Evangelical Alliance; when there's a conflict between Christian leaders and we have been asked to get involved. It's at times like these that I go back to my "Aberdeen moment" and remember it was "God who got me into this".

The weeks that followed involved application forms and statements, two days of interviews, and presentations – all of which led to the day in which I received the telephone call that was to change my life.

It was early evening on 4 December 2008 and I was eating dinner with my family. I decided to take the call, which I don't normally do during a meal. It was Mike Talbot, the vicar of Emmanuel Church, Northwood, north London. He was also the chair of the Board of the Evangelical Alliance.

"I'm afraid I have some bad news for you," he said, following it up with a long silence. "We're going to be seeing a lot more of each other in the coming years."

This was Mike's attempt at humour. He was in fact ringing to invite me to take on the role of General Director of the Evangelical Alliance.

God's hand at work

As I look back – on the events of both 2008 and the years that preceded it – I now see the hand of God preparing the way. I feel honoured and privileged to be serving the church across the UK, and particularly the evangelical community. But one of the great delights of my role is to work with some amazing people, both inside the organization and outside. I work with a staff team and leadership made up of incredibly gifted individuals doing some wonderful work, and they are not in the Alliance simply to pay the bills but have a very deep conviction that this is God's calling on their lives at this time.

I also now look back on thirty years of church leadership and recognize God's preparation – you could say God's personal discipleship programme. I can now see that although it felt as if there was so much that might disqualify me from leading a UK-wide evangelical movement, I realized God's hand was on my life. When asked, I invariably describe myself as a church leader who has stumbled into other areas of work and ministry over the years. You might remember March for Jesus in the 1980s and 90s. I was the international chair, and it was an extraordinary privilege to work with Graham Kendrick, Roger Forster, Sandy Millar, Erica Youngman Butler, Laurence Singlehurst, Gerald Coates, and Lynn Green in bringing leadership to what turned out to be a global phenomenon, with more than 60 million people in 180 countries marching for Jesus. Here was the church out of our buildings and on the streets, united in our worship and celebration and agreeing together in our words of prayer. March for Jesus took place in all kinds of settings across the UK: small gatherings in villages and towns; enormous marches in London and our big metropolitan cities. While we officially stopped organizing March for Jesus after the 2000 global march, it continues around the world with enormous events taking place in South America. It really was a gift from the UK church to the church across the world. I began to wonder recently whether much of the activity and unity that we now see in communities across the UK is at least in part an answer to the prayers we prayed as we marched for Jesus. It certainly was a powerful image of the church united in our desire to see transformation across the UK.

As I look back now on my involvement in Soul in the City in 2004, with 11,600 delegates – mainly young people – working in nearly 600 teams with 432 projects spread across thirty-four London boroughs for ten days, supported by 772 partner churches, resulting in a million delegate hours worked, and of course HOPE 08, I recognize that God was taking me beyond my Pioneer "new-church" family through, for example, meeting up with national leaders at the Evangelical Alliance Council and speaking at Spring Harvest. Both initiatives required me to connect, to build relationships with leaders from right across the spectrum of the church. Although the vast majority would be evangelicals, they would come from many different denominations, networks, and theological persuasions. Of course, what we discovered as we gave ourselves to God's mission was that the things we disagreed on were far less important than the things we agreed on. In the words of Jesus' prayer in John 17, we really did want "the world to know". It increasingly began to dawn on me that this unity of God's people, which we knew was a biblical priority, seemed best expressed as we focused on the mission. It felt as if unity really did have a purpose. We wanted the world to know.

In 2008, in my leadership role within HOPE 08, I had travelled the country and seen the church working. I saw the church demonstrating the gospel, as well as proclaiming it. We were being good news, as well as preaching good news, through citywide events and small-scale community projects and school missions, by digging neighbours' gardens, clearing rubbish, and cleaning off graffiti. It was so encouraging to see the church with fresh confidence, doing the business of church, positioning itself at the heart of communities.

In taking on this new role at the Evangelical Alliance, I was determined that a significant part of the work would be about encouraging this to continue. Our unity, which was central to the Alliance's mission, was not unity for unity's sake, but for a purpose – the mission of God. We also wanted these stories to be told to the wider society. So often the attitude to Christians in the press, and even in government, is negative. But these stories point to a very different picture. The Christian faith and Christians working in unity together are good news for the health and well-being of our nation – physically, emotionally, and spiritually. I'm absolutely convinced that Christ has called us to be the hope of our nation.

So it began

Little did I realize that evening, as I put the phone down on Mike and went to tell the family the news, how much life was going to change in the following months and years. I thought I knew what I was letting myself in for, but I now realize I had no idea. Over the last years, as I've occupied this role, I have so often returned to the "Aberdeen moment". But I'm also enormously grateful for those wonderful Christian friends, most of them leading significant works in their own right, who have been there for me with a word of encouragement and advice and counsel. They've expressed through their words and actions the love that Jesus calls His family to.

As we explore the call to unity in the following chapters, we will return to this theme and indeed to a number of lessons I learned while God was preparing me to take on this role.

In reflecting on the journey that led me to that first speaking engagement at Bradford Cathedral, I'm overwhelmed by the picture it represents of a Father in heaven who has proved Himself faithful over the years; who was whispering in a still, small voice that there will be a day when there is a new heaven and a new earth – a day when He will make all things new.

Questions

- As you reflect on your own history, where do you see God at work?
- Have you sensed God speaking to you about acts of obedience He is asking of you?
- What's the good-news story of God at work through His people in your church and wider community? Is that story being told? If not, could you be a part of the process of getting the word out?

Chapter 2

One: Becoming who I am

"May the God who gives endurance and encouragement give you the same attitude of mind toward each other that Christ Jesus had, so that with one mind and one voice you may glorify the God and Father of our Lord Jesus Christ."
Romans 15:5-6

"He is our companion in prayer, He says to us, 'I'll pray for you...', and does it."
Eugene Peterson, Foreword to *The Church Jesus Prayed For* **by Michael Cassidy**

"Finally, all of you be like-minded, be sympathetic, love one another, be compassionate and humble. Do not repay evil with evil or insult with insult. On the contrary, repay evil with blessing, because to this you were called so that you may inherit a blessing."
1 Peter 3:8-9

As I look back on my life, there have been certain moments or periods of time when I realize God was grabbing my attention. On some occasions it has meant being taken to a fresh place of understanding. On others, God has put His finger on an area of my life in which He is requiring a response of obedience, a fresh step of faith.

Hayling Island was the setting for one of these moments. Ann and I had been married for around seven years and were living just south of London in a small Surrey town called Cobham. We had married immediately after finishing theological studies at London Bible College (London Bridal College, as it was often called), and had then moved to Yorkshire while Ann studied drama and I trained as a teacher. Here we got involved in what was the first stage of a church plant, but as Ann concluded her studies we very clearly felt Bradford was not where God wanted us. Initially the plan had been to work in Scandinavia with Youth With A Mission (YWAM), but after an exploratory trip to Sweden we were not convinced that it was the right place for us, despite our having a great deal of affection for the Swedish people.

So we returned to the UK and stopped off in Cobham to visit some old friends, including Gerald Coates, who led what was known as the Cobham Christian Fellowship. I'll never forget the conversation Ann and I had with Gerald outside Cobham's "patisserie", which had a very posh title but looked remarkably like a bog-standard café to me – perhaps owing to my Yorkshire roots. We were talking to Gerald about our Swedish trip and midway through the conversation he stopped us and said he wondered whether we should be moving to be with them in Cobham. The house-church movement, as it was then known, was beginning to emerge in various places around the country. Cobham Christian Fellowship was still taking shape. Moving to Cobham had certainly not been on our agenda, but as Ann and I returned to Bradford we had a growing sense that this was what God was asking of us. It proved to be a significant move, as the network of churches known as Pioneer, which gathered around Gerald, and that particular church in Cobham, were to become a spiritual home for Ann and me.

And so we moved, selling our house in Bradford and establishing a home in Cobham. We both got jobs. Initially, I was a salesman and then a teacher, while Ann was pursuing work in the theatre. While there was much to appreciate about our new base, it also took some getting used to. Both Ann and I are city people; we love the life and energy of the city. But here we were in a small commuter town. I was a northerner with a heart for the poor and marginalized. This was very much the south and the millionaire belt. But we sensed that this was of God and so we dug in and discovered that there was so much God wanted to do in us as we built relationships in the church. I look back with gratitude for the times I would spend with people who were mature in the faith and from whom we both had so much to learn.

At the same time, there was a growing sense of dissatisfaction. What were we doing stuck here? There was a whole world to be reached. And here we were gathering moss in rich, middle-class, suburban England. I didn't think this was what I had signed up for. I was finding success as a teacher; I almost couldn't stop getting promoted. But this wasn't where my heart was. And while the church was a place of blessing to us, it was also a source of frustration. We weren't reaching out effectively beyond ourselves. We were far too inward-looking.

I thought God had called me. I wanted to speak for Him. I wanted to influence the church. I wanted the church to reach the lost. I was ambitious. I called it "the curse of my ambition". This sense of dissatisfaction grew. What was going on? I thought God had led us to this church, but maybe we had got it wrong. As I moaned to Ann, she would remind me of those who had been called, yet for whom God had taken His time in turning that calling into action. Abraham, Joseph, Moses, David: the list goes on. But the list only helped me for a while. Ann would state with confidence that I would look back on these days and be thankful to God, as it was part of His training for me. Eventually I knew I couldn't leave it like this and simply live as if nothing was going on. So I packed up a tent, my sleeping bag, and a few essentials, jumped on my motorbike, and drove to Hayling Island on the south coast of England. I pitched the tent and started a conversation with God that was at times an argument. I asked God what was going on. I told Him I had really thought He had more for me than this. I told Him I couldn't go on like this.

I have learned over the years that it's best to be open and honest with God. He knows what's going on inside anyway, so there's no point in pretending. Even if you do step over the mark, as at times I did, He is so willing to extend grace and forgiveness.

The conversation/argument went on for a few days. It wasn't until the last day that anything happened. The majority of the time was taken up with me moaning at God. And then... Without any drumroll or flashing lights, the words of a psalm came to my mind. It had been turned into a worship song that we sang at the time: "I would rather be a doorkeeper in the house of my God than take my fate upon myself." If I am totally honest, these were not the words I had wanted to hear. I was hoping for "relocate", "church plant", or "international ministry" to be spoken by God.

I walked around Hayling Island on the last day I was there with clenched teeth, making the statement of prayer to the Lord, "I'd rather be a doorkeeper in the house of the Lord than take my fate upon myself." If that meant spending the rest of my life sorting out the chairs for our meetings, handing out the news-sheet, supporting others in the ministry that God had called them to, well that was the deal I had signed up for. I had agreed He was the boss, the master, the Lord, so He got to decide. As I returned on my motorbike to Cobham, the truth was that nothing had really changed as far as outward circumstances went. But actually, deep down, at the core of me, Steve Clifford, something profoundly significant had happened. Something had been put to death. There were new areas in which the lordship of Christ was being worked out. Sadly, the relationships, the oneness, that God has called His people to are so often impeded by the baggage we carry with us as we relate to each other in the family of God. My baggage, which I carried in those early years of the Christian faith, left me with that sense of dissatisfaction in the place God had sent us and the relationships God had given us. I lived with the need to prove myself, the need to be recognized and appreciated. As I look back now, I'm convinced that the death of my father at such a young age was still having an impact. I had come to the amazing realization that God was my Father in heaven, my Dad, but there was more work to be done. Still more prayer was needed. My identity, my security, my acceptance was not to be based on my performance or position but upon my heavenly Father as He spoke over me His love and acceptance.

In the months and years after Hayling Island, in the midst of prayer and fellowship, what had happened on my camping expedition was being worked out in the everyday stuff of life. And increasingly, without my kicking at them, doors of opportunity began to open. It was almost as if God were saying, "Now I can trust you with the calling I have placed on your life." Hayling Island caused me to face my baggage, or at least some of it. I dread to think what my life and ministry would have been like without God's patient intervention. How important it is for all of us to face up to our past and the challenge it presents to our future. Something of the old Steve Clifford had to die for the new Steve Clifford in Christ Jesus to emerge more fully.

When I was baptized as an adult in a large Pentecostal church in the centre of Copenhagen, it was a response of obedience. I didn't at that time understand what was really going on. The apostle Paul describes our baptism in Romans 6:3–4: "[A]ll of us who were baptized in Christ were baptized into his death. We were therefore buried with him through baptism into death..." When I became a follower of Jesus and when I was baptized, I was dying to my old self so that I might become alive in a new life in Christ Jesus. Thank God that Jesus died in my place, taking what I should have faced. He died so that I could live a new life in Him, both in the here and now and also in the age to come. But there is an ongoing work to be done for me to become who I am in Christ Jesus. The apostle Paul puts it like this in Galatians 3:26: "So in Christ Jesus you are all children of God through faith, for all of you who were baptized into Christ have clothed yourselves with Christ." Imagine for a moment that every one of us lived in the reality of who we are in Christ. What a difference it would make to our relationships, our shared lives. How much historic pain would have been avoided in the life of the church?

Agree with God

If only we could agree with God on how He sees us in Christ Jesus.

- We are children of God, priests, kings, friends, holy people
- We are his workmanship
- We are partakers of the divine nature, created in Christ to do good works
- We have God's Spirit dwelling in us
- We have a guaranteed inheritance
- We share a heavenly calling
- We are ambassadors

We share all this because of what Jesus has already done for us. He works with us to see the reality of all this worked out in our day-to-day lives; our identification with Christ in His death and resurrection, our oneness in Christ, affects everything – our relationships with God and those around us, our relationship with ourselves, and our eternal destiny. Over the years, I have become more and more convinced that if only we as a church could grasp the truth of who we are in Christ, our oneness in Him, it would radically transform so many lives. The trouble is that so many of us believe the lies that come at us from so many directions. While God speaks over us all the wonderful truths of how He sees us, we would rather hold on to the baggage of our past, which tells us we're useless, that nobody is going to love us. *Who do you think you are? You're so ugly. You don't even think straight. Why would anybody love you? You need to prove yourself. Just give up. You will never change.* The lies are endless. But they ring so loudly in our ears. They attack our self-worth and they undermine our relationships. As I have taught on this subject over the years, I have heard so many stories in which people have shared some of their baggage; stuff from the past which is affecting their present. Some of it is devastating, life-changing, and some of it is seemingly innocuous. Yet it lives on, affecting their lives in the decades that have followed.

Day-to-day living

In Paul's letter to the church in Philippi, he develops the theme of our oneness in Christ and the impact it has on our relationships with those around us. Perhaps there was some danger Paul had become aware of that was threatening the unity of the church there. In Philippians 3:2–4, Paul refers to people coming into the church who need to be watched out for because of their false teaching about circumcision. Paul makes it clear to his readers that it is the example of Jesus Christ that is the only reliable foundation for unity within the church. It is because we are members of the same spiritual family that we share the same DNA; however, that unity needs guarding. It must never be taken for granted. We have already gained so much, according to Paul, as we have come to Christ. We know encouragement and comfort from knowing God's love, from sharing the Holy Spirit, and of course from experiencing the deep compassion of Jesus. Philippians 2:1–4 puts it like this:

> Therefore, if you have any encouragement from being
> united with Christ, if any comfort from his love, if any
> common sharing in the Spirit, if any tenderness and
> compassion, then make my joy complete by being like-
> minded, having the same love, being one in spirit and
> of one mind. Do nothing out of selfish ambition or vain
> conceit. Rather, in humility, value others above yourselves,
> not looking to your own interests but each of you to the
> interests of the others.

Paul is answering the question: What does being united with Christ look like in the day-to-day life of our relationships with each other?

The list is wonderfully challenging:

- Like-minded (verse 2)
- Same love (verse 2)
- One in spirit (verse 2)
- One in mind (verse 2)
- No selfish ambition (verse 3)
- No vain conceit (verse 3)
- Humility (verse 3)
- Valuing others above ourselves (verse 3)
- Not looking for our own interests but each of us to the interests of others (verse 3)

Sounds impossible, doesn't it? And of course it *is* impossible without the aid of the Helper, the Holy Spirit. Only God at work in us can enable us to relate like this. It's vital as we relate to each other with the words of the apostle Paul echoing in our ears that we don't become paralysed by the fear of mixed motives, the fear of looking after our own interests rather than the interests of others, the fear of selfish ambition. I'm not convinced any of my actions are 100 per cent pure, but God is still in the business of refining me by the power of the Holy Spirit, bringing to light attitudes, responses, and actions that are not like Christ's. And, as He brings them to my attention, I'm able to apologize and ask for His help in readjustment. Philippians goes on, as the apostle Paul draws on what was almost certainly an early church song of worship, to answer the question: How did this work out in practice in the life of Christ? Paul introduces the song in chapter 2, verse 5: "In your relationships with one another, have the same mindset [or attitude} as Christ Jesus."

So let's ask the same question as it relates to ourselves, as we bring our oneness in Christ into our relationships within the twenty-first-century church. As the Evangelical Alliance, we've agreed together to work with four core values that reflect how we wish to relate to each other and also to those around us. We want to be Christ-centred, relational, servant-hearted, and wholehearted. Part of my role as General Director is to champion these values and to make sure we hold ourselves accountable to them. The call to be relational and servant-hearted challenges me almost every day as we attempt to serve the church in the UK.

Let me give you a flavour of how this works in practice for us as a team. We don't always get it right, but this is how we aspire to live and work:

- *We celebrate what others are doing*, telling their stories and making sure they get the praise. We are the good-news people, so we want to get the good-news stories out and there are amazing stories to be told and for us to celebrate. There have been occasions when we have not told the story in such a way that the right people have received recognition, and when that's happened we have worked hard to put it right.

- *We speak well of others*, even when things aren't going well, when there are things that need to be sorted out. We will always attempt to speak about a person or an organization as if they were listening in on the conversation. I'm amazed just how much gossip goes on in the Christian world, talking behind a person's back, discharging information which is not really ours to share. Stealing a person's reputation by the things that we say. Social media is an area where particular diligence is needed.

- *We listen well.* It's so easy – particularly for those of us with strong opinions, which is true of most leaders – to be really poor listeners. That's because we feel we have important things that we need to share. Listening well even when we disagree is a mark of respect for the person we are with.

- *We invest in relationships.* Relationships are not a means to an end; they are an end in themselves. They have value in their own right. For leaders, it's so easy for our relationships to be simply a means of getting a job done, of seeing our vision realized. We relate on the basis of our amazing church or ministry. We do not meet people as people, but as human projects. Relationships are complex. They are the very heart of church. They come in all kinds of shapes and sizes and should carry different expectations according to the depth of the relationship and its context. But, whether they are superficial or deep, relationships need respecting and nurturing.

- *We realize we could be wrong.* As people of passion and faith, who have confidence in God, it's also helpful to recognize that we don't always get it right. I look back on times when I have gone into a meeting absolutely convinced by my interpretation of a certain set of events, only to discover as the conversation progressed that I really don't have all the facts, or I have misinterpreted a piece of communication or behaviour. I have got it wrong. When going into those meetings, it's really helpful to recognize from the very start that I'm not always right.

- *When we get things wrong*, there is an amazing word that has the ability to turn even some of the worst situations around for good: "Sorry."

- *We are faithful.* If we say we're going to do something, we'll do it, and we'll try our best to do it in the time frame we have agreed. I personally hate being late for an appointment. My lateness I fear will be interpreted as a sign of disrespect to the person I'm meeting. As part of my commitment to faithfulness, I'm willing to have the hard conversations about an issue I might perhaps wish to avoid. But if I avoid it, I know my relationship will be undermined.

- *We forgive.* I try to develop forgetfulness when it comes to hurtful issues of the past that have now been worked through. In 1 Corinthians 13 we are encouraged to "keep no record of wrongs". That sounds like a wonderful way to live; so much better than harbouring a long list of wrongs done to us.

- *We honour those we work alongside* and those who influence and bless us, and honouring those who work behind the scenes, who don't get the recognition I get, is particularly important. We really couldn't do what we do without them, so it's vital that others know and appreciate what they do.

- *We believe the best.* I would rather operate on the basis of believing the best rather than believing the worst. It means that at times I'm disappointed. I'm let down. I'm even taken for a ride. But it does give space for God to be at work and to draw out the best in the people that I'm relating to.

- *We are who we are in Christ.* This is the foundation that affects everything. Without it, all our aspirations for unity across the body of Christ will hit the buffers of our petty ambition, our arrogance, our pride, our need to be right, and our desire for recognition and status. Without it we will struggle with an inability to forgive and find it hard to believe the best.

Becoming who we are in Christ Jesus means the hallmark of Christ will take centre stage in our lives and transform our relationships. John sums this up in 1 John 4:8–9, 11: "Whoever does not love does not know God, because God is love. This is how God showed His love among us: He sent His one and only Son into the world that we might live through Him... Dear friends, since God so loved us, we also ought to love one another."

So what does that love look like? Paul sums it up famously in another letter, this time to the Corinthians:

> Love is patient, love is kind. It does not envy, it does not boast, it is not proud. It does not dishonour others, it is not self-seeking, it is not easily angered, it keeps no record of wrongs. Love does not delight in evil but rejoices with the truth. It always protects, always trusts, always hopes, always perseveres. Love never fails.
>
> **(1 Corinthians 13:4–7)**

Let's learn to live like this!

Questions/actions

- As you have read this chapter, have you sensed God challenging you in certain areas? If so, make a note. Take it seriously. It could be a Hayling Island moment.
- What do you believe about yourself that God might disagree with? Who are you going to believe?
- Why not go through the New Testament making a list of the ways in which God sees you, and make it a spiritual discipline regularly to confess these truths to yourself?

Chapter 3

One: The heartbeat of God

"John 17, without doubt, is one of the profoundest chapters in the Bible. Whole books have been written to expound it. There are depths here we will never fathom; all we can do is paddle in the shallows. Here are heights we cannot scale; we can only climb the foot hills. Nevertheless, we must persevere. For if the upper room discourse (John 13–16) is the temple of Scripture, John is a sanctuary of the Holy of Holies. Here we are introduced into the presence, mind and heart of God. We are permitted to eavesdrop, as the Son communicates with the Father. We need to take off our shoes, since this is holy ground."

John Stott, *The Contemporary Christian*

"What is unique about this prayer rests neither on form nor on literary associations but on him who offers it, and when. He is the incarnate Son of God, and he is returning to his Father by the route of a desperately shameful and painful death. He prays that the course on which he is embarked will bring glory to his Father, and that his followers, in consequence of his own death and exaltation, will be preserved from evil and for the priceless privilege of seeing Jesus' glory, all the while imitating in their own relationship the reciprocity of love displayed by the Father and the Son."

D. A. Carson, *The Gospel According to John*

I took up the role of General Director of the Evangelical Alliance on Wednesday 1 April 2009 – April Fools' Day. I certainly hoped this was not a sign of things to come. Embarking upon this challenging new role, I quickly realized how much I had to learn. I felt as if I wanted to walk around wearing L plates, making it clear to all I was very much a "work in progress". However, in those early weeks and months, there was one overriding passage of Scripture I just felt I couldn't get away from. It was almost as if I'd been ambushed by the great John 17 prayer of Jesus. Wherever I went, it seemed as if this prayer followed me. As I read Scripture and devotional books, and listened to other preachers, I kept being drawn back to the prayer. Encouragingly, as I spent time delving into the Alliance's history, I discovered that right from the very beginning – in both planning and executing the great 1846 assembly out of which the Alliance was formed – there the prayer was to be found. It seemed that John 17 was in the very DNA of the Alliance and particularly the call Jesus made within the prayer for unity among His followers: "I in them and you in me – so that they might be brought to complete unity. Then the world will know that you sent me and have loved them even as you have loved me" (John 17:23).

Throughout my time at the Alliance, I feel I have lived in that prayer. Almost every time I read it, I discover fresh insights into the heartbeat of God. John 17 is like a treasure hunt with wonderfully precious gems to be discovered and enjoyed. The treasure is to challenge, shape, and refine us. I trust that this chapter and the next will at the very least provide some clues for your own treasure hunt within the prayer. I've found it helpful to print the prayer out, leaving lots of space to explore its themes and then link the themes across the page. You might wish to read it very slowly, taking time to dwell on a simple phrase or verse. Or perhaps read it in one go, imagining you're in the room and that Jesus is praying for you (which of course He was and indeed continues to do). Enjoy the prayer, look at it from different angles. It's us, His church, that He is praying for. Hours before He goes to the cross, He has us in mind.

Backdrop

By the time we get to John 13, the crowds have gone; Palm Sunday is behind us. It's just Jesus and His disciples celebrating the Passover meal. And He's preparing them for His departure. In chapters 13–17 of John, Jesus is giving them some final instructions, and some very focused prayer. John introduces us to what is happening in John 13:1: "It was just before the Passover Festival. Jesus knew that the hour had come for Him to leave this world and go to the Father. Having loved His own who were in the world, He loved them to the end."

Around the table with Him were the people Jesus loved. They had spent three years together. There had been great highs and deep lows. It wasn't perhaps the most illustrious group of followers that a rabbi of the time might have chosen. Even in the previous few weeks, they had shown themselves to be not the most promising material for leading a worldwide movement. But then out of the blue, as they sat around the meal table, the most extraordinary event took place. The rabbi, teacher, master, the one they called Lord, took off His outer clothing, wrapped a towel round His waist, and washed their feet. This really shouldn't have been happening. The disciples were shocked, and we as observers are shocked. This was the one we would come to know as the creator. This was the Son, the one who stands alongside the Father and the Holy Spirit as part of the triune God, taking on the role of the servant of the house, washing the dust and dirt from the guests at the meal. The significance of this prophetic act is clear. Despite Peter's objection, this is Jesus demonstrating to the church that would take up His name that this is the way they were to work. This is how they were related. This is how leadership was to be done. Jesus explained it in John 13:12: "When he had finished washing their feet, he put on his clothes and returned to his place. 'Do you understand what I have done for you?' he asked them. 'You call me "Teacher" and "Lord," and rightly so, for that is what I am. Now that I, your Lord and Teacher, have washed your feet, you also should wash one another's feet. I have set you an example that you should do as I have done for you.'"

Clearly, as the early years of the church unfolded, this story alongside many others was told and retold before being captured and written down by the Gospel writers. But we get an insight into its impact as we read Philippians 2, which was almost certainly an early church hymn. Speaking of Jesus, Paul instructs them in Philippians 2:5–7,

> In your relationships with one another, have the same mindset
> as Christ Jesus:
> who, being in very nature God,
>   did not consider equality with God something to be used to
> his own advantage;
> rather, he made himself nothing
>   by taking the very nature of a servant,
>   being made in human likeness.

When I arrived at the Alliance, one of the first jobs I felt it was important to do was to spell out our values. We needed to be clear, both to ourselves internally and also externally, about how we wanted to be and how we wanted to relate to those around us. Through a process that involved lots of conversations right across the organization, we came up with four values which are now slapped in large letters across the wall right next to my desk at our London headquarters.

To each of these values was attached a short, practical strapline. The value of servant-heartedness, we agreed, was best summed up by the words: we do the washing up. It seems our team kitchen had a perennial problem: people would have a cup of tea or maybe their lunch and then just leave stuff in the sink for someone else to sort out.

Doing the washing up is not quite the same as washing the disciples' feet, and indeed is insignificant when compared to the great sacrifice Jesus was about to offer, but doing the washing up is important for all of us. It's very important for leaders like me not to slip into a mindset that says we are an exception to the rule, that someone else can do the dirty jobs. I'm not an exception to the rule. As a leader, I'm called to live out and model the rule just as Jesus did.

Over the years, I've had the privilege of working alongside some amazing leaders – men and women in whom I have seen Christ exemplified before my very eyes. Sadly, I've also observed leaders who have been far from Christlike. There are two extremes. First, there are the leaders who have acquired a title and been given a role but then have not brought leadership. They are doing a job but are not providing anything for people to follow. At the other extreme, sadly, I've met leaders who are definitely leading but their quest for title, status, and respect requires a great deal of service from those around them. This kind of leadership might get the job done, but I'm left wondering whether it reflects the one who got His hands dirty washing His disciples' feet.

As chapters 13 and 17 unfold, Jesus is preparing the disciples for what is to come. He's going to be betrayed by one of those sitting round the table. Another is going to deny Him. All of them will fall asleep when they should be praying. But they mustn't be concerned because they are not going to be left on their own. Even when they are persecuted and hated as He is. There will be an advocate who will stand alongside them, the Holy Spirit. In the midst of these final instructions He slips in a defining command, which is to shape everything they do in the future – John 13:34: "A new command I give you: love one another. As I have loved you, so you must love one another."

Put another way: now it's your turn. As you've seen Me love, now you need to love. But then He takes it further. "By this everyone will know that you are my disciples, if you love one another," He says in verse 35. This is a theme that is to be developed later in the prayer. "Loving each other" does not seem to be simply a nice aspirational strapline that Jesus is leaving with them and the church who will emerge from them. No, it seems more than that. It seems that it carries a missional imperative, but we'll come to that later.

As chapter 16 draws to its conclusion and the great prayer comes towards us, we find a wonderful insight into the humanity of Jesus. He knew what was coming. The betrayal. The unjust court. The unrighteous judgment. The beating, the terrible pain, the humiliation. The Son of God crucified naked on a Roman cross. He knew they would all disappear; loyalty overwhelmed by fear. Perhaps to Jesus their desertion was one of the greatest pains. His friends, the ones He had invested so much in. The ones He loved. But they weren't going to be there when He most needed them. But then Jesus pulls Himself together, reflects again on what is about to happen, and then reminds them (verse 32), "Yet I am not alone, for my Father is with me." Paul sums this up in 2 Corinthians 5:19: "God was reconciling the world to himself in Christ."

So it is that the prayer starts. Jesus, says John, looks towards heaven and the first word that comes from His mouth is "Father". We're about to listen in on an intimate interaction between Son and Father just hours before what we now know was the watershed of human history. There are many names the Bible uses in reference to God, but "Father" is by far Jesus' preference. It's the sign of relationship, of intimacy. We translate it "Father", but Abba, the Aramaic word, could be translated "Dad" or "Daddy". It's the name a young Jewish boy would call out as his father came home after a long day's work. It's the name Jesus taught His disciples to use. The prayer we know as the Lord's Prayer, though it's ours too, starts with the same words, "Our Father in heaven".

Isn't it amazing that we get to call God Father? One of the defining moments of my childhood occurred when I was five years old. My father, a young and relatively new vicar in inner-city Bradford, West Yorkshire, was killed in a motor accident by a drunken lorry driver. The next morning, after the accident, I came downstairs to be met by my mother, who told me my dad had gone to be with Jesus. As I look back on the weeks, months, and years that followed, I realize my mother was in survival mode. As a Christian community in those days, we didn't know how to grieve well. Neither I nor my younger brother went to the funeral. But life changed big time. For my mother there was so much uncertainty. The home we lived in belonged to the church. Would we be allowed to stay there? Where would money come from? My mother was a full-time mum. What would life look like now my dad had gone to be with Jesus rather than stay with us? But God looked after my family. A generous benefactor bought the house for us. My mother went back to work as a teacher. My three-year-old brother went to nursery and I started primary school. We were OK. We survived, although I'm not sure my mother even to her dying day ever really processed her grief. And of course I never knew what it was to have a father.

Our home was a place of faith. My childhood was full of church activities: Sunday School, Boys' Brigade, Christian camps. But by the time I was a teenager there wasn't a lot of faith left in my life. All that changed for me, however, at the age of seventeen. While working over the summer holidays on a farm attached to a Christian conference centre – Capernwray Hall – I heard the gospel, not for the first time, but that night I knew deep down that it was true and I gave my life to Christ. As the following months and years unfolded, my journey in the faith took me to work in Scandinavia with Youth With A Mission, and on to London Bible College to study theology. But there was a significant issue I had to face. I came to the realization that I found it easier to talk to God the Lord, the creator, the all-powerful one, but I really struggled with God as my Father, God my Dad. I remember one evening in my bedroom realizing that this needed my attention. So I began to pray. I so struggled over the words. It really didn't come easily. I'm not quite sure how long it took. It seemed like hours as I struggled to call Him Father. Dad. But eventually I got there.

Dad; yes, He was Lord, master, creator, all-powerful one. But He was more. He was my Father. He was my Dad in heaven. As I now look back on that time alone with God and some subsequent prayers in the area of my father's death, I regard them as perhaps the most significant in my spiritual journey. While the death of my father was the defining moment of my childhood, the defining revelation I live with concerning who God is, is God as my Father. I love the way the apostle Paul sums it up in Galatians 4:5–7: "That we might receive adoption to sonship. Because you are his sons, God sent the Spirit of his Son into our hearts, the Spirit who calls out, 'Abba, Father.' So you are no longer a slave, but God's child; and since you are his child, God has made you also an heir."

As we listen in on the John 17 prayer, we are listening to family business. But we're also invited to enter into it ourselves, to join the family. We enter into the very relationship of the Godhead. So the Son prays, "Father, the hour has come. Glorify your Son, that your Son may glorify you" (John 17:1). He can also pray regarding His future. In verse 22–23, He says, "I have given them the glory that you gave me, that they may be one as we are one – I in them and you in me – so that they may be brought to complete unity." This is family pushed to a deep level. It seems as if in some extraordinary way we are to participate in the divine unity.

As a Christian leader, I have benefited a great deal from those who have written on the subject of leadership and management, both Christian and secular. However, I have recently grown a little concerned that, in our attempts to organize ourselves well and bring effective leadership, we can end up forgetting that as a church we are first and foremost a family, not a business. So, while there are helpful principles and lessons to be learned from the realm of business, we always need to be prepared to challenge ourselves and those around us with the question, "Is this how family works?" Or, perhaps more pointedly, "Is this how the Father works?"

As Jesus prays, He prays for Himself, but then He turns His attention in our direction. To both those in the room with Him and those who would follow them. He is entrusting us back to the Father. Isn't it an amazing thought that in that room, just hours before the cross, Jesus was thinking also about us and He was talking to the Father about us, those who would follow in the centuries and millennia to come?

This kind of unity is beyond simple doctrinal agreement or indeed a mutual appreciation of love. It seems as if we are being called to participate in the unity of the Godhead, out of which we discover our true identity and a unity in love, in truth, in mission. It's a unity that is impossible independent of God.

Expressing our unity

Over the last few years, as I have explored Jesus' call to unity, I've been influenced by many who have written on the subject, but there is one book that I wish I had written myself and I commend it to you. *The Church Jesus Prayed For* by Michael Cassidy (Lion Hudson, 2012) provides us with a wonderfully in-depth insight into John 17, and reflects on Jesus' vision for His church amidst the reality we face in the twenty-first-century world. Michael Cassidy's insights have helped to shape my own, so I honour him as we explore further the wonderful challenges John 17 brings to us.

As we have already observed, the prayer takes us to a place of recognizing our unity as we are caught up in the unity of the Godhead. Such a desire for unity is, of course, very countercultural in our twenty-first-century world. We live in an age of increasing fragmentation as we separate ourselves into self-defined groups built around age, ethnicity, culture, class, wealth, educational achievement, and profession. In fact, for many, individualism reigns supreme. I am the centre of my universe. I am all that really matters. My needs must be met. And so it is that this "I" occupies my time, filling my life with stuff that will both supply my material needs and help define for the world around me who I really am. It is in such a world that Jesus is committed to building His church, a church of in-depth relationships, of preferring and sharing. A church of such diversity that finds a unity which crosses all divides. What does such a church look like? John 17 takes us into new depths in the areas of unity and oneness, which we are exploring in this book. However, there are other characteristics of such a church. Cassidy helpfully identifies from John 17 ten marks that Jesus wants to characterize His church.

- Truth – a coherence with rational and factual realities of God and His world
- Holiness – a human character conforming in measure to the divine
- Joy – as being Jesus Himself and given from His heart to those who love and obey Him
- Protection – as deliverance from both the power of evil supernaturalism and the ways of the world
- Mission – as Christian labourers carried out in the manner in which Jesus fulfilled His own
- Prayer/prayerfulness – as constant communication with and dependence on God
- Unity – as exists within the Trinity, to be striven for and maintained by Jesus' disciples
- Love – as the active and bonding emotion between the persons of the Godhead and the supreme requirement of us, His disciples
- Power – as released in us by the Son through the Holy Spirit
- Glory – as reflective of the radiant character and multicoloured dimension of God shining through[1]

Such a church requires supernatural intervention. It's beyond human endeavours. This is eternal life at work in the here and now. In John 17:2 Jesus develops the theme: "For you granted him [Jesus] authority over all people that he might give eternal life to all those you have given him. Now this is eternal life: that they know you, the only true God, and Jesus Christ, whom you have sent."

Church as outlined above is experiencing the power of the age to come in the here and now. God at work among His people. Knowing God the Father, knowing Jesus the Son, and knowing each other in the community of faith (the church). Such a church loves the truth of God, and wants and pursues a holiness that is pleasing to Him. Joy is a hallmark of such a church, which makes it wonderfully attractive when put alongside its passionate commitment to God's mission in the world.

Such a church recognizes the need for constant prayerfulness as its members are in a battle and are in need of divine protection and the Holy Spirit's power. Love is centre stage and draws them back continually to a place of unity with one another and with the Trinity. Glory fills such a church as they reflect back to the world who God really is in all His beauty and wonder. Michael Cassidy helpfully points out as we look at his ten marks that "there really are in many ways two poles to this prayer – with truth and holiness at one end and unity and love at the other". The church Jesus is building requires us to live with both; truth and holiness alone will see a church with little grace and lots of legalism. On the other hand, love and unity alone means we discover a church where anything goes and we lose the power to see lives changed. To hold these two poles in tension, we desperately need the power of the Holy Spirit, who makes Jesus known in all His love and fullness and who leads us into all truth. We also need a commitment among the church community to "speaking the truth in love, [so that] we will grow to become in every respect the mature body of him who is the head, that is, Christ" (Ephesians 4:15).

Brought to complete unity

The prayer builds to a high point as we get to verse 23: "I in them and you in me – so that they might be brought to complete unity. Then the world will know that you sent me and have loved them even as you have loved me." So it seems there is something for His followers to recognize: that's their "familyness", their oneness. But there is also something to be developed or built. They are to be "brought" to complete unity.

How easy it is in the context of church life for our relationships to go wrong. An unhelpful comment passed on, a piece of gossip which travels like wildfire around the church. A disagreement at a church meeting, which is not resolved and takes on a life of its own.

Our child not being treated fairly. Some biblical teaching that does not quite fit in with our view of Scripture. A new leader appointed, but "I'm just not sure they're the right one for the job". Church money spent, "But was it spent wisely?" Changing the time and structure of our services. I have heard of more than one church that split over whether the pews should be removed to allow for a more flexible space.

It seems that we may be brought to "complete unity", but there's still something to be maintained, developed, and protected.

So many of Paul's letters focus on this theme. In Ephesians, he spells it out in chapter 4, verses 3–6: "Make every effort to keep the unity of the Spirit through the bond of peace. There is one body and one Spirit, just as you were called to one hope when you were called; one Lord, one faith, one baptism, one God and Father of all, who is over all and through all and in all."

Paul is determined that we should recognize our "oneness". Seven "ones" in two verses: one body, one Spirit, one hope, one Lord, one faith, one baptism, one God and Father. Paul has begun with an exhortation, perhaps reflecting some difficulties in the church to which he is writing: "Live a life worthy of the calling you have received." In other words, be true to who you are. He then gets very specific: "Be completely humble and gentle; be patient, bearing with one another in love." It sounds like a great way for a church to relate to one another. This is where Paul is leading us: "Make every effort to keep the unity of the Spirit in the bond of peace." It seems there's work to be done to maintain the unity that Jesus both prayed for and then, through His death and resurrection, made a spiritual reality. So our "oneness", says the apostle Paul, is not in doubt, but it needs looking after, nurturing, protecting – in other words, unity has to be worked at.

David Coffey, in his book *All One in Christ Jesus* (Keswick Ministries and Authentic, 2009), helpfully provides his readers with a long list of "one another" verses from the New Testament, emphasizing the unity to which we are called. He asks the challenging question, "What would be the impact on our friendships, local churches and indeed among national leaders if we were to submit our lives and fellowship to these scriptures?"

Let me give you a flavour of the challenges these "one another" verses bring to us:

> A new command I give you: love one another. As I have loved you, so you must love one another.
>
> **(John 13:34)**

> Be devoted to one another in love. Honour one another above yourselves.
>
> **(Romans 12:10)**

> Live in harmony with one another. Do not be proud, but be willing to associate with people of low position. Do not be conceited.
>
> **(Romans 12:16)**

> Therefore, let us stop passing judgment on one another. Instead, make up your mind not to put any stumbling block or obstacle in the way of a brother or sister.
>
> **(Romans 14:13)**

> Greet one another with a holy kiss.
>
> **(2 Corinthians 13:12)**

> [Speak] to one another with psalms, hymns, and songs from the Spirit. Sing and make music from your heart to the Lord.
>
> **(Ephesians 5:19)**

> Submit to one another out of reverence for Christ.
>
> **(Ephesians 5:21)**

> Encourage one another and build each other up, just as in fact you are doing.
>
> **(1 Thessalonians 5:11)**

Let us consider how we may spur one another on towards love and good deeds.

(Hebrews 10:24)

Offer hospitality to one another without grumbling.

(1 Peter 4:9)

When things go wrong

The story has been told of a large gathering of evangelical leaders at which representatives had come together from all over the world in an amazing celebration of the global nature of the church. However, as the assembly progressed, tensions began to emerge. One session involved different delegations sharing what God was doing in their nation. It came to the turn of one South American country and they brought to the stage with great excitement a member of the delegation who had recently won the main beauty-queen competition in their nation. It was seen by them as an indication of God's blessing and as an opportunity for the gospel. That sentiment was not, however, shared by others who were part of the gathering. So it was that a significant group of leaders from one European nation left the room, protesting against the whole beauty-queen industry and the exploitation of women and their bodies that it represented. As you can imagine, the assembly was in a state of shock, and particularly the South American delegates. The meeting continued and, as it came to a conclusion, the delegates filed out for a break to find the European delegates who had left the meeting sitting in the conference centre reception drinking beer – and some were smoking pipes. These were two actions that most of the southern-hemisphere delegates would have found quite shocking.

What do we do when things go wrong? It's strangely encouraging to realize that, alongside the New Testament's emphasis on the unity of God's people, there is also a great deal of practical advice about how to handle things when our unity is being challenged. Paul's first letter to the Corinthians stands out among his writings as one which gives the greatest attention to this matter. Paul states in 1 Corinthians 12:12–13: "Just as a body, though one, has many parts, but all its many parts form one body, so it is with Christ. For we were all baptized by one Spirit so as to form one body – whether Jews or Gentiles, slave or free – and we were all given the one Spirit to drink."

Paul is here using his favourite metaphor for the church – a body made up of many parts, with different jobs to do yet still one body; coming from very different backgrounds and cultures, yet one body. All given the same Spirit, sharing the divine unity. Part of the family.

But the Corinthians are in need of serious correction. After some warm opening remarks, as Paul so often gives, he quickly gets down to the issue that will dominate the book. "I appeal to you, brothers and sisters, in the name of our Lord Jesus Christ, that all of you agree with one another in what you say and that there be no divisions among you, but that you be perfectly united in mind and thought" (1 Corinthians 1:10). So Paul is setting out clearly from the start his reason for writing. He wants to challenge all division. He wants to see the church united in mind and thought. As the book unfolds, we begin to realize that Paul has got his work cut out, or, perhaps more accurately, the Corinthians have some serious work to do as they submit to the guidance of Paul and the work of the Holy Spirit among them. What are the issues?

- They have taken sides (1 Corinthians 1:12): "One of you says, 'I follow Paul'; another, 'I follow Apollos'; another, 'I follow Cephas'; still another, 'I follow Christ.'"
- They have not matured (1 Corinthians 3:2): "I gave you milk, not solid food, for you were not ready for it. Indeed, you are still not ready. You are still worldly. For since there is jealousy and quarrelling among you, are you not worldly? Are you not acting like mere humans?"
- They are dishonouring their father in the faith, Paul (1 Corinthians 4:15): "Even if you had ten thousand guardians in Christ, you do not have many fathers, for in Christ Jesus I became your father through the gospel."

- They have failed to handle sexual immorality in the church (1 Corinthians 5:1–2): "It is actually reported that there is sexual immorality among you, and of a kind that even pagans do not tolerate: a man is sleeping with his father's wife. And you are proud! Shouldn't you rather have gone into mourning and have put out of your fellowship the man who has been doing this?"
- They have taken lawsuits to local courts rather than settle them among themselves (1 Corinthians 6:1–2): "If any of you has a dispute with another, do you dare to take it before the ungodly for judgment instead of before the Lord's people? Or do you not know that the Lord's people will judge the world, and if you are to judge the world, are you not competent to judge trivial cases?"
- They are unclear whether it's good to marry or remain single – chapter 7 gives us a long exploration of this theme.
- They are unclear whether they should eat meat offered to idols or not (1 Corinthians 8:1): "Now about food sacrificed to idols: we know that 'We all possess knowledge.' But knowledge puffs up while love builds up."
- They have got it wrong in the relationships of men and women (1 Corinthians 11:11): "Nevertheless, in the Lord woman is not independent of man, nor is man independent of woman."
- They are abusing the Lord's table (1 Corinthians 11:19): "No doubt there have to be differences among you to show which of you have God's approval." Verse 20: "So then, when you come together, is it not the Lord's Supper you eat, for when you are eating, some of you go ahead with your own private suppers. As a result, one person remains hungry and another gets drunk."
- They are expressing their disunity in their use of spiritual gifts (1 Corinthians 12:19–20): "If they were all one part, where

would the body be? As it is, there are many parts, but one body"; "... so that there should be no division in the body, but that its parts should have equal concern for each other. If one part suffers, every part suffers with it; if one part is honoured, every part rejoices with it" (verses 25–26).

- They are disorderly in their public gatherings (1 Corinthians 14:26): "What then shall we say, brothers and sisters? When you come together, each of you has a hymn, or a word of instruction, a revelation, a tongue or an interpretation. Everything must be done so that the church may be built up." "But everything should be done in a fitting and orderly way" (verse 40).

- They are unclear about the resurrection of the dead (1 Corinthians 15:12–14): "If there is no resurrection of the dead, then not even Christ has been raised. And if Christ has not been raised, our preaching is useless and so is your faith."

As we look through this list, most of the points seem fairly obvious, and we are left wondering how they could have failed to see things more clearly. However, the same challenges remain today. How do we make sure that we don't start taking sides with our favourite writer or preacher, or a particular theological position against others? In our relationships, are we honouring those who have gone before us and have been spiritual fathers or indeed mothers to us? When issues arise in our church, there must come a point when, as the apostle Paul does to the Corinthians in chapter 5, we say, "Enough is enough". We have to draw a line. This unrepentant behaviour means you can no longer be regarded as part of this church. You might be able to attend public gatherings but, until there is a change of behaviour or attitude, you can't be part of the family business.

How does this relate to Jesus' teaching on church discipline in Matthew 18, where reconciliation is to be sought with a wrongdoer one to one and then with witnesses before any expulsion from church is considered? If we are charismatic Christians in a charismatic church, are we exercising the gifts of the Spirit for the common good? And what about how the rich and poor are treated in the Christian community? Is there mutual respect? I wonder what other issues the apostle Paul would highlight if he were writing to the church in the UK today.

Let's return for a moment to our international assembly of evangelicals. Some of the delegates were offended by the parading of a beauty queen before the conference. Others were offended by the practices of smoking and drinking alcohol. How do we respond to this kind of situation? Returning to 1 Corinthians, Paul's long and at times complex argument in chapters 8 to 10 gives us some guidelines. We seem to have here a special category of unity-keeping, where care and great wisdom are needed. Paul seems clear in chapter 8, verse 4, that "'[a]n idol is nothing at all in the world' and that 'There is no God but one'". So, in Paul's view, he is himself free to eat meat that has been sacrificed in a pagan temple and then sold in the butcher's next door. But Paul recognizes that while he is clear about it on his own account, some fellow believers might not be as clear, and he might encourage them to eat such meat against their conscience, and indeed damage their conscience in the process. Paul sums up his position in verse 13: "Therefore, if what I eat causes my brother or sister to fall into sin [by going against their conscience], I will never eat meat again so that I will not cause them to fall."

Paul is thus limiting his freedom out of respect for those with a weaker conscience than his own. Some care needs to be taken, however, with the "weaker conscience" argument, that it doesn't become a theological weapon aimed automatically against the amazing freedom that we have been granted in Christ (Romans 8:21; Galatians 5:1). Over the years, it's been remarkable to consider prohibitions that have been presented by some evangelicals either as biblical absolutes or as protections for those of weaker conscience, but which in the process have restricted other Christians' freedom to pursue legitimately what they might see as abundant life in Christ: the wearing of jewellery and of certain hairstyles and clothes; the adoption of body art and tattoos; dancing, cinema-going, and rock music. Yet, while the "weaker conscience" provision cannot be a "game, set, and match" argument applied in a blanket way, it does call us to give due regard to others in the body of Christ. In 1 Corinthians 10, Paul takes the argument further and explores the "eating of meat" issue as it relates to an unbeliever who has invited a Christian to a meal. This time, however, regard for the other extends to taking care of the conscience of the unbeliever, as well as one's own Christian conscience. So, to honour the unbeliever's hospitality Paul's first advice is, "Don't ask where the meat came from." Yet if the unbeliever ventures that it came from a pagan temple, then, for their conscience's sake, don't eat it. Paul sums up his position in 1 Corinthians 10:31: "So whether you eat or drink or whatever you do, do it all for the glory of God. Do not cause anyone to stumble, whether Jews, Greeks or the church of God – even as I try to please everyone in every way. For I am not seeking my own good but the good of many, so that they may be saved. Follow my example, as I follow the example of Christ."

So how does all this work out in practice? What does it mean for me as General Director of the Evangelical Alliance in the twenty-first-century UK? My behaviour varies according to my context. For example:

- I'm a charismatic Christian, but I choose not to speak in tongues or indeed raise my hands in a non-charismatic setting.
- My style of dress is casual, but if I'm speaking in certain settings or visiting Downing Street or the Palace of Westminster, I will wear a suit and tie.
- I feel free both at home and when out with family and friends to drink alcohol, but in certain settings with friends where alcohol is culturally not acceptable, I will only drink soft drinks.

- I'm committed to women in ministry and leadership, but in certain settings I will not raise the subject, as I recognize the biblical interpretations that other Christians have adopted on this matter.
- I have gay friends. They know the position that I have taken on human sexuality, but when I'm with them I don't keep returning to that subject, as I want to help deepen their love for Christ first, rather than define our friendship only in terms of my views on sexuality.
- There are certain subjects on which people take different theological positions that I will avoid when preaching, teaching, writing, or in general conversation, because I know that they could hinder my relationships with fellow Christians:
  * End times
  * The state of Israel
  * My membership of a political party

Paul, at the end of a passage exploring similar issues to those in 1 Corinthians, summarizes these themes as follows: "May the God who gives endurance and encouragement give you the same attitude of mind toward each other that Christ Jesus had, so that with one mind and one voice you may glorify the God and Father of our Lord Jesus Christ" (Romans 15:5–6). Paul does not, however, leave his readers at this point. Recognizing that there are some points on which we will never agree, Paul poses a challenge that speaks to the tone of our disagreement and debates: "You, then, why do you judge your brother or sister? Or why do you treat them with contempt? For we will all stand before God's judgment seat" (Romans 14:10).

While, back in Corinthians, his clarion call in all of this is the call of love: "Love is patient, love is kind. It does not envy, it does not boast, it is not proud. It does not dishonour others, it is not self-seeking, it is not easily angered, it keeps no record of wrongs. Love does not delight in evil but rejoices with the truth. It always protects, always trusts, always hopes, always perseveres. Love never fails" (1 Corinthians 13:4–8).

If only this were true of us today as a church across the world.

Final comment

As we explore unity/oneness, let's be aware that while we worship a God who calls us to participate in the unity of heaven, there is also a battle being waged against us – by an enemy who loves disunity, who relishes division, who celebrates broken relationships. Jesus has already prayed for us in the prayer we've been considering: "My prayer is not that you take them out of the world but that you protect them from the evil one" (John 17:15). God knows that we need protection. Our struggle to maintain the unity of the Spirit is not a battle merely against flesh and blood; it's not a matter of simply getting our attitudes and behaviour right. There are powers at work in the world – and indeed targeting the church – that love nothing better than to see the Christian community falling out with one another, speaking ill of one another, and competing with one another. There is spiritual warfare to be undertaken, as Paul concludes in his letter to the church in Ephesus. Having outlined the spiritual battle they (and we) face, he ends by giving them these instructions in Ephesians 6:18: "And pray in the Spirit on all occasions with all kinds of prayers and requests. With this in mind, be alert and always keep on praying for all the Lord's people."

Questions

- Read John 17 slowly, imagining that you are in the room and Jesus is praying for you.
- Photocopy John 17, leaving lots of space around the prayer to connect the main themes that run through it.
- Allow the "one another" verses to challenge you and help you consider your relationships with fellow Christians. Are there steps you need to take in order to respond to their challenges?

Chapter 4

One: The invisible made visible

"The very event by which the son was being 'lifted up' in the horrible ignominy and shame was that for which he would be praised around the world by men and women, whose sins he had borne... The cross and Jesus' ascension/exaltation are thus inseparable. The hideous profanity of Golgotha means nothing less than the Son's glorification."
D. A. Carson, *The Gospel According to John*

"Our unity not only commends the gospel, it proclaims it. Our unity does not just support our witness, it is our witness. A major purpose of our unity is evangelistic."
Michael Cassidy, *The Church Jesus Prayed For*

"The hard fact is the lack of Christian unity in the Church destroys our credibility in the world."
Michael Cassidy, as above.

"Without true Christians loving one another, Christ says the world cannot be expected to listen, even when we give proper answers. [So] after we have done our best to communicate to a lost world, still we must never forget that the first apologetic which Jesus gives us is the observable love of true Christians

for true Christians. As with the Early Church, so with us, people should say above all 'Behold how they love one another'."
Francis Schaeffer, *The Mark of the Christian*

"Give your church power to preach the gospel of Christ and grant that all Christians may be united in truth, live together in your love, and reveal your glory to the world."
Anglican Prayer Book

Events in recent years have brought to the surface great divisions across UK society. Perhaps they were always there. The two most recent referenda – in Scotland and then the whole of the UK – have each in their own way revealed major differences in how various sections of the population view their current lives and, more importantly, the kind of nation they want to be part of in the future. The vote to leave the European Union, despite so much money and energy having been spent in an attempt to obtain a vote to remain, exposed differences between young and old, the big metropolitan centres and the rest of the country, the working class and the middle class, and Scotland, Northern Ireland, and the rest of the UK. Despite the perceived wisdom that such votes are always about the economy, a large number of people seemed to be less concerned about the economy than they were about taking back control of borders, control of law-making, and control of future direction and policy.

It seems clear that large sections of the "Leave" camp reflected a vote of no confidence in the political class that has governed our country for years, but from and by which large sections of the population feel disconnected and indeed disrespected. The rise of radical Islam and the fear of radicalization have also brought to the surface deep anxieties about the nature of British society and the foundations upon which it is built. This book is being written to the church, but is perhaps a challenge to us as a Christian community. At times such as this, when there is such uncertainty, we must speak and indeed model to a disunited UK a better way to live.

Significantly, one of the dominant themes that run through the John 17 prayer is "the world". It occurs sixteen times in twenty-six verses and carries three different meanings: one, the world as a planet within a physical universe (verse 5: "the glory I had with you before the world began"); two, the world referring to humanity – a human community (verse 6: "those whom you gave me out of the world"); three, the world as that which can be recognized as a society organized in opposition to God's purposes (verse 14: "the world has hated them, for they are not of the world...").

It's these latter two uses of the word to which we will begin to pay particular attention in this chapter. Jesus is sending us to reach out to the world of people who inhabit this God-created planet, but as we go we recognize that it is not without opposition. There is a world's system which is hostile to God and His people, and the gospel message that we bring. It's the same hostility that Jesus faced, so we shouldn't be surprised that we will at times face opposition. And let's not forget that Christians in other parts of the world face it to a far greater degree than we do.

As we have discovered already in the prayer, our oneness in the family is of critical importance to Jesus. He says (verse 21 onwards) "that all of them may be one"; "May they also be in us..."; "that they may be one as we are one..."; "so that they might be brought to complete unity".

As we listen in on the prayer, there can be no doubt that Jesus wants us to share in the divine family unity that He experiences with His Father. But, as we dig deeper, we discover that Jesus has more than simply oneness in mind. This is unity for a reason, and it's all to do with the world: (verse 21) "so that the world may believe that you have sent me"; (verse 23) "[t]hen the world will know that you sent me and have loved them even as you have loved me". This is a unity with a purpose, a unity which carries a missional outcome. A wonderful story is told of a late-night conversation between a dad and his three-year-old son. The lights have gone out and the young lad calls out, "Dad, Dad, I'm scared of the dark." Returning to the room, the father explains to his son that there's no need to fear because he is not on his own; God is with him. Without hesitation, the response comes back, "But Dad, I want someone with skin on their face."

This story carries the profound truth that goes at least some way towards explaining the incarnation and very practically explores the place of the church in the world. God knows that, for most of us, in both finding faith and maintaining our faith, words – even wonderfully true words – are not enough. We need people with skin on their faces.

In the last chapter, we celebrated our participation in the family of God, our invisible union with the Father, the Son, the Holy Spirit, and indeed our brothers and sisters in Christ. However, as we explore the prayer, we discover that this invisible union is not enough, as it has to become visible for the sake of the world. It really does need people with skin on their faces, like you and me.

Called to display His glory

The word "glory", which appears eight times in the prayer, is a bit of an old-fashioned word. It doesn't tend to crop up in general conversation these days. My football team might be aiming for glory. I might on occasions comment on a glorious sunset. The Last Night of the Proms in the Royal Albert Hall still involves the audience singing "Land of Hope and Glory". And some of the older members of the congregation might refer to someone as having "gone to glory". But, theologically, what is glory? It is a theme that runs throughout Scripture. *Kabod*, in Hebrew, carries the sense of being laden with riches, while *doxa* in Greek refers to honour, recognition, and acclaim. This deeply rich word leaves theologians struggling to capture its essence. Denzil Tryon describes glory as "the radical character of God shining through".[1] And Jesus at the very beginning of the prayer picks up the glory theme: (verse 1) "Father, the hour has come. Glorify your Son that your Son may glorify you..."; (verse 5) "glorify me in your presence with the glory I had with you before the world began".

It seems clear to us that Jesus saw as a key part of His ministry on earth the public demonstration of the character and greatness of the Father. This is glory displayed for the world to see. But now we move into shockingly dangerous territory. In verses 9–10, Jesus says, "I am praying for them [speaking of His disciples in the room]. I'm not praying for the world, but for those you have given me, for they are yours. All I have is yours, and all you have is mine. And [here comes the shocker] glory has come to me through them."

The glory of Jesus – the Son of the creator God – is in some mysterious way affected by His relationship with this uneducated, irreligious bunch of followers that He called to be with Him. But it gets worse. In verse 20, He's now praying for those who will follow in the years to come – that's us. Those who will "believe in me through their message" (verse 21). "I have given them the glory that you gave me, that they may be one as we are one" (verse 22).

We are given His glory. We are called to display that glory, to make visible that glory; and it seems that our oneness is an essential part of this process. In John's amazing introduction to his Gospel, he has already introduced us to the theme that he will explore throughout the Gospel (John 1:14): "The Word [speaking of Jesus] became flesh and made his dwelling among us. We have seen his glory... full of grace and truth."

It seems from John that the two words that best describe the character of Jesus are "grace" and "truth". As I reflect on the church through the centuries, I realize that, unfortunately, we have often tended to emphasize one or the other. But in Jesus we find both personified. Even as I write these words, I feel as if I have painted myself into a corner of the room and there's no way out. How can this be? We know how often we get things wrong. How un-Christlike, unloving, our church communities can at times be.

Sadly, as we look back over church history, we find it littered with schisms, corruption, and the abuse of power, yet we have been given His glory and we can't carry it on our own. We have to do it together. As I stand back and reflect, I begin to realize it's true. I've glimpsed His glory as I've committed myself to His people, the church. As we have gathered as church, I have felt His presence and experienced the Spirit of Jesus at work, speaking, healing, setting people free. As we have cultivated a culture of worship and adoration, teaching and prayer, we have grown closer to each other and to Him. In the context of church, I've experienced love and seen love demonstrated to those around me. I have known church with a great banner proclaiming "All welcome and nobody excluded", a place of compassion and forgiveness. At its best I have known church as a truth-learning and truth-telling community where sin is taken seriously, but grace is always available yet never cheap. The churches I've been part of have been places of mission, agents of change in the world that surrounds them, witnesses for truth that prophetically challenge the powers that be. But, alongside all this, church has been a place of fun, eating together, drinking together, and lots of laughter, together with some tears.

As I write these words, I reflect again on how grateful I am for the church and for a God who took the risk of entrusting His glory to us. Every so often, I'll hear someone saying, "I've given up on church" or "I'm taking a rest from church" or "I don't need church to be a Christian". And I want to shout out, "No, no, no; you've missed the point." It's really not about you having your needs met and having a nice time on a Sunday morning. Church is not just an alternative to a lazy Sunday-morning lie-in. We have an amazingly high calling. We have the privilege of making visible His glory, and we can't do it on our own; we have to do it together. The invisible is made visible and something of His glory is revealed.

The concept of churchless Christianity would have been unthinkable to our early church forebears. Church was central to their understanding of the faith. In becoming a follower of Jesus, you were joining a community of faith. The two went together; they couldn't be separated. For the early church, their life and faith depended upon it.

Cyprian, an early church leader and theologian, wrote, "He who does not have the church as a mother does not have God as his father."[2]

Called to make Him known

What do people in the UK really know and believe about Jesus? What do they really think of His followers? Are we talking about Jesus enough, and, when we are, are we drawing people closer to Him or further away? These are just some of the questions that we at the Evangelical Alliance, along with the Church of England and HOPE, commissioned the Barna Research Group to ask on our behalf. We were hoping and praying that this study, the first of its kind, would be a major catalyst for effective, focused evangelism in the years to come. It all began in March 2015 in the Lake District when we gathered more than forty key leaders of denominations and networks, as well as a few key influencers from across the spectrum of the church. For twenty-four hours, we prayed, we talked, and we shared our concern for mission, our collective longing to see God move in the UK. We reflected on the research we had commissioned Barna to undertake. There are rare moments in church history when the unity of God's people is tangible. This was one of those moments. The leaders who gathered for those twenty-four hours at that hotel in Windermere agreed to put down some benchmarks based on the research, and to work to see significant progress made towards achieving these goals, looking towards 2050 – thirty-five years from that gathering. What was particularly encouraging, as we planned for the twenty-four hours together, was the realization of just how diverse the meeting would be. Here was the church in most of its denominational expressions, meeting with a common purpose. It was wonderful to realize just how ethnically diverse the church was, with a significant number of denominational heads present from the migrant church. Their voice and their passion were particularly influential as the time together developed. On the final morning, one leader, Bishop Wilton Powell of the Church of God of Prophecy, a large, predominantly Caribbean denomination, addressed the meeting. He told the moving story of his father arriving in the UK in the 1960s and not finding a welcome in the British church. So it was that their own denomination was established. Bishop Powell went on to tell how his father outlined a vision he had, which he sensed was from God. He had a vision that, one day, British leaders and leaders from the migrant church would meet together to pray, to strategize, and to plan for the evangelization of the British Isles. Bishop Powell concluded that what he sensed at this gathering was a fulfilment of his father's vision. Here was unity being worked out, the church in its oneness focusing on its mission to reach the world.

So what did the research show? If you want the details, you'll need to go to the *Talking Jesus* website (www.talkingjesus.org). But let me give you some headlines. (Feel free to move past this bit if statistics are not for you.)

We surveyed 3,000 people across the UK, with an oversampling of 1,500 practising Christians, to ensure we had a big enough sample when it came to asking questions regarding Christians' commitment to sharing their faith. We discovered that while 57 per cent of people in the UK describe themselves as Christians, the majority of those are "survey Christians": when they turn up at hospital and are asked what religion they are, they say "Christian". When it comes to practising Christians, those who regularly read the Bible, pray, and attend church at least once a month, we're down to 9 per cent of the UK population (although the figures vary greatly across the UK, with larger attendance still in Northern Ireland).

What we are discovering from this and other surveys, which are broadly in line with these findings, is that nominalism in the UK is dead. With a few exceptions, it's no longer socially advantageous to occupy a pew or a seat on a Sunday morning. I have to confess that I don't mind the death of nominalism, as it is nominal Christianity that can so easily be an antidote to real Christianity. What we now know is that around 9 per cent of the UK population are the committed ones. The research reveals some good news, some challenging news, and some shocking news. Let's start with the good news: 67 per cent of non-Christians know a Christian, and when we asked what they thought of the Christians they knew, the feedback was encouraging. Words like "friendly", "caring", "good-humoured", and "generous" scored really high, with negative words such as "hypocritical", "uptight", and "homophobic" really low. So it seems that non-Christians, when they know a Christian, tend to like that Christian, which has to be a good start.

We also discovered, much to our surprise, that practising Christians are talking about Jesus to non-Christians far more than we thought. Some 33 per cent had spoken about Him in the last week and a further 33 per cent in the last month. When we asked non-Christians about those conversations, the good news was that one in five said they were open to experiencing an encounter with Jesus for themselves.

So if that's the good news, what about the challenging news? Well, despite the one-in-five positive figure above, a larger number – two in five – reflected on those conversations and concluded they were glad they didn't share the Christian faith of those they were talking to. So we do need to know what's going on in those conversations. But let's not get too depressed, as these people are part of the 43 per cent self-selecting non-Christian population, who have already in some way decided they are not Jesus followers. Let's also remember that Jesus Himself was not always well received.

The survey also revealed that while practising Christians are sharing their faith more than most Christian leaders anticipate, there is still significant anxiety in Christian witness. Around 33 per cent are afraid of causing offence and 35 per cent think others are better equipped than they are to share their faith.

And now to the shocking news. Well, again, despite the high level of Christians talking about Jesus, 61 per cent of all UK non-Christians have never had a conversation with a Christian about Jesus. And even when the non-Christian knows a Christian, the figure only goes down to 42 per cent. So it seems as if we are talking to the same people about Jesus and not breaking out of a narrow circle of close friends and family. This is confirmed by the shocking news that 81 per cent of practising Christians are educated to degree level. This compares with 41 per cent of the UK adult population. It seems that we as a church are very poor at reaching out in particular to those within cultures where educational achievement is not a priority.

The final, and perhaps the most shocking and challenging, statistic is that 40 per cent of the UK population are not convinced that Jesus was a real person who actually lived. This question was not exploring whether He was the messiah or the Son of God or whether He rose from the dead, but simply whether Jesus actually lived as a real person in history. This has to provide us as a church with an enormous challenge for decades to come. How can somebody become a follower of Jesus if they're not convinced He existed? Incidentally, it also has to be a challenge to the British education system and indeed the BBC, both of which have responsibility for educating the UK population.

The impact of the Windermere leaders' gathering and the Barna research has been extraordinarily encouraging. As we had hoped and prayed, it has provoked strategic conversations in all kinds of settings – individual churches and large networks and denominations, and indeed churches working together across cities and towns. The key question that has emerged has been simply, "How do we, looking forward to 2050 and beyond, make Jesus known to our generation?" How do we become a making-Jesus-known church? At the Evangelical Alliance, our response has been to create a one-stop website, www.greatcommission.co.uk, where the church, or indeed individuals, will access inspiring stories of lives changed by Jesus. They will be signposted to a wide range of evangelistic initiatives, tools, and resources. Our prayer is that it will help us talk about Jesus more and with even greater effectiveness.

Despite the shock of some of the negative statistics, I have been encouraged by some stories I have heard from Christians who have been challenged by the *Talking Jesus* results. I shared the challenge of the research in one particular church and I was back there the next week. On my return, a relatively young secondary-school religious education teacher came up to me at the end of meeting and said, "Steve, I've risen to the challenge that you gave us last week, the making-Jesus-known challenge." It transpired that what she had done in her lessons for the whole of the previous week had been to start most of them with the statement, "You do know that Jesus was a real person, don't you?"

She said the conversations that had followed had been extraordinary. Kids would say to her that they thought people had disproved His existence. She corrected them by telling them the fact that He really did exist. "But what about miracles," some asked; "we know they don't happen." "We can talk about miracles later," she would say. "But for now I'm simply telling you that Jesus was a real historical character." At the end of lessons these days, pupils have to write a little assessment which says what they have learned during the lesson. It was very encouraging for her to read so many of her pupils' feedback, which said they had learned in the lesson that Jesus was an actual person who really lived.

Well, there's a start.

Making Jesus visible

As we read and reread the prayer, we can't avoid the conclusion that simply affirming our invisible union with or membership of the one family with God as our Father is not enough. The invisible has to become visible if we are to fulfil the Great Commission, if we are to make Jesus known. Verse 23 says: "I in them and you in me – so that they may be brought to complete unity. Then the world will know that you *sent* me and have loved them even as you have loved me." The "sent" word is one of the big themes that run through John's Gospel. In almost every chapter, we find Jesus making it clear that

He is the one who has been sent. The Father has sent Him with a job to do. He is not there with human authority, or on the strength of His own words or teaching. He is there to do the will of Him who sent Him and He is returning to the one who has sent Him. It seems that to Jesus it was vital that the world knew that His mission was not His alone. This is a mission of the Father who had sent the Son and would of course eventually send the Holy Spirit. This is the mission of God, and of course, it begins to dawn on us that we are invited to participate in this mission. Jürgen Moltmann put it like this: "It is not the church that has a mission of salvation to fulfil in the world; it is the mission of the Son and the Spirit through the Father that includes the church."[3]

In this rescue plan for creation, this is the great arc of history that the Bible reveals to us. Genesis 12:1 reads like this:

> The Lord had said to Abram, "Go from your country,
> your people and your father's household to the land I will
> show you. I will make you into a great nation, and I will
> bless you; I will make your name great, and you will be
> a blessing. I will bless those who bless you, and whoever
> curses you I will curse; and all peoples on earth will be
> blessed through you."

Abraham is being told to go. He's being sent from his country, his people, his household. And yet out of Abraham's family line would emerge a clan, a tribe, a nation; and from this nation, despite all their disobedience, trials, and testing, would come the messiah, the saviour, Jesus, who would make it possible for the covenant of Abraham to be fulfilled: "All peoples on earth will be blessed through you."

Jesus has already spelled it out to them as He has prepared them for this moment. The call to be with Him was not a call to an easy life. There were all kinds of troubles, trials, pains, and even eventually death, ahead of them. What had been the experience of Jesus was to be their experience. "As you sent me into the world" [says Jesus],

"I have sent them into the world" (verse 18). Their relationship with the world is going to be complicated. They are called to love the world (humanity, the human community) because God loves it. But verse 14 states, "The world has hated them, for they are not of the world" (meaning society organized in opposition to God). So how should they respond? They will remain in the world (verse 15): "My prayer is not that you take them out of the world but that you protect them from the evil one." Our relationship with the world remains complex, not easily navigated. The danger is that we go to one of two extremes. We can be so "not of the world" that we have little or no engagement with the wider community. In a quest to keep ourselves pure, separate, and holy we become irrelevant – unable to communicate with the world that surrounds us. On the other hand, we have Christians who feel so called to the world that it becomes increasingly difficult to differentiate them from that world, and their lives and messages become compromised. There is no chance that the world would ever hate them.

However we navigate our relationship with the world – and we all come to different conclusions – it's important that we recognize that there is "a world" (the opposed-to-God world) that is opposed to us and our message. For us in Western Europe, it's important to understand how we are bombarded with messages that are built upon a world view which assumes there is no God. The TV soap operas, the news broadcasts, the Hollywood films, the newspapers, and the social media that we watch and read mostly come to us with one prevailing world view – secular humanism. Its starting point is simple: there really is no God, and the world that surrounds us is the result of an enormous cosmic accident. As we track the impact of that view, it leads us to a series of outcomes that shape the decisions the world makes and with them our lives. Materialism, consumerism, individualism, humanism... I could go on.

Of course, as followers of Jesus, our starting point is diametrically different. We start with God. He really does exist, and the world we live in is the work of a creator, not an accident. And, despite humanity turning its back on the loving creator, He is at work, turning things around for good. This is the mission of God with an end in mind – a new heaven and a new earth. (Peter Lynas, our Northern Ireland Director, greatly helped me to see the conflict of these two world views.)

So it is to this world that we are sent: a world that we are called to love and a world which at times, owing to its opposition to God and His mission, will hate us and what we represent.

It's some time now since I caught on to that word "sent" in a new way. I had obviously read it before, and probably spoken on it, but, at a time of some pain and pressure, it was as if God were implanting that word into the core of my being. I had been "sent"; I was being "sent" – all this was not a terrible mistake or an accident, but was by divine appointment. It's amazing what impact this truth began to have on me. I would wake up and one of my first thoughts of the day would be: "sent". I would shower, reflecting on the day to come, and would find faith rising as I acknowledged God sending me into the day. As I opened the front door of my home and stepped out, my confession became, "I am sent by the Father and the Son into this day." As I faced the challenges of the day, I would find myself also acknowledging again, "I am 'sent' but I am not on my own, because the 'sent one', the Holy Spirit, is with me."

It's strangely encouraging when we track the people that Jesus called and sent. They were people like you and me, arguing who was the greatest; wanting to do a building project on the mount of transfiguration. Trying to do a deal over who would sit on either side of Jesus in the age to come. Falling asleep in the garden and, of course, at the first sign of trouble, all disappearing. They were very much works in progress, yet it seems Jesus was trusting them.

I've spent some time recently reading some of the biographies of the great Christian leaders who have gone before us – Whitefield, Wilberforce, Wesley: eighteenth- and nineteenth-century evangelicals, or "enthusiasts", as they were called (as an insult). So many of them in the midst of wonderful ministries, yet while shaping British history they lived with their own insecurities, doubts, and fears. God doesn't wait until we're perfect to use us. It's also good to know that He doesn't send us out on our own. In the build-up to the John 17 prayer, Jesus has been preparing His disciples and at one point He comes out with what has to be one of the most remarkable statements in Scripture. He makes it clear to them that they're going to be better off because He is leaving them. In John 16:7 He says, "But very truly I tell you, it is for your good that I'm going away." I have to confess, if I had been one of the disciples who heard Jesus say that, I think I would have had an argument with Him. "How could it possibly be better that You go away? We have learned so much from You. We will be lost without You." But Jesus is insistent: "It's good that I'm going away. Unless I go away, the Advocate will not come to you; but if I go, I will send him to you."

Jesus is clear that it's going to be better for them with Him gone because of who is being sent (that word again) to them. I have come to the conclusion that this Christian life is absolutely impossible without the help of the Holy Spirit. One of the most dangerous states we can find ourselves in as someone who has been a Christian for a while, or if we're in Christian leadership, is beginning to think that we know what we're doing. We'll never publicly admit it, but we have got pretty good at doing this Christian thing. I have been in full-time Christian ministry for more than thirty years. I get paid to read the Bible, pray, and talk about Jesus. The danger is that I can get into the habit of doing things, speaking or leading meetings, and losing that sense of depending on the Holy Spirit. I have begun to make it a discipline to confess that I don't know what I'm doing unless God intervenes.

John's Gospel is drawing to a conclusion in chapter 20 and we have what some describe as John's "great commission". The resurrection has taken place, the disciples are together behind closed doors, and Jesus appears to them. His first words to these fear-filled disciples are: "Peace be with you! As the Father has sent me, I am sending you" (verses 21–22). We can't get away from it.

And then He breathes on them and says, "Receive the Holy Spirit." Luke recalls in Acts 1 some of Jesus' final instructions. First, they mustn't rush off; they're not to leave Jerusalem yet. Yes, there's a whole world to be reached, but they haven't got what they need, so they are to "wait for the gift my Father has promised", namely the Holy Spirit. And further down the chapter, He makes it even more specific: "But you will receive power when the Holy Spirit comes to you. And you will be my witnesses in Jerusalem, in all Judea and Samaria and to the ends of the world" (verse 8). This mission of God, this Great Commission, is impossible without the Holy Spirit.

The work of the Holy Spirit has been an area of some significant disagreement in the church over the last 100-plus years, but wherever we stand on the gifts of the Holy Spirit, or the miraculous work of the Spirit in healing and deliverance today, and whether we believe in a separate experience of filling or baptism of the Holy Spirit from our experience of conversion, we would all agree that we need the Spirit to work in and through us to enable us to be effective in our Christian growth, ministry, and witness. In Jerusalem, Judea, Samaria, the ends of the earth, but also in our workplace, neighbourhood, school, or college and among our family and friends. We need the Holy Spirit. In the everyday things of our lives, we need the help of the counsellor, the friend, the advocate, the one who stands alongside: the Holy Spirit. What are the right words to say; the right actions to take? What wisdom or understanding can the Spirit give us that might change a situation around for good? And of course the great good news is as we perhaps in our stumbling words and clumsy actions attempt to demonstrate the love of God and to introduce the saviour of the world, God is already at work doing what we could never do – speaking to the very core of a person's being. Thank God His mission is not solely dependent on us. Chris Wright, in his wonderful book *The Mission of God's People*,[4] attempts to summarize the mission of God like this:

It is the story of how God in his sovereign love has
purposed to bring the sinful world of his fallen creation
to the redeemed world of his new creation. God's mission
is what spans the gap between the curse on the earth of
Genesis 1 and the end of the curse in the new creation
(Revelation 22).

The mission is big enough to encompass every area of our lives. God
is concerned about everything. So, as I travel the country and see
the church at work, I'm proud of the contribution we are making.
The foodbanks, the night shelters, the Street Pastors, the debt
counselling, the work among the elderly and the young and those
with special needs, the work in prisons and among the unemployed,
and with those who are living with addictions. Thank God for the
church; the invisible is being made visible. Thank God for all those
members of the church who, day in and day out, are going about
their work, not simply to pay the bills at the end of the month
but because they sense God has called them to make a difference
for good. These are educationalists, health workers; those in the
leisure industry, in business, in banking, working for government
and manufacturing; those caring for children or the elderly. We are
sent into all these places as agents of good and for God. As we go,
we carry with us a message that is one of amazing good news, which
only the followers of Jesus can bring. And while others can provide
foodbanks and debt counselling and night shelters, it's only the
church that can bring the good news of the gospel of salvation.

John 17:23 says, "Then the world will know that you sent me
and have loved them even as you have loved me."

So what do you see?

Some time ago, I was at a leaders' conference and Ann joined me
for the weekend. It was at a conference centre that had a swimming
pool, and so we decided to go for a swim before the evening meal.
We went down to the pool and Ann went into the ladies' changing

room while I went into the men's changing room, I guess as you would expect. I got into a conversation in the changing room and was therefore delayed. I arrived at the side of the pool to be met by a perplexing scene.

You know those occasions when you walk into a room and you just know that something's not quite right. Well, it was one of those moments. There was Ann in the water, and swimming away from her at some speed was a man.

It turned out that what had happened was that Ann had arrived at the side of the swimming pool and, seeing me in the water with my back to her, had sought to surprise me by diving in and swimming up behind me. She began to embrace me, starting from the shoulders and working her way down to the waist. Fortunately, by the time she got to the waist, she realized it wasn't me. It turns out that the person she was embracing – the man who was now travelling at some pace away from her – was a young man in his early twenties. He was 5'10". I'm 6'4". He weighed around 11 stone. I weigh around 14 stone. The next morning, I got both of us to stand and I asked the conference whether he looked anything like me.

You see, Ann was convinced that she had seen me in the water. It was only as she began to embrace me that there was a growing realization that it actually wasn't me. It's not easy when you normally wear glasses and you've taken them off to swim.

We all live with a filter system that is in danger of distorting our view of the world. We think we see things clearly, but the truth of the matter is, the messages that bombard us profoundly affect our spiritual eyesight and influence our view of our faith, the church, and indeed the world we live in. It's a key question for us to face: "What do we see?" Early in John's Gospel, in chapter 5, Jesus is in conflict with some Jewish leaders. He has healed on a Sabbath. By way of defence, Jesus explains, "My Father is always at his work to this very day [including the Sabbath], and I too am working." In verse 19 we read, "Jesus gave them this answer: '.. I tell you, the Son can do nothing by himself; he can do only what he sees his Father doing, because whatever the Father does the Son also does'."

It is clear that Jesus is continually looking out for where He sees the Father is at work. I am convinced that one of the greatest challenges of Christian discipleship is learning to see things as God sees them. Paul takes this further in Ephesians 1:18, as he prays for the church in Ephesus: "I pray that the eyes of your heart might be enlightened [or opened] in order that you might know the hope to which he has called you, the riches of his glorious inheritance in the holy people."

Paul is making himself clear. He wants them to see things clearly. He wants them to know the hope to which they are called. These are eyes of faith, eyes that see God at work in and through His people. Eyes that see beyond the cynical mindset which is like a cancer within our culture. Desmond Tutu explained it like this: "Hope shouldn't be confused with optimism. Hope is a choice. Hope believes despite the evidence, then works to see the evidence change." We are the people of hope, the hope-carriers. Hope in a God who has not abandoned humanity. Hope in a God who is committed to His church. Hope in a God who is at work in His mission and invites us to participate. Hope in a message of salvation where people can come into a living relationship with Jesus, and know sins forgiven and lives turned around. Hope that, in the years to come, we will see millions coming to that place of new birth, entering for themselves into the family of God and becoming part of a glory-displaying church. A church in which the invisible union of the family of God's people has become visible and with that visibility the good news of the gospel will be both seen and heard.

Questions and calls to action

- When you look at your church, what do you see?
- When God looks at your church, what do you think He sees?
- Who are you going to agree with?

- When you look at "your world" (or the bit of the world that is closest to you), what do you see?
- When God looks at your world, what do you think He sees?
- Who are you going to agree with?

Look again at the *Talking Jesus* research. What steps could you take to see:

- Your church becoming a church that makes Jesus known?
- Yourself becoming a person who makes Jesus known?

Chapter 5

One flesh: Marriage

"God has called us to live in peace."
1 Corinthians 7:15

"That is why a man leaves his father and mother and is united to his wife, and they become one flesh."
Genesis 2:24

"The disciples said to him, 'If this is the situation between a husband and wife, it is better not to marry.'"
Matthew 19:10

Over the years, Ann and I have had more than sixty people live with us. Some stayed for a few weeks or months, but most of them lived with us for years. The record is Martina, who came for three months and stayed for nine years.

It all started by accident, with Mal. We were newly married, in our first proper home – a two-up, two-down in Bradford, West Yorkshire – and I had a temporary job working at a discount electrical retailer. Mal, a colleague who had become a friend, confided that he was facing conflict at home. He was a Yorkshire lad in his early twenties, born and brought up in Bradford, but from a traditional conservative Pakistani background. His mother and father were planning an arranged marriage for him, but Mal really wasn't sure it was right for him.

"Why don't you come and live with us for a while?" I asked. "See if you can sort it out without the pressure of living together." Opening our home to him seemed the obvious response.

"A while" turned out to be two years.

Mal just fitted in. It was easy having him around. He gave us a fascinating insight into Pakistani culture and we were introduced to his family. It was also amazing to watch him return from the local Indian takeaway laden with a better and cheaper curry than we would have managed.

Over the years, the people who lived with Ann and me came from all kinds of backgrounds and were with us for all kinds of reasons. As we look back on what is now over forty years of married life, we reflect on the richness of those relationships and how they have influenced and shaped our lives.

In the next two chapters, we will explore oneness, unity, as it touches on our marriages and our family life. But we will also look beyond that to our household – a household which for us includes a marriage – Ann and me – and the family, our two children, Jake and Jordan, but beyond that the wider household, including the people who have lived under our roof. They have shared our meals and we have celebrated birthdays, weddings, anniversaries together. They have enjoyed Christmas with us, but together we have also navigated some of the hard stuff of life: deaths, redundancies, mental and physical health problems, lost relationships, disappointments, and pain. If we're serious about the biblical exhortation to oneness, it has to have, as a foundation, a unity that begins at home. This cannot be a unity that stands with folded arms, keeping people out, but instead one with outstretched hands that are looking to invite people in. We see it in the life of Jesus. It was the practice of the early church, yet it's so easily lost within the individualistic culture of the twenty-first century.

Living another way: A prophetic challenge

The Bible makes it clear that not all of us are called to marriage, and the reality of life is that not all will have the opportunity to marry, even if they would like to. But, whatever the circumstance, we all need home, family, household – however it might be worked out in the complexity of twenty-first-century life. As the modern world unfolded, particularly in the northern western hemisphere, so this trend developed: mobility of labour resulted in families moving, sometimes large distances, every few years. Grannies and granddads were left behind. The extended family living within a few hundred yards of each other became a thing of the past; sacrificed for employment, promotion, economic development, and sometimes just survival. At the same time, with a high percentage of young adults going away for the sake of higher education, the assumption began to emerge that children really should be leaving their parents' home by their late teens and early twenties. Even for those who weren't going away – an increasing number now owing to tuition fees and the cost of student accommodation – the assumption was that they really should be leaving and there was something of a stigma attached to those who stayed at home. Parents joked about looking forward to when they were gone. The soon-to-be empty-nesters seemed to have all kinds of plans for their lives without teenagers around.

So, in the early years of the twenty-first century, the UK population is facing a crisis: there simply aren't enough homes to go around. But there aren't enough homes because we're living in smaller and smaller units. Just a quick look at the national statistics in the UK paints a picture: 12 per cent of adults live alone; another 12 per cent head single-parent families; 25 per cent are couples living together; 45 per cent are in a nuclear family. Even the nuclear family statistics are getting smaller owing to decreasing family sizes, particular among the indigenous white population. Is a husband, wife, and 1.8 children living in a small box otherwise known as a flat or house the best environment for a healthy marriage or bringing up a healthy family? It all feels a bit claustrophobic to me. Were we really meant to live like this? It certainly doesn't seem to be a biblical pattern, and perhaps reflects an enormous social experiment. We are in uncharted territory in the building of a healthy society. The New Testament writers have a great deal of practical guidance on relationships within the family, outlining the attitudes and actions that should be manifest between husbands and wives, children and parents – and indeed between slaves and masters. For Ann and me, the little phrase used in 1 Corinthians 7:15 sums up our aspirations for how we wish to live: "God has called us to live in peace."

That word, "peace", takes us beyond simply a lack of conflict. In fact, it doesn't preclude conflict, which is faced and worked through. But it's a peace, a shalom, which speaks of order, harmony, being in unison with one another. It sounds to me like oneness. It's fascinating when we explore Paul's instructions to Timothy and to Titus about the qualifications for eldership (in other words, leadership) in the early church. One might have expected the list to include "great preacher", "charismatic leader", "brilliant understanding of Scripture". But we have very little of that. Paul's main focus is not gifting, but character, character which is worked out in relationships within the family. The list includes: faithful to his wife, hospitable, managing his own family well, and having children who obey him. Paul sums up the qualifications with this reflection in 1 Timothy 3:5: "If anyone does not know how to manage his own family, how can he take care of God's church?" It seems that, for Paul and the other New Testament writers, what happens in the home either qualifies or disqualifies a person for leadership and ministry in the church.

It is perhaps sad to reflect that in recent years the church has given more attention to gifting and charisma than to character. The catalogue of scandals that have dogged the church could have perhaps been limited if we had taken more seriously the Bible's "person spec" for the leaders, pastors, bishops, and reverends who have led our churches. Perhaps when leaders are reviewed (assuming they are), questions should be asked not just about church attendance, pastoral care, and church finances, but about how their relationships are at home.

Becoming one

"That is why a man leaves his father and mother and is united to his wife, and they become one flesh." This passage in Genesis 2:24 has to be one of the most quoted from the Old Testament. Both Jesus and Paul refer to it. But also in wider society, virtually every church marriage service I attend or participate in quotes from it, not only in the liturgy but also in the talk. It's even more remarkable as it comes out of the creation narrative and places centre stage this coming together of a man and a woman in a committed, loving relationship. The "unity" words jump out at us. This is a relationship implying a deeper level of togetherness.

Once this new relationship begins, historical relationships with father and mother need to change. This relationship involves man being united with his wife as expressed in the sexual act. But it seems to go beyond simply sex, as important as that is. It seems to take us deeper, reflecting some spiritual union. In 1 Corinthians 7, Paul explores this theme with his warning to the Corinthians about sexual union with a prostitute. This short Genesis passage provides us with the framework for our understanding of this building block of society: marriage. It presents a challenge about the relationships we are going to build. However, when Jesus talked on this passage, He provoked a different reaction. I don't think I have ever heard anyone speaking at a marriage service on Matthew 19:10: "The disciples said to him: 'If this is the situation between a husband and wife, it is better not to marry.'" It's not quite the piece of wise advice the bride and groom are looking for on this special day.

Jesus is engaging in a debate with the Pharisees, who are pushing Him on the issue of divorce. Jesus takes them back to Genesis, refusing to be swayed by the exceptions provided by Moses. There is of course a theological debate still raging around divorce in the church, but here it is the disciples' response that is fascinating. While the church has through the centuries argued about the circumstances in which divorce can be permitted (if at all), the disciples take it in another direction. "Based on what You've been teaching," they effectively say to Jesus, "we're wondering if we would be better not getting married at all."

Be assured, I am not advocating that we shouldn't be marrying. I am, however, pleading for us to think very seriously about whether, and, perhaps most importantly, whom, we marry. I have observed over the years a number of marriages about which, when I stood back and reflected, I was forced to wonder whether they should really have got together. One of the difficulties often faced within church communities is that people can be almost thrown together by circumstances, or indeed some kind of corporate peer pressure. If there aren't many eligible men or women in your church, it might seem as if you don't have much choice. When you add to this the fact that pre-marital sex is discouraged, rightly from my understanding of Scripture, living together before marriage is therefore also frowned upon. It's thus very easy for a young Christian couple – and Christians do marry a lot younger than the rest of society – to rush into an ill-considered marriage. They haven't had enough time to build friendship or explore visions, passions, or aspirations for the future. One of the observations I've made in our church is that we all seem to benefit from pre-engagement preparation courses. The trouble with the usual pre-marriage course is that it's taking place as all the plans are being made. Rings are usually on fingers, dates have been set, venues booked; even honeymoons planned. It's very hard to say "Stop". It's so much easier to have had the opportunity to explore the viability of the relationship before any commitment is made. Having said all this, I'm convinced that God is able – with the commitment of both parties – to make a marriage work, whatever the seeming incompatibilities. If we are willing, He will work alongside us to meet some of the greatest challenges.

When oneness doesn't last

As I look back on more than thirty years of church leadership, I reflect on a whole mixture of memories and emotions. Fun, laughter, and great joy, but also real pain. Some of the greatest feelings of disappointment and anguish come as I reflect on close friends, fellow church leaders. We prayed, planned, and dreamed together, spent Christmas together, and yet today they are no longer with their family. Wives have been left, their children having to come to terms with two new homes. They have walked away from leadership and shown little evidence of faith. These memories raise all kinds of issues for me. How did this happen? Why didn't I see it coming? What more could I have done? Faced with these questions, I look at my own life, thankful to God for my marriage to Ann and our family life, but also recognizing my own vulnerability to the temptations I face every day. In the sex-mad world we live in, how do I respond to the daily opportunities I get to undermine my relationship? I'm not planning on walking out of my marriage any time soon, but I know that, given a series of what might appear to be small and insignificant choices that I decide to make, I could fatally wound my marriage in the future.

Looking back on those broken relationships, I see that for some it was a gradual drifting apart to the point at which there was very little holding them together. But, for others, it was simply a moment of madness, the pressing of a self-destruct button. Yet, either way, the damage done was enormous. Rebuilding a marriage when it gets to a certain tipping point is hugely challenging. We've journeyed with some couples seeking restoration and it is wonderfully rewarding when you see one of these marriages not just survive but flourish. Of course others don't make it, and the consequences are immense. When these people made their vows to each other, the vast majority meant it. They expected their marriage to be for life. But now it is broken. The family split. Children's loyalties tested. Trust eroded. Homes lost. Divorce should carry a government warning: it's seriously bad for your health.

The reasons marriages break down are complex. We all know that being in a Christian marriage doesn't automatically prevent us from experiencing deep pain and sadness. We may even know Christians who have had to leave their marriage for their own safety or the safety of their children. But in general, when I'm talking pastorally to a couple facing divorce, I often start with the statement, "A marriage breakdown is never just one person's fault." There's always at least some responsibility on both sides. When it comes to attributing blame, only God knows the percentages, and He's not telling us. There can in some cases be one decisive act, one act of stupidity, but usually it's a series of little choices – actions, attitudes – that have slowly and disastrously undermined the marriage. Friendship has been lost and they have drifted apart. Marriages need attention, investment, and taking seriously; otherwise, failure is a risk for us all.

Good foundations

A few years ago, a small group of us – all married couples – got together specifically to talk about our relationships. We agreed some rules: we were going to be honest. We could say anything and it was OK. And anything that was said stayed within the room. As we talked, we recognized that most of us had encountered, or were still dealing with, very similar problems. We also realized that we were at times in danger of believing two big lies when it came to the issues we faced. First, the lie that made us think what we were feeling or going through was "not all that important", or "didn't really matter", or was "not worth talking about". Second, the lie that told us there was no way out, and that we were trapped. Both of these lies were powerful because they stopped us from having open, honest conversations. The very thing we needed to be doing was acknowledging our struggles and sins, sharing our vulnerabilities, refusing to allow secrets to control our lives, and recognizing that God is interested in every area of our lives and our relationships.

The agenda we set for the series of conversations around our large dining-room table included money, sex, communication, planning, and children. There was so much common ground between us. We realized how we had all brought baggage into our marriages: past relationships, our experiences of our parents' marriages, and presuppositions about handling money, the bringing up of children, and sex. We also realized we had been fed a diet by the media of how relationships were "supposed to be", and our experiences showed us that it just wasn't like that in real life.

As we talked, we realized how important it was to build good foundations for marriage, but also that those foundations needed regular, sustaining, intentional maintenance. And at times of pressure and stress, they needed protection. Building, maintaining, and protecting our foundations was essential if we were to be united in our marriage, thriving not simply surviving. Sadly, some marriages just survive even though they don't end in divorce. Survival is not the goal. Flourishing, healthy, rich marriages are God's intention even if there are days, months, and even years in which we might be struggling and in need of help to work things through. Thank God for the helpful resources that are available these days, from marriage preparation courses, to marriage enrichment courses, books, videos, marriage counselling, psychosexual counselling, and computer software designed to keep us off pornographic sites.

While Ann and I have availed ourselves of many of the resources mentioned above, just as important – if not more so – have been the lessons we have learned from those around us. I'm convinced we were never meant to do this marriage thing on our own. We need people around us. We have watched and admired marriages that are flourishing and have thought: how can we learn from them? We have observed marriages that have failed or are failing and asked ourselves: how can we avoid going down that path? We've asked for help. In the early days of married life, we faced some big challenges in the building of the foundations. Our friends Martin and Sue were there for us throughout it all. We would meet once a week, have an early-evening meal, and just chat. Some of the baggage Ann and I had brought into our marriage got looked at, challenged, and dealt with. Because of the conviction we had that we couldn't do this thing on our own, Ann and I agreed that if we faced a conflict and just couldn't sort it out between the two of us, either of us could say – and the other would agree – that someone else should come in and help us sort the issue out. I can't tell you what an amazing safety net that has been. We have rarely used it, but it has meant we weren't locked into having to sort it out between the two of us.

As the conversations around the table continued, certain themes emerged, including the need for honesty and a willingness to give our very best, investing our time and energy in our relationships. We also acknowledged our need to keep God centre stage. While we needed people around us, we also at times needed divine intervention. God was an anchor that held our marriage in place. Without Him, we faced the danger of drifting into the choppy seas of society, where marriage breakdown is fast becoming a norm. Some practical suggestions began to emerge. We drew up the rules for a "good argument". Disagreement and conflict don't have to be a problem. They can be creative and positive. We recognized the need to handle arguments well. Our rules for a good argument are:

- No hitting, kicking, biting, or spitting.
- Listen to each other.
- Believe what the other says.
- No emotional blackmail.
- Don't let the sun go down on your anger. In other words, don't turn the light down on an argument.
- Don't brush things under the carpet and then bring them up regularly.
- Don't get locked up in each other. Get help. Everyone needs it.

Simple. Yet profound. I wish we had agreed on them earlier. We talked about the practical matters: how to find a rhythm of living in the midst of our busy lives and demanding jobs. Some around the table were facing the arrival of children and in the light of this had to revisit how their marriage was to work. How do couples adapt to a world that is changing around them? Time together, date nights, maintaining romance all needed to be planned if they were to happen. We recognized that if they weren't planned, they wouldn't just happen. For some, holidays were vital. For others, planned weekends or simply nights in together were what was needed. We weren't all the same. Our stages of family life were different and therefore the solutions needed to vary.

We also talked about sex and temptation. In our sex-saturated world, how could we not talk about sex? Hollywood and the media provide us with a window into the world of fantasy sex, media sex, supremely beautiful bodies in luxurious hotel rooms. Soft background music and multiple orgasms. In media sex, there's not a hint of awkwardness. There are no disappointments and there's no need to talk about it; it just happens. Despite our sex-obsessed media, I was amazed by a recent survey of British couples which showed just how little sex was actually going on.

Despite the rumours to the contrary, God's a big fan of sex. It was His idea from the start: "United to his wife, and they become one flesh." In our conversations with couples over the years, Ann and I have regularly reminded them of the importance of sex. It's important to God, so it should be important to us. It should be frequent and it should be fun.

Now there are all kinds of practical issues to be faced in this area. Sometimes health problems can get in the way. Sometimes help is needed, but it's important, and without it we're vulnerable. We're vulnerable because, in our sex-soaked society, temptation is everywhere and the opportunities to get into trouble are endless. If we're to protect the foundations of our relationship, we need to be able to talk about our temptations. It's easy for them to sneak up on us. I live in London, and as I travel around on the underground as a heterosexual male – particularly in summer – it seems I'm surrounded by attractive, scantily clad women. But what do I do with those images? How do I discipline my thinking? The teaching of Jesus in Matthew 5, "Anyone who looks on a woman lustfully has already committed adultery with her in his heart", takes us to a completely new level. It's not just about my actions; what goes on in my head matters too.

Ann and I have an agreement. We will talk about temptation. It's part of our commitment to an open, honest relationship, and we find it breaks the power of temptation by bringing it into the light. It's been a lifesaver for us – for me as a church leader working closely with both men and women, and also for Ann, working as she did in the theatre. The opportunities for getting into trouble are always there. On numerous occasions, Ann and I have had the conversation, "Watch out for me here" or "I find that person attractive" or "I'm not sure I would feel comfortable with that person living with us". It's amazing where these thoughts, attractions, and temptations can come from, even in the most surprising context – such as a church service. But they're just temptations, warning signs – they're not real; it's what we do with them that counts.

I remember vividly in the early years of my church leadership role, driving home from a daytime meeting and realizing that a female member of the congregation would be at home and I could just pop in for a "pastoral visit". We got on well; she and her husband were friends of ours. She would be home with their toddler and her husband would be at work; nobody would think there was anything amiss if I just popped in for a cup of tea. But as I drove past her house, slowing down for only a moment, I just knew it would be wrong. Not that anything would have happened over an afternoon cup of tea, but it could have been the beginning, the top of a slippery slope that might have ended in a disaster. I have learned to listen to the little voice in my head that on occasion says, "Warning: keep out" or "Danger: don't go there". I have come to believe it is the voice of God, which I ignore at my peril.

Men and women relating together is complex and at times unexpected. I have over the years had numerous women friends and colleagues, and have devoted a whole chapter in this book to men and women working together. But such relationships must be clean, clear, and honest, and we must give no ground to the enemy who would love to destroy our marriages and our ministries.

The unwelcome stranger

We cannot talk about temptation without mentioning the "P" word: pornography. Alongside drugs and oil, this multi-billion-pound business has become a dominant force in the world economy. It's wrecking the lives of millions. Before we talk about our marriages and porn, let's not forget those who for the sake of the "industry" perform in the most dehumanizing, degrading way, selling their humanity to satisfy sick fantasies. Porn is different from Hollywood media fantasy. It takes us to dark places, it's brutal, and it was never part of God's plan for sex.

While it's mainly feeding male fantasy, it's increasingly developing a market that appeals to women – *Fifty Shades of Grey* being one such publishing phenomenon. I'm grateful that my teenage scrapes with porn were of the magazine variety, passed around in the playground or at a party. Today's porn is to be found everywhere. It's available at the press of a button, on our phones and computers, easily addictive and so damaging to real-life sex: husband-and-wife sex. On more than one occasion over the years, a good friend has taken me aside to share something of their journey. Particularly in their struggles with pornography. Whenever this has happened, I've been faced with a variety of emotions. Along with sadness, disappointment, and sorrow for them in their difficulties, my most overwhelming sense has always been one of thankfulness. I've listened with a sense of privilege that this friend has trusted me enough to want to share their struggle. They want to be free, to be accountable, and don't want this secret sin to be a secret any more.

We all understand that the power is in the secret, and the journey to freedom begins with transparency. I know this story can be retold so many times – individuals and couples seeking help, recognizing their struggles, and finding a safe place to talk, seek guidance, and find a way forward.

Porn is the unwelcome stranger in so many marriages. The third person in many marital beds. It needs to be faced, brought to the light, talked about by husband or wife. And it will often involve a need for the help of others; for an accountable relationship that will regularly ask questions. As we build, as we maintain, and as we protect the foundations of our marriages, we do so with the shared commitment that our unity, our "one-fleshness", will not be affected by this virus. And, if it has been, we will do all we can to see the virus killed off.

Shared vision

Ann and I recently celebrated our fortieth wedding anniversary. We decided we would make the most of it by having a series of celebrations, which would include as many people as possible. As we were making our plans, inevitably we took the opportunity to look back on our forty years together. We have so much to be thankful for. During our reflections, Ann reminded me of the most embarrassing aspect of our engagement. We had taken time to pray separately about whether we felt God was bringing us together, whether we had a future or not. Once back together, we came to the conclusion that there was a future, and so it was that we started to plan. However, during one of our now-famous walks through Sandpit Woods in Northwood, north London, Ann stopped me in the midst of our planning for the future to make it clear that I had forgotten one vital thing. I had never actually asked her to marry me.

Ann's and my recollection of what happened next differ significantly. As I recall it, I immediately fell to my knees and, taking Ann by the hand and looking up into her beautiful green eyes, told her how much I loved her and asked if she would do me the honour of becoming my wife. Ann doesn't quite remember it like that (but, as I'm writing the book, I get to tell the story). Whatever the truth or otherwise of how I asked the question, what Ann and I would both agree on is what kind of conversation we were having at the time. Yes – we loved each other; we loved being together, Ann was great fun to be with; she was introducing me to the arts and the theatre, and I was introducing her to the delights of Yorkshire cricket. But our conversations were about our desire to serve God together; where God was calling us, who were the people God was calling us to work alongside for the advancement of His kingdom. You see, for the two of us, our marriage really wasn't just about us. We wanted our coming together to be a source of blessing to those around us. We wanted to make a home where people would come to know Him and would grow and mature in Him. Wherever He wanted to take us, we were willing to go.

In Ephesians 5, in talking about the marriage relationship, the apostle Paul quotes from Genesis, and then takes it further in Ephesians 5:31: "For this reason a man will leave his father and mother and be united to his wife, and the two will become one flesh. This is a profound mystery – but I'm talking about Christ and the church." This is indeed a mystery, but it seems Paul is calling us to that same sacrificial love that brought the Son of God to earth and made it possible through His sacrifice for salvation to come to the world. Could it be that our loving, sacrificial relationships might have an effect on those who surround us? Wouldn't it be amazing if the church was known as a group of people who model a different way of doing marriage? That's not saying we won't face our struggles and pains, and indeed some of us will fail. But what if as a church we were the people who created little expressions of heaven here on earth in the homes so that we establish and the families we raise that the communities around us are blessed? Is that really a pipedream or could it be a God-inspired vision?

Questions

- Think about the marriage of a couple you admire. What could you learn from it?
- Where you've seen a marriage in difficulty, are there lessons you could learn?
- How do you deal with temptation?

Questions for married couples

- Who do you talk to about your marriage?
- How do you handle conflict in your marriage?

Chapter 6

One: Unity begins at home

"But as for me and my household, we will serve the LORD."
Joshua 24:15

"Unless the Lord builds the house, the builders labour in vain..."
Psalm 127:1

If oneness is a challenge when there are just two of you, add a child or two or three (or maybe more) and it becomes even more complex. Suddenly, husband and wife gain new roles: mum and dad. When Ann and I married, we weren't convinced about children. We were too busy wanting to save the world. But six years into the marriage something changed and, after an emotionally painful miscarriage, very quickly our son Jake, and three years later our daughter Jordan, arrived.

Of course, children aren't a given. Our story has not mirrored the experience of some of our friends. Some, despite numerous IVF interventions, have faced involuntary childlessness. For them, all kinds of questions have had to be faced. How long do they keep trying? How many rounds of IVF do they submit to? When NHS funding stops, do they start paying? What about adoption and fostering? Or do they build a marriage that makes the most of the freedom offered by not being parents?

For us, the challenge was not childlessness, but two children. We quickly realized that these two wonderful bundles of humanity, these demanding and at times exhausting individuals, would provide a wonderful addition to our family of two. But they would also be the source of incredible challenge.

The foundations of our marriage would be tested. Would they be strengthened or would they crack? Sadly, for some, the arrival of children is the beginning of the end. The foundations aren't strong enough. Husband and wife simply become Mum and Dad. The unity, the oneness, is undermined. The marriage becomes secondary to the role of parent. How many marriages begin to disintegrate in those early months and years after the children arrive? All the attention, the effort, goes into providing for – and maybe surviving – this new arrival. Romance, friendship, and togetherness are lost. The cracks in these foundations might not become apparent for years, maybe not until the children, now young adults, begin to leave home. And suddenly the realization comes for husband and wife that there's nothing left.

It's amazing how children bring to the surface both the best in how God has made us and the worst of our character. Nobody prepared me for just how much I would love this little human being, how much I would be willing to fight to protect and work to provide for this new member of my family. But the new arrivals also bring to the surface areas that need work. It's amazing how sleepless nights, bouts of sickness, and the need for constant attention can bring out the worst in us and perhaps highlight some areas that God wants us to pay attention to.

Ann tells a story of a shopping trip to Tesco with our eighteen-month-old son. As she wandered along the aisles picking out her weekly shopping, with Jake in the trolley, she suddenly realized that he had turned red. His eyes had rolled back and he was having a fit. As far as she was concerned, at that moment Jake was about to die. Abandoning her shopping, she picked him up and bolted out of the store, running through the streets of Cobham, where we lived, to the health centre. An ambulance was called. As she sat in the ambulance with Jake, Ann had no idea whether he would live or die. She picked him up, held him up, and committed his life to

God. Despite her natural dread of losing Jake, Ann accepted that he was God's, not hers. His life was in his Father's hands.

As it turned out, this was the first of what would be a series of febrile convulsions that Jake suffered over the next four years. We discovered that it's not uncommon. He grew out of it, but for Ann and me it brought to the surface a number of areas we needed to give attention to. It was amazing how often Jake would have a similar attack when I was away leading a team or speaking. It seemed like a spiritual battle as well as a physical problem. We sought all the right medical help, but it was also the motivation for a great deal of prayer.

Our starting point as we considered family life was that children are a gift from God. And He was trusting us with the privilege of partnering with Him in parenting Jake and Jordan. It's a great place to start, because it recognizes our need of Him. After all, He knows them far better than we do. He knows what's going on inside even before they can verbalize it. He knows the plans He has for them, and what experiences will help to shape them for His purposes in their life. But how does it work out in practice? I had come from a single-parent family, my father having died when I was young. I certainly hadn't experienced fathering first-hand. Ann came from a broken family, her mum and dad having divorced when she was in her early teens, and her relationship with both mum and dad had been problematic. So what would living in peace look like with these two new arrivals?

As I look back now, it was that sense of desperately needing God's help that laid the foundations for the next season of our lives. I can't think of any area that Ann and I prayed more about or indeed talked more about. It was clear from the start that we had to be in it together. It had to be a team effort, and although Ann was the primary carer in the early years, there could be no abdication of my responsibilities.

Keys to parenting

Over the years, a few keys to our parenting began to emerge. I'm sure there are more, but these are ours.

Consistency

If we were in this thing together, our children needed to know it. Playing one parent off against the other wasn't going to work. If we agreed something, it was agreed and followed through, and reversed only with further agreement. Consistency, however, didn't mean Jake and Jordan were always treated in the same way. Fairness was important. Fairness is close to justice, and children have a strong sense of justice. But, within fairness, there was flexibility to adjust to the different personalities and priorities of our kids. Jake and Jordan were so different. For example, as far as Jake was concerned, any publicity was good publicity. So he was delighted that my being a preacher meant that I would use illustrations from his life, often his mishaps, to make a point. With Jordan, on the other hand, as she was a far more private person, I agreed that I would obtain her permission to tell any story publicly if it referred to her. Even in writing this chapter, I have checked whether she is happy for these stories to be told.

Jake, like Ann and myself, was naturally tidy. When you lived the way we lived, with so many people coming in and out of the house, it was kind of necessary. Jordan, however, never quite saw the importance of a tidy bedroom. Ann and I tried everything: threats, bribes, parental support in tidying her room. Eventually we came to the conclusion that there was only one solution: to close the door. We decided it was a battle we couldn't win, and really there were far more important things for us to worry about.

Deciding which battles to fight is such a critical thing for parents. I remember one family who lived with us for a while desperately trying to make their children eat food that they obviously hated. I have observed so many parents fighting battles that they were never going to win, and which frankly weren't all that important.

Kindness

Early on in our parenting, we discovered an amazing word, which began to take centre stage in our family life. It became a touchstone for so much of our interaction. That word was "kindness". It's a word that is close to love. And while "love" is a wonderful word, it's in danger of being overused and can get lost in translation. So much of our children's behaviour, and indeed also Ann's and mine, could be measured against the question: was that kind? Jake pulling Jordan's hair like that, was that kind? Jake annoying Jordan with that water pistol, was that kind? I have to confess that the question was most often brought as a challenge to Jake. Not that he wasn't fundamentally a very kind boy, but he had a particular gift of annoying his sister and mother.

Encouragement

Challenging the attitudes behind the behaviour began to be a key for us. It meant that inappropriate behaviour could be dealt with, but, at the same time, good behaviour could be praised. The "kindness" word allowed us to focus on encouragement. We wanted to have a home where encouragement was the air that we breathed. We were cheering each other on, seeking out the best in Jake and Jordan, and looking to reinforce and support it.

I have over the years visited some homes where sadly the reverse is true. The focus is on what the children are getting wrong. The bad attitudes, the unacceptable behaviour, the terrible report from school, the awful friends, the horrid music they listen to. It has to be the adults' responsibility to create the culture of the family, the atmosphere in which family life is conducted. There are some parents who get this so right. I remember visiting one family a few years after the arrival of Jake and Jordan. I walked in one early evening and here were the family – mum, dad, and three children – seated around the table having a meal. I was invited to join them. It was amazing. The day's activities were discussed, along with what was happening around the world. As I sat there, I realized this wasn't part of my family's rituals of life. We would usually eat together, but it would invariably be short and sharp and often disturbed by a phone call (this was before the time of social media). When I got home I told Ann what I had just observed; it was like a flash of lightning. We knew it needed to be installed as part of our family life. It took a while to get used to, but the evening meal became a cornerstone of family-building. Sometimes it was just a quick fifteen minutes, other times it could last over an hour. But it became the context for talking, for sharing life, for laughing, for being encouraged. It shaped our family culture.

Respect

As I walked through the supermarket one day, there was a parent–child confrontation going on before my very eyes. A young lad was being dragged along an aisle by his frustrated mother, who was shouting at the top of her voice. A public display of anger, frustration, and embarrassment. It's not an uncommon event. But, as I reflected on it, I realized that the word "respect" works both ways. It's usually used by a parent to a disobedient child: "Show some respect". But we as parents carry a responsibility to respect our children, even when they are at their most frustrating. How can we teach respect if we don't model it? How can we expect our children to respect those in authority, which is a biblical requirement, if we speak ill of their teachers, the police force, or the government? I'm not talking about blind and uncritical respect, but, nevertheless, respect.

Ann and I realized that respect had to begin at home. Jake and Jordan needed to know that although Mum and Dad were in charge, they had a voice. Their opinions would be heard and taken seriously. The meal table was a good place for those voices to be heard, and indeed an institution known as our "family conference" was instigated, in which any member of the family could raise an issue of concern which they felt needed consideration.

Family conferences sometimes resulted in apologies being made, including by Mum and Dad. It was to a family conference that

Jake eventually brought what had become a big issue for him, and indeed was to become an issue for the whole family. Jake was twelve years old and had come to the conclusion that he wanted to buy... a gun. An air pistol. You can imagine the reaction from Ann and me. We had tried to discourage guns as a childhood toy, not always successfully. It's amazing how adaptable bits of wood and metal (and indeed human body parts) can be in creating imaginary guns. The conversation started with Ann. She wisely said when asked, "If you push me on it now, Jake, the answer is no. But if you give me time to consider, that could change."

So it was that the process of negotiation took place. Guidelines and rules of engagement were drawn up, and eventually at a family conference over an evening meal the purchase of a gun was agreed. I can still remember the scene as the four of us arrived at the specialist gun shop in Chichester, West Sussex. Jake led us into the shop and, having considered the merits of various pistols, eventually purchased a top-of-the-range sparkling red gun.

As Jake handed over his hard-saved money and we walked out of the shop, his face was a picture. He had argued his case. He had changed the minds of his parents. He had agreed with the whole family, including his sister, on how the gun was to be used safely. (A matter of real concern, it should be said, for his sister, who feared she might become a target.)

Respect had worked both ways.

Building memories

The story of the gun lives on in the repertoire of our family's corporate stories, which are periodically brought out and rehearsed at family gatherings. Ann and I realized we wanted to build memories that our children would take with them into their adult lives. In the early days of our marriage, money was tight. There wasn't a lot splashing about. But we still worked hard to build the memories. Trips to the woods, climbing trees, a day at the sea, collecting wood, making a fire, toasting marshmallows, and an annual overnight camp in a farmer's field. When the snow came down, we were out in it throwing snowballs, riding sledges. We were looking for adventure, with the occasional hint of danger.

The children also shared our spiritual adventures. They would travel with Ann and me and a team as we took theatre productions on the road. They would join in local evangelistic events we were running, and they were with us as we led conference events and festivals.

Back in 1988, at the beginning of March for Jesus, we were facing some difficulties in negotiating permission to march in the centre of London. A meeting had been planned with an Inspector Divine – that really was his name – at New Scotland Yard. Our fear was that they could ban the march, or make the route impossible for us to take. It was therefore decided that the four of us would do our own March for Jesus, so accompanied by a close friend, we marched with eighteen-month-old Jordan in the pushchair along the route that we wanted to take before I went into the meeting. And so we started on the Embankment and walked down Whitehall, round past the Houses of Parliament, down to Victoria, round the back of Buckingham Palace, and into Hyde Park. We prayed our way around the march and, as we arrived at Hyde Park, Jake wandered off a little way and the adults continued praying. After a few moments, Jake came back, and we asked him the question, "What do you think God says?" And he asked us in turn, "When God speaks to you, does He speak inside you?" We said He did. "Oh, well, God says yes, yes, yes," he said, and ran off again. As it turned out, the "yes" from God was actually right. My meeting at New Scotland Yard with Inspector Divine went remarkably well. The route was agreed and so it was that 55,000 marched for Jesus on an amazing day in May. We've often told that story. Jake was part of the adventure of March for Jesus. He had heard from God, and God had answered his prayers.

Granting freedom

I share these stories not to suggest that we got everything right. I'm sure we made many mistakes and our children have been very forgiving. However, I'm so grateful to God for two children who have developed into wonderful adult followers of Jesus, who are trying to make a difference in the world. But there is, as we know, no guarantee. Relationships go wrong. It doesn't always work out as we hope, or indeed pray for. I know from conversations with many Christian parents, and indeed sometimes their children, how painful that can be. I've watched some of those relationships from a distance. When asked, my plea has been, "Whatever you do, however much you disagree, do all you can to hold on to the relationships."

For some, the process of transition into adulthood can be particularly challenging. Allowing these young adults to leave, even if they stay, is a principle we have tried to adopt. Jake and Jordan needed to know that we weren't holding them back. We wanted them to be free. We wanted them to fly. By the age of thirteen, Jordan was on mission trips without Mum and Dad. By eighteen, she was in China teaching English as a second language before travelling the world and returning to start university. While all kinds of negotiated safety measures were put in place, she knew we were releasing her with our blessing. The amazing thing is that both of them have felt free to come back, having been released, and in one notable period we had all four of them – each having by now married – living with us as part of our household.

It's now over forty years since Ann and I married. At a recent celebration, among the many generous and kind things that were shared by friends, Jake spoke about our relationship and how much it meant to him, saying that as he looked at our life and marriage, we were the most genuinely authentic couple he knew. And as he said these words, we felt so humbled and blessed. It had been worth all the hard work.

The household

We decided early on in our marriage that we wanted our home to be a place that extended beyond simply our marriage or our immediate family. It all started by accident, but we quickly realized this was the way we wanted to live. We wanted others to be welcomed, and in a measure to share life with us. The people who have lived with us have come from all backgrounds and cultures. They have been mainly single people, but we've occasionally had married couples and indeed families. The majority have been Christians, but not all. Most we have known and had some degree of relationship with. But two or three have come because there just wasn't anywhere else for them to go.

As our concept of household developed, we realized it extended beyond merely those who slept under our roof. There was a wider network of friends who shared our lives, our meal tables, our celebrations. As we explored Scripture, it seemed that this was far closer to a biblical norm. This was church in the home. A household of faith. One of the questions often asked was, "What about the children?" The vast majority of the people who lived with us enriched our lives and we were sad to see them move out. Twice we ran into conflict, and for the sake of our children, who were always our number-one priority, it was necessary for us to ask them to leave. On a number of occasions, our children were asked, "What's it like living with strangers in your home?" A very twenty-first-century question, with a number of presuppositions underlying it. Their answer was always fascinating. Shaking their heads, they would confess that they didn't know anything different. For them, living in community was just the norm. As Ann and I have reflected on the impact on them, we've realized how socially able both of them are, how instinctively they adapt to social settings, how easily they are able to relate to people of all kinds of backgrounds. And they have learned to read people, to recognize vulnerabilities and needs.

One added benefit for us when they were teenagers was that, when they were fed up with Mum and Dad, there was always someone else around who appreciated and respected the two of us, yet to whom Jake and Jordan could moan about us. It was brilliant as they grew up to be able to provide a place where they could have a space, a home, for their friends to share.

How did it work out in practice?

We settled on the word "household". We avoided the language of extended family. It seemed to raise all kinds of questions and, although people could choose to speak of themselves as part of the Clifford family, we didn't want to impose it. We also avoided the word "lodger". This was for us far more than the provision of accommodation – a friendly bed and breakfast. "Household" seemed to work. People who joined us were participating in our home. Ann and I had the final say. We had learned early on that we couldn't expect people to read our minds. So spelling out expectations was essential. Everyone was given and talked through an A4 sheet that explained how we wanted the house to run. We very rarely had to refer to it but it was there just for clarity, to leave no room for misunderstanding.

Living like this wasn't without its challenges – the stuff of lives which became part of our concern: cleaning, washing, eating, parenting, health issues, physical and emotional relationship problems, employment and unemployment, alongside all the practical aspects of just living together: shopping, cooking, cleaning, and mending. But we ensured there was always a place – usually our bedroom – where Ann and I could escape. And where Jordan and Jake could do their own thing without being disturbed. At one stage, we ran out of space, and we took what was for us an enormous step of faith and bought a significantly bigger house. When conflicts came, as they did from time to time, we were committed to open and honest conversations. Living like this means you can't allow problems to remain unresolved.

As we look back on the sixty people we have lived with, many of whom we still have contact and a relationship with, I'm so grateful for the friendships. But I also recognize that in God's economy it has provided a place of safety where problems could be faced and healing brought. A place of discovery, finding God, and hearing Him speak on what was next in their journey with Him. A place of learning and discipleship. For some it was a place where they found Christ. Others grew closer to Him. It was a place of joys, pains, parties, and celebrations.

A home for good

As I conclude this chapter, I do so aware that while for Ann and me exploring unity in our marriage, family, and household has taken us down one particular pathway, others have made the journey with other outcomes. The amazing response of Christians to the needs of children in the care system remains to some degree an untold story. As the Evangelical Alliance launched a campaign a few years ago, along with Care for the Family and the churches' Child Protection Advisory Service, to highlight this issue, little did we know just how much was already happening and how open the church was to doing more. Home for Good was the campaign, and as it drew to a close, we just knew it couldn't end there. So it was that the Alliance launched Home for Good as an independent charity, still closely related, still based in our building, but dedicated to supporting the Christian community in extending their families and including some of the most vulnerable.

Other experiments are emerging. Modern-day monastic communities: a group of people living together, sharing life and faith and a commitment to reaching out in a missional way to the communities that surround them. Open homes, open tables: they are all part of the same aspiration to reach beyond our small family unit and create something bigger.

As part of my role, I have the privilege of visiting many different parts of the UK and indeed many parts of the world. Yet I must admit that my favourite place in all the earth is my own doorstep. I love coming home. We might not always have people living with us, but I don't want my home to be an exclusive place occupied only by Ann and our immediate family. We're so blessed. And so, in the spirit of relationships and hospitality, we want to be a blessing to others. What an amazing statement we as a church make when we live like this. It's not always easy and we do need to be creative, but we can do it.

I recently visited a small church in Kensington. Although in a tough area, this relatively small group have been faithful for years. It is now the hub of many activities in the community. Alongside Alpha and Journey are English conversation classes, line-dancing, cooking, craft classes, and other activities. However, one initiative caught my attention: they were recently joined by an Eden team run by a young couple. They really missed their family lunches. Rather than feeling miserable, they invited the teenagers they were working with for a sit-down Sunday lunch and were amazed by the response. The table quickly filled up and the kids behaved well and participated in the "God slot" between courses. It was such a success that these lunches have become a regular occurrence. On hearing this, I was profoundly moved. Here was the family of God extending the boundaries and including others at the table to hear and experience the story of God.

Families need help

I'm not sure there has ever been a more challenging time to parent a growing family than the one we are in right now. So many norms of parent–child relationships are being challenged, by marriage breakdown, government intervention, social media, and new norms of behaviour that are emerging. Parents desperately need our support and also our prayers. The family unit remains God's building block for healthy societies and indeed for the development of mature, healthy individuals. As family units get smaller, and often more isolated, so the pressure upon them increases, and the danger is that children will get damaged in the process. This is an area where the voice and the work of the church must be heard and seen.

Questions

- Could God be speaking to you about how "household" might be expressed in your life?
- What are the key words that reflect how you wish to bring up your children?
- Are there any suggestions in this chapter that you could try in your family life?
- With whom do you talk about family life?

Chapter 7

One: In the local church

"To him be glory in the church and in Christ Jesus throughout all generations, for ever and ever! Amen."
Ephesians 3:21

"I will build my church"
Matthew 16:18

"I believe that the greatest tragedy of the Church in our time has been its failure to recognize the importance of the spiritual gift of leadership. It appears to me that only a fraction of pastors worldwide are exercising the spiritual gift of leadership: organizing Church around it and deploying members through it."
Bill Hybels, *Courageous Leadership*

"It is not so much the case that God has a mission for His Church in the world, as that God has a Church for His mission in the world. Mission was not made for the Church; the Church was made for mission – God's mission."
Chris Wright, *The Mission of God*

I have to confess that, when I'm asked what I do for a living, my answer varies somewhat according to who I'm with. When I'm standing in a neighbour's garden enjoying a barbecue, saying that I'm General Director of the Evangelical Alliance is a bit of a mouthful. It's also a conversation-stopper. When I speak at churches, someone else normally introduces me with my full job title. But no matter the setting, I go on to explain that, a bit like the proverbial stick of Blackpool rock, if you cut me in half, running down the centre is the word "church". Deep down, I am a church leader. It's what I have occupied myself with since the 1980s: churches in all kinds of different shapes and sizes.

As I write this chapter, I do so with an unapologetic bias. I love the church. I thank God for the church. I celebrate God's gift to us of the church. Over the years, the church has been for Ann and me the place where we have celebrated with others births, marriages, jobs gained, promotions achieved, new homes, answers to prayers, projects completed, exams passed. But we have also shed tears and grieved over deaths, miscarriages, failed interviews and exams, redundancies, sicknesses, broken relationships. Church for me has been the place of my greatest joys and hopes but also the place of my greatest pains and disappointments.

Central to God's plan

As we explore the full arc of biblical history, we discover that God's mission on the earth has always had at its heart a community of faith that would work under His direction to see His purposes fulfilled. God calls to Abraham in Genesis 12 and puts down a marker: "I will make you into a great nation, and I will bless you; I will make your name great, and you will be a blessing. I will bless those who bless you, and whoever curses you I will curse; and all peoples on earth will be blessed through you" (Genesis 12:2–3).

God is calling Abraham and his wife Sarai, and promises that from their family what will prove to be His rescue plan for all humanity will be worked out. Out of this family, clan, tribe, and eventual nation will come a blessing to all the peoples on earth. Out of this family will come the messiah whose life, death, and resurrection give birth to this amazing global family, this new humanity. This body of Christ: the church. The apostle Paul can summarize his preaching as "mak[ing] plain to everyone the administration of this mystery, which for ages past was kept hidden in God, who created all things. His intent was that now, through the church, the manifold wisdom of God should be made known to the rulers and authorities in the heavenly realms, according to his eternal purpose that he accomplished in Christ Jesus our Lord" (Ephesians 3:9–11).

It's almost as if Paul is shouting at us down through the years: "It's about the church, stupid!" Over the years, the church has received some bad press. Not only in the mainstream media but also sadly among ourselves. It's become almost fashionable to knock the church, to rehearse the stories of how we have failed. The truth of course is that often we *have* failed. We haven't always been what God intended the church to be. In fact, as the stories emerge of the church's being complicit in some child abuse scandals and then covering up those tragic events at the highest level, we acknowledge that some of our number have been a disgrace to the name of Christ and have damaged the reputation of the church for many and eroded our good-news message to the world. Despite these and indeed other scandals, I still strongly affirm that there is another story to be told. It's the story of the church across the UK, and across the globe, living as a genuine community of faith and being good news to those around them as well as speaking good news.

When we read the New Testament writers, we discover church expressed in a variety of settings. The books of Ephesians and Revelation introduce us to the global church, made up of people from every tribe and nation, while in the final chapters of Romans we have Paul sending a greeting to the church meeting in the home of Priscilla and Aquila. In between these two extremes, we discover that for the New Testament writers the churches in the towns and cities and indeed regions were all church, and we need to appreciate all these expressions.

Without a picture of the global church, we miss out on God's big-picture kingdom agenda for the whole of creation. But, on the other hand, without the local, the small, the church in the home, the town, the city, we fail to put flesh and blood on our message. It doesn't have an impact on the day-to-day lives of the Christian community.

One of the things we can be certain of is that, for the New Testament writers, the idea sometimes articulated by twenty-first-century Christians of "churchless Christianity" would have been unthinkable. Churchless Christianity can sound so reasonable. Churchless Christians say they love Jesus, pray, read Scripture, and find Christian literature so helpful. They read blogs, download sermons, and occasionally chat to their friends about their faith. Sometimes they even pray together. But church, they say, is not really for them. They may find it demanding or simply feel that church doesn't meet them "where they are at". Their lives are so full and they feel they don't really have time for church.

I am convinced we all need church. It's a necessity, not an option. The very presupposition of this book, and the title itself, assumes that the challenge of being "one" with others means we simply can't do this on our own. Church will come in all kinds of shapes and sizes and cultural expressions, but it is still church – the followers of Jesus coming together to fulfil His purposes in the world.

Paul writes to the Ephesians (4:3–5), "Make every effort to keep the unity of the Spirit through the bond of peace. There is one body and one Spirit, just as you were called to one hope when you were called; one Lord, one faith, one baptism." He means that all of us, in some amazing mystery of God's grace, are drawn together in the "unity of the Spirit"; we become one, not in isolation, not each doing our own thing, but one body in Christ Jesus. In becoming a follower of Jesus, the very process of salvation is to be made part of this new family. A new people, the body of Christ. It's not an optional extra. It's not a case of "take it or leave it". God knows we need it, and He also knows that the world needs the church to be the church if Jesus is to be made known. We really can't do it as individuals.

This lays down a challenge to all of us. First, are we a committed part of a community of faith, connecting with people we believe God has joined us to? Second, are we being the kind of welcoming, hospitable, Christlike community where people can find a home regardless of their background and culture? As a church leader, I feel this challenge acutely. Is my church a place where "oneness" is expressed? The answer is probably yes and no, depending on which direction you look in and probably who you speak to. Over the years, I've found so many books on leadership and management that have helped me – both those written by Christians and those by mainstream experts. While I continue to appreciate the insights, disciplines, and helpful advice they bring, I'm increasingly aware that if we are to be true to our calling, it's vital that as a church we express ourselves not so much as an organization or an institution, but first and foremost as a family.

One of the wonderful New Testament terms used to describe the loving, intimate relationships within the early church is the word "fellowship". This rich word has a far deeper meaning than simply getting on well together. J. Schattenmann describes it as "the expression of an enthusiastic love".[1] This kind of relationship cannot simply be the result of hard work or the legalistic following of the laws of good church membership. There is a supernatural element to the New Testament "fellowship". This theme is explored in 1 John 1:3–6, declaring that our fellowship with brothers and sisters in Christ is dependent on our relationship with God. David Coffey[2] explains it like this:

> At the heart of our life together is a "sharing in" fellowship with the Father and the Son and the Holy Spirit. This is our secret. With God's help, we have to work to establish meaningful fellowship with other believers. Without the work of the holy trinity, there can be no fellowship in the church. Without the active participation of a community of believers, God's intention for his church can never be realized.

We can never truly be God's family without divine intervention.

Our unity in the local church should not be based on our commitment to a particular structure, style of worship and ministry, or even theological distinctive. If we are to be church, we need first and foremost to be family. This provides enormous challenges for some churches on account of size or turnover of membership. Large metropolitan churches can see 30–40 per cent leaving and joining each year. But, even in these settings, being family and expressing family is critical.

The challenge of church as family

As I look back on my life, I realize the rich variety of church life that I have enjoyed and am able to thank God for. As the son of a vicar, my early years were spent in an inner-city Anglican church, and although my father died when I was five we as a family continued to attend for some years. Although as a child I didn't always appreciate it, I look back now with thankfulness for the grounding in the biblical narrative that I gained through Sunday School, Pathfinder camps, and Scripture Union notes. The stories of scriptural heroes helped to shape my view of the world, and although by the time I was a teenager there wasn't a great deal of faith left in my life, I couldn't deny my deep-down conviction that there really was a God.

After becoming a Christian, I returned to Bradford, my home town (I had become a follower of Jesus while working away from home). Somehow I found myself joining an independent Methodist church called Sunbridge Road Mission, led by Pastor Douglas Evans. Here was a church passionate about seeing people come to Christ. A city-centre coffee-bar outreach was run, and kids' holiday clubs and outreach to the Asian community, among other missionary activities, were all part of the church's commitment to the gospel. Those early years as a Christian at Sunbridge Road Mission under the watchful eye of Pastor Evans were so influential for me. And while the church was non-charismatic and probably verging on anti-charismatic, I'm grateful to God for their care for this new convert and the opportunities they gave me to push out in leadership, preaching, teaching, and developing the passion to see people come into relationship with Jesus.

It was only some years later that the issue of the gifts of the Holy Spirit became a point of difficulty. After a time with YWAM (1972–73), an international mission agency in Denmark, and then three years (1973–76) studying theology at London Bible College (London School of Theology, as it is now), Ann and I – newly married – found ourselves moving to become part of what we now know as a new church, but which was referred to then as a house church. We really did meet most of the time in homes.

It was only as cinemas, community centres, and warehouses became our meeting places that the name "new church" emerged. (I guess there will have to be another renaming soon. How long can a new church remain new?!)

In 1979, Cobham Christian Fellowship, renamed Pioneer People, became home to us. I'm deeply grateful for our years as part of Pioneer People. It became our family, our spiritual home. Our children grew up and came to faith in that church. There was a strong emphasis on community, the gifts of the Spirit and prophetic ministry, and eventually church-planting and evangelism. It was in this setting that my passion for church took root. It was a fellowship wanting to learn from the experience of the early church and see it lived out in a twentieth-century United Kingdom. To do this, relationships were seen as the key. Anything that undermined those relationships was faced and where necessary challenged. This unity in relationships expressed itself through shared homes, cars, and DIY and garden equipment. Hospitality and generosity were values expressed in everyday life around meal tables, on holidays, and in home improvements. I'm deeply thankful for those days. In the context of our strong commitment to corporate worship, prayer, and ministry, this was a church that eventually began to send teams to plant churches and to engage in local evangelism and international mission. But it was also a church that looked broken marriages in the face. I remember a group of around twenty of us friends meeting with Luke and Jo (not their real names). Luke confessed that he had been unfaithful to Jo and was seeking forgiveness and the restoration of his marriage. This was part of the rebuilding of their marriage, the next step in Luke's journey of repentance. As we heard from both Luke and Jo, the room was filled with a whole mixture of emotions, yet as we prayed together and agreed to meet again in the not-too-distant future, we did so with a deep sense that God was at work. Around a year later, that same group were present as Luke and Jo repeated their wedding vows and we celebrated a marriage saved.

This was a victory, but as a church community we also encountered tragic loss. Together we faced the pain of death. Matthew – a much-loved teenager – was found in bed having died from an aneurysm in his brain. How the church grieved. This was the most heartbreaking of losses for his family – his mum, dad, and sister – but also for the whole community.

This was the stuff of life. It was in facing it together that we found strength. The stuff of life included homes lost owing to repossession, bankruptcies, miscarriages, redundancies, and much more. Of course, in the midst of the stuff of life, we didn't always get it right. Marriages weren't always saved. Not all children or teenagers became followers of Jesus. Some church plants didn't work out as we'd hoped.

Were we a little too local-church-focused? Certainly, in the early days. We didn't always handle prophetic ministry well; and when leadership conflict came, while it was faced, it wasn't always resolved as well as it could have been. I thank God for the local church and recognize all that it has done in shaping my life – the people who have influenced me not just through the things they have said, but the lives they have lived. However, I accept that it's also been a place of pain, and of learning in and through that pain.

During a time of leadership conflict, I remember sitting with Ann in our lounge after what had been a difficult church meeting.

We were reflecting on what had happened and were both close to tears. Neither of us knew quite how it would be worked through in the weeks and months to come, but it was at that point that I had what I can only describe as a divine insight. The words of Proverbs 4:23 came to mind: "Above all else, guard your heart, for everything you do flows from it."

I just knew this was a watershed moment. In the hurt, the pain, and the disappointment, it would have been easy to allow our hearts to be damaged and hardened, to become resentful of people and perhaps even of the church as a whole. I can't tell you how often Ann and I reminded ourselves of this truth over the weeks and months that followed. I've met so many Christians over the years who have been hurt in the context of church. If we're honest, we realize that it wouldn't hurt as much if it wasn't so important to us. But in the context of hurt their hearts (the core of their being) have been damaged – and it's crippled them for life. (In a recent piece of research we conducted among young adults aged eighteen to thirty-seven, nearly half – 48 per cent – had been really hurt by others in the church they attended.[3])

I love the fact that the Scriptures weren't written by spin doctors. The great men and women of faith are also shown at times with distinctly ungodly attitudes and actions. They face conflict and do not handle it well. We find one of those incidents in Acts 15:36–41. Paul and Barnabas have developed into a formidable church-planting team. As we know, Barnabas, the "son of encouragement", had "discovered" Paul, spoken up for him, and even risked his reputation by backing Paul as a credible convert and now church leader and apostle. Their first missionary journey had gone well, except for the unexpected departure of John, also known as Mark, who had returned to Jerusalem early in the journey. By the time we get to Acts 15, Paul and Barnabas are planning another journey with the aim of revisiting the cities where churches have been planted. Barnabas, the encourager, wants to give John another chance, whereas Paul is convinced this is too much of a risk.

As so often in situations like this, there isn't necessarily a right and a wrong answer to the question, yet it becomes so easy to make the issue a matter of "rightness". For Paul, it was too much of a risk. There could be trouble in the communities they were visiting. They needed people they knew they could trust, who wouldn't let them down. Barnabas, however, with his pastoral heart, was convinced John had changed. He could be depended upon, and he felt that Paul really should trust him, Barnabas, on this one – just as the apostles in Jerusalem had trusted him when he introduced Paul to them in the early days.

The resulting row was full-on. It was not a mild disagreement. Tom Wright, in exploring the Greek word *paroxysmos*, which is used to describe the "huge row", says, "It carries overtones of severely heightened emotions. Red and distorted faces. Loud voices. Things said that were better left unsaid."[4] Not the greatest advert for these two early church apostolic ministries. I'm grateful that Luke included this sad, perhaps shameful, account in Acts. It serves as a warning to all of us but perhaps also as an encouragement. If two of the early church heroes could have got it so wrong and yet kept going, "guarded their hearts", and remained true to their calling in God, perhaps we can as well. Even when things go wrong.

The church at work

It was early on in my current job that a young creative guy called John and I were sitting having coffee in a London hotel. He asked me, "What's your theory of change?" I wasn't sure I had one, but I wasn't going to admit it. He realized I was struggling so began to explain by way of a story about a young North American business executive whose life was turned upside down by the death of a close family member in a random shooting. He felt that he had to do something about it, and a conversation some months later with a young mother shaped his strategy. The mother revealed her concern about her child visiting other homes that might have guns in them. So a theory of change began to emerge. Perhaps mothers asking other mothers if there was a gun in the house could create a climate in which people began to feel embarrassed and put pressure on the owners of the guns – usually the fathers – to get rid of the weapons. In this case, maybe mothers could help change a culture. "So," said John again, "what's your theory of change?" Suddenly it became easy. "It's the church," I said.

I believe that God's primary agent for change right across our society is the church. God's committed to change and instigated His change theory thousands of years ago in His people, empowered by the Holy Spirit to bring change to the fallen world we live in.

One of the amazing privileges I have in my role at the Alliance is to travel the country and see first-hand the church at work. Despite rumours to the contrary, I've discovered that the church is alive and making a profound contribution in some of the most challenging contexts in our society. It's wonderful to observe all the church gets involved in in communities up and down the country.

But let's also not forget the Christian community who go to their places of employment day in and day out, not simply to pay the bills but with a sense of God's calling to make a difference for good in business, the health service, police, legal and social services, media, hospitality, entertainment, etc. These are missionaries, agents for God's agenda, looking for change.

The remarkable Cinnamon Faith Audit in 2015 estimated that faith groups – the vast majority of which are Christian – contribute more than £3 billion per year to UK society through time given to social action initiatives. In an age of austerity and cutbacks, in some communities it's only the churches that remain to provide social cohesion. This is church at its best. Often not simply working on its own but working collaboratively with other churches. This is church not simply concerned for our own church family, although that's important, but looking outwards, following the example of Jesus when He quotes that famous Isaiah passage in Luke 4: good news to the poor, freedom for the prisoners, recovery of sight for the blind, setting the oppressed free. It was the early church who reached out beyond themselves to the sick, the abandoned babies, the slaves. It was the early church who refused to abandon the cities when plagues broke out. And so it was that the church grew. Over the centuries, we have built up such a rich heritage of the church at the very heart of responding to the major needs of society. As we've cared for those in need, and shared the gospel, people have become followers of Jesus.

Why do things go wrong?

It was a few years ago now that I heard of a newly-planted church that they called "One". I have to confess, when I heard the name, my first response was to smile. It seemed to reflect a significant limitation in their aspirations for growth. Of course, the name was nothing to do with numerical growth; it was a statement of intent. If they were to be true to their name, the quality of their relationships had to reflect how the New Testament writers saw the church – many people, certainly, but with such a shared fellowship and life that it could be said of them that they were one.

As a church leader and someone who has provided support and oversight for a number of churches, I've seen so many things "go wrong" in the local church when our unity is threatened. There's probably a book to be written exploring just this subject. A good place to start is a recognition that we live in a fallen, sin-filled world. And that we are sinners whom God's in the process of sorting out. We are saved by His grace but we are still very much a work in progress. So, as a church member, and church leader, I bring my whole self, with all my strengths and weaknesses, but also my struggles and even at times my sin, into my participation in this wonderful God idea, the church.

We must also recognize, as the apostle Paul tells us, that we are in a spiritual battle. "Our struggle is not against flesh and blood, but against the rulers, against the authorities, against the powers of the dark world and against the spiritual forces of evil in the heavenly realms" (Ephesians 6). If unity, oneness, is so important, we can be certain that Satan, the prince of darkness, will do everything he possibly can to undermine and destroy unity and sow seeds of division. Unity must be a matter of prayer in all our churches. It should never be taken for granted. It must also be a priority for the church leadership. It must never be assumed. Unity among the leadership team must be a foundation for any local church. Regularly asking "How are we getting on?" is such an important thing to do, as it implies taking some time to reflect and making sure there are no outstanding issues

Over the years, I've picked up countless stories about church divisions, sometimes over what appear to be the most insignificant of issues. The church divided over the position of a projector and screen because it involved moving a cross. Arguments about the colour of a carpet or the removal of some pews. How is it possible that this global movement committed to changing the world can be reduced to this? But for churches that primarily look inwards, who fail to see the bigger picture, it's so easy to become obsessed with what frankly in the light of eternity is really insignificant. It's in settings such as these that we have to conclude there is very little vision for the future – just a history of what has been. How did churches like these find themselves in such a situation? Was it down to poor leadership, which failed to paint a bigger picture of what could be? Or did these churches kill off effective leadership? Sadly, the history of the UK church in recent years is littered with church leaders, pastors, and vicars who have found themselves worn down and burnt out, unable to bring the leadership they sensed the church needed. Those who have attempted to provide leadership in the context of church know that it's perhaps one of the most challenging settings in which to do this. Fostering the most skilled, equipped, trained, recognized, and empowered leaders in our church has to be the key to ensuring the health of the church here in the UK in the years to come.

Let's also recognize that some of our church structures and models of decision-making do not make leadership easy. The various church traditions all bring with them a variety of approaches, each with a theological framework and history to explain and support it. I would suggest that this is the time to review some of these models, and that perhaps a radical rethink is needed. As one who stands back and observes in some networks and denominations, I can see it's not working. Questions need to be asked when the future direction of a church is decided by a 51-per-cent vote at a church meeting. When a leader is moved on from a church every five years regardless of the condition of the church. When a trustee can overrule an eldership team on the priorities of church expenditure. The church is suffering. Leaders are losing faith and potential leaders are staying well clear.

I'm fascinated by the fact that Jesus only refers to church on two occasions. And on one of these occasions, in Matthew, he does so in the context of church discipline. It's amazing how many churches I've come across that have what I can only call a "shove it under the carpet" approach to church life. So church life works a bit like this: some misunderstanding or disagreement takes place; it might be between two members of the children's work team or worship team. But, rather than sort it out, it gets "shoved under the carpet". Two friends fall out over an invitation to a party. Rather than talking it through, they let it get "shoved under the carpet". I'm sure you get the idea. Of course, after a few years of such an approach to church life, there are whole sections of the church that are impossible to navigate. There are so many unresolved problems and damaged relationships under the carpet. And it's almost impossible to get anything done. Jesus' teaching in Matthew 18 refuses to allow us to get away with this approach to church life. Jesus requires us to have the honest conversation, to bring the issues to light.

> If your brother sins against you, go and tell him his fault, between you and him alone. If he listens to you, you have gained your brother. But if he does not listen, take one or two others along with you, that every charge may be

established by the evidence of two or three witnesses. If he refuses to listen to them, tell it to the church. And if he refuses to listen even to the church, let him be to you as a Gentile and a tax collector.

(Matthew 18:15–17, ESV)

Some use the word "confrontation". I prefer the word "faithfulness". I don't like those hard conversations. I prefer to live a quiet life. But I want to be faithful to those who are part of my church, who I'm in danger of losing relationship with. And I also want to be faithful to Jesus, whose church it is anyway.

Sadly, in some churches, gossip has become a substitute for honest conversation. Rather than speaking directly to the person concerned, we talk to others; we gain their support, their sympathy. Often gossip steals the reputation of the person we're talking about. It's a form of theft and it's certainly not faithfulness. Jesus requires us to start off with just the two people involved. I've discovered that when we start between the two of us, if I go with the right attitude – humble, eager to listen and learn – I often come to the realization that I haven't fully understood the situation. It wasn't quite as I thought it was. I leave with the distinct impression that it's been resolved. Matthew 18 provides us with a framework. If we can't sort it out just between the two of us, we might need others to help, "two or three witnesses". Perhaps even the whole church, or at the very least the part of the church that has been most affected. I'm not convinced we are as faithful to each other as we should be. We so easily make the excuse "Oh, it's not all that important" or "Oh, it doesn't really matter". But maybe it does matter. Perhaps if we were a bit more faithful, some of the jealousies, petty rivalries, and power games that have undermined our churches and challenged our unity would have been nipped in the bud very early. Perhaps some of the moral failures that are so damaging to church life would have been challenged by faithful friends before they destroyed marriages, families, and indeed whole communities.

I remember to this day the phone call, the drive to my friend's house, and then the walk round the block. The previous evening, I'd been at a social gathering and was making my way to the toilet when I looked across and thought I saw, but couldn't quite be sure, a friend of mine almost out of sight. But he seemed to be kissing someone who was not his wife. Was it a figment of my imagination? By the time I returned, there was no one to be seen. But overnight, what I thought I had seen just wouldn't go away. So I was faced with a choice: should I simply ignore it, push it under the carpet, but always wonder; or should I pick up the phone, make a call, and ask to meet him? I chose to call, and as we walked and talked he admitted it had actually happened – my eyes hadn't been deceiving me. He couldn't explain it. He was so sorry. He wanted to sort it out and I could help him do that because I had been willing to face the pain of being faithful to my friend.

Unity, oneness, at a local-church level is not an optional extra to our faith. It sits centre stage. It requires our attention and at times our hard work. Either our relationships (because that's what we're talking about) are part of God's process of drawing us closer to Him and then to each other, or we're being pulled apart. They are practical witnesses to the world that the members of this Christian community really do love each other. The words of Jesus echo in our ears: "By this everyone will know that you are my disciples, if you love one another." When our relationships as a church family do not demonstrate this love, we undermine our message and therefore our saviour.

While my current role at the Evangelical Alliance takes me to many parts of the UK and beyond, and I get to visit a whole variety of churches, I remain a committed member of a local church – a Pioneer church in west London. For me, it's important. My commitment to the local church is not a nice theological principle. It's worked out as part of my everyday life. Around half the year, I'm there at our Sunday gatherings. I'm part of a home group and act as advisor to the leadership team. It's my church and I love it.

Well, perhaps more theologically correct is that it's Jesus' church and it is a wonderful privilege to be part of it.

Questions

- Can you make a list of all the things you love about your church? If you can't, ask God to help you.
- What's your vision for your church? If you're not sure, who can you ask to find out?
- Are you a "shove it under the carpet" kind of Christian, or a "let's sort it out" one? What about your church?
- Are there areas in your relationship in and around church that need sorting out? What are you going to do about it?

Chapter 8

One: In villages, towns, and cities

"The Church must be seen as the company of pilgrims on the way to the end of the world and the end of the earth."
Lesslie Newbigin, *The Household of God: Lectures on the Nature of the Church*

"Society is not to bring its worldliness into the Church, but the Church is meant to bring its godliness into the world."
Michael Cassidy, *The Church Jesus Prayed For*

"Whatever happens, conduct yourselves in a manner worthy of the gospel of Christ. Then, whether I come and see you or only hear about you in my absence, I will know that you stand firm in the one Spirit, striving together as one for the faith of the gospel."
Philippians 1:27

"But I do more than thank. I ask – ask the God of our Master, Jesus Christ, the God of glory – to make you intelligent and discerning in knowing him personally, your eyes focused and clear, so that you can see exactly what it is he is calling you to do, grasp the immensity of this glorious way of life he has for his followers, oh, the utter extravagance of his work in us who trust him – endless energy, boundless strength! All this

energy issues from Christ: God raised him from death and
set him on a throne in deep heaven, in charge of running the
universe, everything from galaxies to governments, no name
and no power exempt from his rule. And not just for the time
being, but forever. He is in charge of it all, has the final word
on everything. At the centre of all this, Christ rules the church.
The church, you see, is not peripheral to the world; the world
is peripheral to the church. The church is Christ's body, in
which he speaks and acts, by which he fills everything with his
presence."
Ephesians 1:18ff., *The Message*

Every Christian believes that the church should be united. I have
yet to meet anyone actively campaigning for a divided church –
although there are some whose behaviour suggests that they might
be. But if we're serious about unity, what does this look like on the
ground? How is unity expressed in towns, villages, and cities where
the theological, practical, and personal challenges of church unity
are played out? How do churches work together for the sake of the
places in which they live?

There is hope

It was early in 2005 and someone had come up with a crazy idea:
that what had happened in London as part of Soul in the City in
July 2004 should be happening all over the country. I have to
confess that my first thought was: *You must be mad.* Soul in the City
had been incredible, but it had nearly killed us. It had consisted
of more than 11,500 delegates from across the country, indeed
across the world, working with 9,500 local churchgoers in fifty-
two partnership churches across thirty-four London boroughs. The
impact had been amazing. Churches that hadn't even known each
other existed before the mission worked together as part of the
event. It saw the young and the old working together, too. There

was such creativity in mission: words and actions put together to proclaim and demonstrate the gospel. We saw more than a thousand people making a response to Jesus. But we were still recovering. How could we do it all again? And how on earth could we possibly do this right across the country?

Though it seemed impossible to me, the idea just would not go away. In fact, it began to gain traction. I'm sure my early reticence was in part due to the fact that I had a sneaky suspicion that if this was going to happen God would want me involved.

Gradually, as 2005 came to an end, there was a growing sense that God was in this. Of course, it couldn't be exactly the same as what had happened in London, but some of the key elements would be the same. It was about the whole church – not just part of the church – working together to see their communities impacted by the love of Jesus. It was about mission being through both words and actions. If this was a God idea, not just a good idea, we needed to test it. So the next months involved loads of conversations with leaders from across the full spectrum of the church: heads of denominations and networks, and influential church leaders. But we also needed to seek the input of heads of key agencies and ministries. If this was of God, we needed the church across the UK to pull together, willing to converge their vision and agenda in a larger collective venture.

As the spring of 2006 arrived, there was a growing sense that we should be going for this crazy vision. The decisive meeting took place in the Birmingham Prayer Centre, right in the heart of the city. We reported back on what we had been hearing. We prayed and we agreed. So it was all systems go and 2008 was to be the year – twelve months of co-ordinated mission. But what would we call it? Some strong voices advocated keeping the Soul in the City brand. But it was clear that this would never work. It was too closely aligned with one city and one ministry. It needed to be a new name – a name the whole church could own. A name filled with possibilities for the future. So it was that "HOPE" was born.

The next two years felt like a whirlwind. A leadership team was put in place. Roy Crowne (who was at Youth for Christ at the time), Mike Pilavachi (Soul Survivor), and Andy Hawthorne (The Message) were at the heart, with others drawn in to provide expertise and energy. If HOPE was to have the impact we were praying for, it needed committed involvement at both a national and a local level. All the indicators were that national leaders were on board. But what about on the ground? We had set ourselves a target of HOPE reaching 500 locations. How on earth would we find and connect with so many leaders? We needed an army of volunteers. Around 150 HOPE champions were recruited whose job it was to promote and support the initiative – at work and on the ground, and also to feed back on what was happening. It was agreed early on that HOPE would not build a large resource base. Although Ian Chisnall was appointed as HOPE national co-ordinator, with a small team around him, we wanted the initiative to be built around volunteers, with churches and organizations donating their services to see the vision realized.

We were also clear from the start that HOPE existed to serve the church, not to dictate to the church. So what happened on the ground was completely up to each church community. They knew far better than we did what their community needed. We gave away the name and the brand identity. We simply asked that if it was to be used, it would be because they were "doing more, doing it together, and doing it in words and actions". This non-prescriptive approach proved to be strategically significant. A HOPE resource book was produced and sold almost 30,000 copies, giving a menu of what the church could choose to do. It gave the national ministries and agencies an opportunity to spell out how they could support the church, alongside lots of other agencies with similarly great ideas. In the end, 155 associate groups registered with HOPE to support the year of mission. One of the building blocks of the HOPE resource book was to support churches in using the church calendar to provide high points. Resources were produced which could be used to galvanize mission. Easter, Pentecost, and Christmas were three obvious starters, but "Fresh Hope" in January and "Hope Explored" in September were also developed.

One of the lessons we had learned from Soul in the City and encouraged in HOPE was to engage with local councils and the police. Early approaches were appreciated and resulted in greater opportunities for joined-up activities and greater impact. I'm also convinced that a significant reason for the impact of HOPE was the wonderful prayer cover, which supported and underpinned all the planning and indeed continued throughout the year. HOPE was launched at an enormous prayer event at the Birmingham NEC, and Jane Holloway and the national prayer networks got behind it from the very start until the finish.

We had no idea what was going to happen in 2008 and, as the 2007 countdown flew by, we could only hope that the word-and-action vision was getting out there. The first few months of 2008 were a revelation. We had dreamed of 500 locations getting involved, but it turned out that about three times that many had signed up. As the year progressed, there was a growing sense of being caught up in something much bigger than any of us could have predicted. And then the invitations started to come in. It was an honour to stand at Downing Street listening to the prime minister extol the virtues of HOPE, and to introduce Prince Charles to the HOPE champions at Clarence House. It was at times like these that we realized this was never our project to control.

Downing Street and Clarence House were fun. But what got me more excited was when the stories began to come in. This is what we had been hoping and praying for. We began to hear reports of big citywide events drawing together thousands of people, alongside small-scale home-group activities reaching just a handful. The churches in Loughborough managed to get themselves into the *Guinness Book of World Records* with an enormous painting-by-numbers depicting the Easter event. Placed in a prominent site on the edge of the town centre, this enormous piece of art measured 25x7 metres and needed two miles of scaffolding to hold it in position. It was painted by around 2,000 people from right across the community, including schools, churches, and community groups. The story of Easter became the talking point of the town.

Easter became a focal point of church activities in the HOPE year, with Passion plays, prayer walks, art exhibitions, a mass blood-donation campaign, and a large-scale outdoor public baptism.

In Manchester, an enormous schools mission took place, with 100 secondary schools participating and 100,000 pupils reached. In Bradford, more than thirty churches worked together and hired a banqueting suite at Bradford City FC. Some 600 people turned up to enjoy live music and a meal, and to hear Wayne Jacobs, the Bradford City coach at the time, share his testimony and invite guests to sign up to Alpha, Christianity Explored, or the NOOMA course. In Cardiff, May 2008 saw close to 500 young people donating three days of their time to throw their lot into Ignite Hope; 6,500 hours of kindness were contributed to the local community and 800 young people attended a citywide gathering for music, worship, and teaching. In Ramsgate, all the churches participating in HOPE decided to focus on one social housing estate. In Bilston, fifteen young people donated their time to transform their run-down community centre. As far as the church across the UK was concerned, 2008 was an amazing year of creativity. Fun days, cake-baking, prayer stalls, garden makeovers, street parties, parenting courses, film nights... the list is endless. As the year came to an end, the Archbishop of Canterbury thanked those involved in HOPE for "waking the sleeping giant", the church.

As a church leader, I've experienced first-hand what can feel like enormous pressure from Christian agencies, ministries, and charities to connect my church with their work, latest initiative, or event. For almost every Sunday of the year, there's an opportunity to have a special church service which focuses on a particular area of opportunity or need. Getting the balance right is not easy; these amazing ministries desperately want to connect with the

Christian community, and the local church is the most obvious route. So, as a church leader bombarded with requests, you'd feel like the miserable gatekeeper who keeps saying "no". One of the great lessons I learned from HOPE and indeed replicated in the "Unity Movement" has been the mantra "We exist to serve the local church". The resource book, the website, and the email communications all indicated clearly what the agencies or ministries could offer the church: their expertise, material, personnel. But it was up to the church to decide what would work in their situation. This non-prescriptive, servant-hearted approach became a key value of HOPE and in fact we ask it to be so of all the agencies that work with us.

As 2008 came to an end, we were deeply thankful to God and indeed to all those who had made 2008 possible. As far as we were concerned, that was it. A report was commissioned by Theos, the public think tank, to evaluate HOPE and to celebrate what was achieved and learn lessons for the future. The office was closed down and we got back to "life as usual". God had other things in mind, however, and by mid-2009 further conversations were taking place about HOPE continuing towards 2014 and possibly beyond. And Roy Crowne had agreed to take on the leadership role.

A taste of things to come

As I travelled the country in my role as chair of HOPE 08, I found it enormously encouraging to see all the activities that were going on. But somehow I sensed there was more than met the eye. Something was happening below the radar, which I couldn't quite put my finger on. It was a conversation with Roger Sutton, the minister of Altrincham Baptist Church, that took me to the next stage. He was on sabbatical at the time and asking questions about his future. At the end of the conversation I asked Roger to contact me when his sabbatical was over as I wondered whether we were meant to be working together. I can't remember ever saying this to anybody in the past. It was as a result of this conversation that

Roger joined us at the Evangelical Alliance and we began to explore whether something was happening across the UK beyond simply a willingness of churches to work constructively together. As we were to discover, an amazing picture was unfolding. Very quickly, Roger began to report back on what we started to call "unity movements". The practical outworking varied from place to place but there were some common factors. These unity movements involved Christian leaders – not just church leaders but leaders in business, charities, social concerns, education, and healthcare.

Here were leaders building relationships with each other. Some had been together for years. The relationship-building usually involved praying together and eating together. Friendships were being nurtured, trust was being built, and out of these relationships a passion for their town and city was emerging – a desire to see transformation, physically, socially, and spiritually. God was beginning to give these leaders prophetic insights into His heart for their community. There was also a growing realization that God was interested in every square millimetre of their area; every activity, every institution, every relationship, all that was going on, either for good or for ill. It implied that if God was interested, they were meant to be too. They couldn't be concerned just about their church or indeed the churches of the city. They were called to be agents of the kingdom. Stories began to emerge of key pioneers in these unity movements: Dave King in Salford was just one of these.

In recent years, Salford has seen a return to its heyday, and so has the church in the city. At the heart of the city's heritage lie Salford Docks, which were opened in 1894 by Queen Victoria and used to be one of the country's busiest ports. Before they closed in the early 1980s, the docks employed around 5,000 people. When the port started to decline in the 1970s because it could no longer accommodate the larger modern container ships, the city changed. Instead of a spirit of pride in the city, there was a spirit of inadequacy.

Dave King, who runs Kingdom Voice Limited and works to unite churches across the city, knows Salford better than most. His father had been praying for the city for more than forty-five years and then the baton was passed to Dave. "I was always brought up to believe that, because I came from Salford, I would never become anything. I always believed that I wasn't worth much."

The city is an area of high deprivation. Government figures in 2011 showed that it ranked in the top twenty worst areas in the country – joint fourteenth with Burnley – for indicators such as poverty and unemployment. The city sees high levels of crime and children failing in education. Dave said he felt challenged by God in the late 1990s to see the church as responsible, and that what was needed was a renewed sense of unity in order to bring hope to the area. "God asked me what the most dysfunctional family in Salford was. I was thinking of big crime families," said Dave, who spoke at one of our Evangelical Alliance conferences in 2012. "But what God said to me was that the church was the biggest dysfunctional family in the city." Churches in Salford were not functioning in unity and so the wake-up call led Dave to work hard to bring the churches together. "God had said to me that people may look to the government, but that His church was the role model family for this city. God was also clearly saying that we should welcome new churches into the city because really there is only one church. We encouraged everyone in the city not to see themselves as isolated cases, but to work together in oneness."

Alongside the renewed sense of unity, which is beginning to bear fruit, have come a regeneration and a rejuvenation of the Salford area. The past few years have seen the redevelopment of Salford Quays, with media organizations such as the BBC moving into the neighbourhood. One of the leaders of a new church in Salford, Victory Outreach, is Pastor Paul Lloyd, who has seen drug addicts, alcoholics, and gang members have their lives completely transformed through its ministry. He commented recently, "If you change the spiritual atmosphere in the city, the church will grow. That's God's economy. Jesus hasn't got many churches. We are one church."

As these unity movements began to emerge and take shape, they brought fresh focus and clarity. Some indeed continued to be Churches Together groups, or local evangelical fellowships (LEFs), or just groups of friends meeting together. In Southampton, three leadership gatherings – Southampton Christian Network, the Churches Together group, and Southampton Pastors Network – came together to form Love Southampton. In that city the church has developed a close relationship with the local council.

Illustrious Southampton, known historically for its bustling trade, job creation, and being the place from which the *Titanic* set sail, has experienced setbacks in recent years. The closure of the Ford assembly plant, a vital source of employment for many since 1939, was just one of those setbacks. Alongside higher levels of job insecurity, the local authority in Southampton was facing a serious funding crisis. Programmes were under threat, something which could have spelled a future with no libraries or youth clubs, no potholes filled in, and no bins emptied. Southampton's council responded, adopting a vision statement that the place would be "good to grow up in and good to grow old in". The churches in the city committed themselves to working together and in partnership with the council in helping it prosper once again and to seeing that vision become reality.

Of course, the church is no stranger to social action and serving the local community. In fact, in 1925 a sign on the part-built Southampton Methodist Central Hall called for workers, not in construction, but for volunteers in maternity care and Boys' and Girls' Brigades, and to assist with food and clothing provision.

In the wake of the cutbacks, £25 million worth of funding and 300 jobs went in just one year, and the council turned to the local churches for help. Key leaders heard from the council that all the youth workers employed by the city would lose their jobs and the children's centres were under threat. A meeting about the cuts was held for church and community leaders and attended by around

400 people. It seemed as if this was a significant opportunity for the church to respond and to make an impact. The churches realized that between them they had seventeen paid youth workers and thirty-seven mother and toddler groups. These were resources and opportunities to serve the wider community. Several working groups were formed to explore ways of addressing the particular areas of need, including open-access youth provision, work with under-fives, fostering and adoption, post-sixteen housing, and hardship. A commitment was made to twenty-one days of prayer, and practical responses were also made. The churches managed to keep the youth service open.

"We all committed to twenty-one days of prayer and then we got practical," commented Paul Woodman, a church leader in the city. "We've managed to keep open the youth services that were to close; youth drop-in centres are open for more sessions, and we've increased output and help for families. Churches are more engaged and the city council has saved a lot of money. I have built stronger personal links with other church leaders when working together in niche and practical ways, like looking hard to find foster carers, rather than planning a basic church event. Unity for a purpose."

Local government had spent £1.2 million a year paying agencies to search for families able to provide a home for vulnerable children in need of foster care or adoption. By establishing Families for Forty, the churches committed to finding the council more foster carers. Within fifteen months more than seventy people have applied to become foster carers. The Alliance's Home for Good initiative, learning from the success of Southampton, is now working with churches across the UK to achieve the same goal.

These stories can be replicated in so many places across the UK. I wish I had time and space to tell them all. Out of the relationships, prayer, and prophetic insights have come shared activities. Many of the HOPE 08 citywide activities were initiated and overseen by these unity movements. Indeed, in Swansea, the unity movement adopted the name and became Swansea Hope.

As Roger Sutton and I spoke, it became clear to us that God was at work. And that we were waking up to what He was already doing. I've personally found that a far better way of working over the years. I've tried the other way – me coming up with a great idea and then inviting God to get involved. Somehow it doesn't work. What was happening in Salford and Southampton was happening all over the UK but there was little if any communication or shared learning, and most of the city unity movements were oblivious to what was happening elsewhere.

So it was that Gather was launched as an expression of the Evangelical Alliance's passionate commitment to unity. The aim was to support and cheer on these unity movements where they already existed, and also to catalyse new movements into existence in places where at present none could be found. Currently, the Gather network consists of over 120 unity movements. In many places these movements are doing locally what the Evangelical Alliance is doing nationally, but on a smaller scale. Over the last four or five years, I've had the privilege of visiting many of these cities and hearing first-hand what's going on. I've valued getting an experience of the depth of relationship that has been nurtured between the Christian leaders. I love the fact that in Chester the churches have agreed that if a church member moves from one church to another, the church leaders will have a conversation before the new church welcomes the person into membership. I love the fact that in York, every Wednesday morning at 7.45, thirty-five to forty-five church leaders meet for prayer and breakfast, and they've been doing it for the last eighteen years. I love the fact that in Croydon church leaders meet three times a year with the leader and chief executive of Croydon Council and ask them what they think is the biggest need in the town. I love the fact that, in Liverpool, the churches of the city are responding to the Talking Jesus research and asking the question together: How do we together work to make Jesus known in our region? I love the fact that more and more initiatives such as Christians Against Poverty, Street Pastors, foodbanks, night shelters, healing on the streets, city-centre chaplaincies, work among young people, the elderly, and the disabled, and employment schemes are going on thanks to the church on the ground. And they're not being run by one church but by many.

This kind of unity does not come without a price tag. As I talk to those who are involved in unity movements, I am reminded that unity is not always easy. There are barriers to overcome, issues to be worked through. In some cities, there has been a history of broken relationships and historical pain that has had to be addressed. It's amazing how the prospect of unity can bring things to the surface. In at least one city I can think of there's been a catalogue of broken relationships among leaders, and this has had a significant impact on the efforts for unity across the city. Some cities have had to work through how unity can be expressed when those of different theological persuasions are around the table, with differing views on women's ministry, human sexuality, the prosperity gospel, the place of the Catholic Church, styles of worship, and gifts of the Spirit. These have required sensitive yet honest conversations. At times it has meant compromise for the sake of unity. But at other times there has been a recognition that, while we can do certain activities together, we cannot unite on all things. In some cities, the smaller and medium-sized churches have found it more difficult to draw in the larger churches, which often have so much going on in and around them that they question the need for joint action.

Drawing in the migrant church leaders has also proved very challenging in many city unity movements. For example, meeting times can present a practical problem, as the migrant church leaders are often also holding down a day job. But there are also lessons to be learned from our experience nationally with the One People Commission, where relationships have to be invested in. Time and commitment are needed. Time and commitment are always an issue for busy leaders. If unity across the city does not become a priority for those at the heart of the unity movement, it will simply become just another diary commitment that can be dropped if a better or more important option comes along.

Many of the unity movements include leaders not just from the church but from key areas of influence right across the city or town. True transformation means that the voice of Christian leaders – not just church leaders – must be heard so that they are able to influence the direction of the unity movements and indeed be supported in their work in the city.

The challenge of unity is particularly marked in the large metropolitan cities such as London and Manchester, where borough-wide unity movements exist and are often vibrant. What a unity movement looks like across London as a whole is an issue some of us have been working on for a while. At present, a network of networks exists, wanting to avoid placing yet more demands on the leaders of the boroughs. This network of networks only meets two or three times a year and focuses on one area – the relationship with the Metropolitan Police Service.

These unity movements require leadership. All of the Gather networks that I have visited have involved a small team who have been anointed and appointed to bring leadership. Without leadership, it's very easy for focus to be lost and for drift to occur. When and if leadership changes, it's vital that new leadership is put in place to carry the respect of the Christian leaders within the movement.

Finally, while the growing respect and relationship that has developed between the church and the civic authorities over the last few years is important and encouraging, care needs to be taken that we are not simply becoming a convenient and cheap means of helping local authorities overcome the implications of austerity. Ultimately, our allegiance is to God's agenda for the city, not that of any local politician or chief executive. Our notion of transformation includes spiritual transformation. We can bring to the city and town what nobody else can bring – the gospel of Jesus Christ.

So, thank God for all that's happened in towns and cities across the UK. Thank God that increasingly we are seeing ourselves as part of one church in the city. While we remain Anglican, Baptist, Pentecostal, Methodist, new-church, or whatever, our denominational branding must not overwhelm our view of ourselves. We are, after all, the family of God in Liverpool, Swansea, Cardiff, Glasgow, Belfast, Southampton, York, Hull, Grimsby, Lincoln, Peterborough, Oxford, Bristol, Reading, Doncaster, Newcastle, Middlesbrough, Sunderland, Bradford, Leeds…

Questions

- Do you know the top three needs of your town or city?
- Is there a unity movement where you live? Do you know what its focus is?
- What would transformation look like where you live, physically, socially, and spiritually? Imagine what your town or city could look like in 2050.
- Do you pray for your city or town and those who are bringing leadership to it?

Note

Through the inspired leadership of Roy Crowne, HOPE continues building on what was achieved in 2008, providing models of what effective mission can look like – motivating and equipping Christians to reach out effectively to their communities: www.hopetogether.org.uk

The Gather network continues to grow, enabled and supported by the Evangelical Alliance, under the leadership of Roger Sutton – similar relationships are now being built with unity movements around the world. Details of resources and events are available via the Gather website: www.gather.global

Chapter 9

One: Men and women

"Joy is a gigantic secret of the Christian."
G. K. Chesterton, *Orthodoxy* (1908)

"May the Lord make your love increase and overflow for each other and for everyone else, just as ours does for you."
1 Thessalonians 3:12

"Perhaps it is no wonder that the women were first at the Cradle and last at the Cross. They had never known a man like this Man – there never has been another. A prophet and teacher who never nagged at them, never flattered or coaxed or patronised; who never made arch jokes about them, never treated them as 'The women, God help us!' or 'The ladies, God bless them!'; who rebuked without querulousness and praised without condescension; who took their questions and arguments seriously; who never mapped out their sphere for them, never urged them to be feminine or jeered at them for being female; who had no axe to grind and no uneasy male dignity to defend; who took them as he found them and was completely unselfconscious. There is no act, no sermon, no parable in the whole Gospel that borrows its pungency from female perversity; nobody could guess from the words and deeds of Jesus that there was anything 'funny' about woman's nature."
Dorothy L. Sayers, *Are Women Human? Astute and Witty Essays on the Role of Women in Society*

As people entered the auditorium, the stewards graciously but firmly directed them to their seats. But there was something strange going on. All the men and boys were directed to the front and the women and girls to the back. People were a little confused, but obediently sat where they were told. We were at a Pioneer conference in a large holiday park in North Wales and this was our evening celebration. The evening service started. I gave a welcome and prayed, the all-male band took up their positions, and the worship began. There was a distinct air of confusion emanating from the congregation. After about ten minutes, at a quiet moment, a male voice came from the side. "This isn't right," he said. "What's going on?" And then a female voice joined in from the back: "I don't like this. We shouldn't be seated like this." Other voices began to be heard, no longer pre-planned. Fingers were pointed. Arms were raised. Others wanted to speak. It was then that I took the mic. I attempted to bring some order, but the disruption continued. Eventually, after two or three minutes, I asked everyone to take their seats. We needed to stop the meeting. It was time to explain.

It had been a risky strategy and we had wondered whether we would be able to pull it off. We explained to the congregation that what they had just experienced – before the interruption – was Jesus' weekly reality as He grew up. The front half of the synagogue occupied by men, who were the ones leading, speaking, and teaching. Meanwhile, women were at the back – silent. An afterthought. Unable to contribute.

The culture that surrounded Jesus in His childhood and early adult years was a patriarchal one in which women were second-class citizens and had few rights but lots of responsibilities. So we suggested to the congregation that they might consider how radical Jesus' ministry was in the light of this.

It was Jesus who had women as part of His travelling band; women who indeed supported His ministry with their finances. Jesus whose very first mass evangelist was not only a woman, but a Samaritan woman. Jesus who encouraged a woman to stop her domestic work and to listen to His teaching. It was a woman who touched the rabbi and was healed. A woman who anointed Him with oil in preparation for His burial. There was a crowd of women around the cross as He died. It was to a woman that Jesus first appeared, following His resurrection. She became the first witness to the watershed of human history.

By this stage, the room was silent. We asked people to look around – to see the great divide. We read a passage from Scripture, from Galatians 3: "So in Christ Jesus you are all children of God through faith, for all of you who were baptized into Christ have clothed yourselves with Christ. There is neither Jew nor Gentile, neither slave nor free, nor is there male and female, for you are all one in Christ Jesus."

As the meeting continued, we encouraged everyone to start moving around the room. To mix it all up. To shake hands, to embrace, to pray with each other. Women came up onto the stage and joined the worship band. Women started to join in leading the meeting. The atmosphere was electric. We hadn't just opened Scripture, or indeed had teaching on unity in the body of Christ; we had experienced it. The radical nature of the life and ministry of Jesus had been brought home to us first-hand.

The big picture

The role of women and men in the life and ministry of Jesus, and the life of the early church, remains an issue of disagreement. However, when we come to how women are treated around the globe, surely there can be no grounds for disagreement. My friend and hero Elaine Storkey, in her recently published book *Scars Across Humanity*,[1] has provided us with a harrowing overview of our world's propensity to inflict an appalling level of violence on women. Of course, when I say our world, I mean in the main my gender: men. It is devastating to think how women are subjected to a long list of injustices: the sex trade and rape as weapons of war, forced marriage, honour killings, domestic violence, selective abortion, infanticide, female genital mutilation. The list goes on. Elaine refuses to accept the commonly held view within academic circles that this violence should be seen as part of the evolutionary process; that we have a selfish gene and that we can't do anything about it. She argues, "Above all, we need a theological framework in which to understand why violence against women happens. Our theological framework is creation and sin. We are made in the image of God to serve and love one another, but sin screws that all up…"

"For me," says Elaine, "the beauty about the Christian analysis is that sin never has the final word because there's always the possibility of redemption."[2]

The Christian charity Restored is an international alliance working to transform relationships and end violence against women. They provide us with shocking statistics. Globally, one in three women have experienced psychological, abusive behaviour on the part of an intimate partner. One in twenty have been raped since the age of fifteen, while in the UK 1,000 women are sexually assaulted every day. On average, 85,000 women are raped in England and Wales every year. Two women a week are murdered by their partner or former partner. And it's starting young. Four in ten teenage girls have experienced sexual coercion. Twenty-five per cent of young women aged thirteen and over have experienced physical violence; 72 per cent emotional abuse in their relationships.[3] And it's happening in our churches as well. The Evangelical Alliance survey "How's the Family?" in 2012 reported that 20 per cent of the women answering the survey had experienced physical abuse in their relationships, with 7 per cent of the men surveyed admitting they had perpetrated physical abuse. These are evangelical Christians.[4]

As we step back and consider these "scars across humanity", we have to conclude that this unequal battle, which has rendered half of humanity vulnerable to the abusive power of the other half, must reflect an enormous cosmic, spiritual conflict. This is not, in the words of the apostle Paul, simply a "flesh and blood" conflict. It's far more than that. Genesis 1:27 recalls the high point of creation.

On day six "God created mankind in his own image, in the image of God he created them; male and female he created them".

We are then told, "God saw all that he had made and it was very good." It's as if God stands back and admires His workmanship. Not just good, but very good. Of course, the events that follow take us down a pathway that we know as the Fall; humanity turning its back on the loving creator God. The outcome of that decision is the world we have today. In our fallen world, men and women made in the image of God live with sin still at work undermining, eroding, and destroying that precious relationship – that high point of creation. Elaine Storkey comments, "There has been a lot of misappropriation of the Bible in relation to women. But there has also been the opposite. Christianity has looked after women and raised their dignity; and that story has to be told as well."

Back story

The global story of how women have been treated and indeed continue to be treated must sober us as we consider the role of men and women in the church, which continues to be a focus of significant disagreement across the worldwide church and indeed among evangelicals. After an extraordinarily lengthy process, the Anglican Communion in England has negotiated a compromise regarding women bishops – the issue of women priests having been settled a few years earlier. Within evangelical churches, our research indicates that just over 70 per cent agree that women should be eligible for all roles within the church in the same way as men (9 per cent were unsure and only 20 per cent disagreed).

Most of the large evangelical denominations would now recognize women in all areas of leadership and ministry, although some remain theologically unconvinced. As the Evangelical Alliance, we have not taken a position in this theological debate. And indeed this is not the time or the place to enter into the theological merits of both positions. While I personally am an egalitarian and would be supportive – indeed encouraging – of women in all areas of leadership and ministry, the

Alliance has council members and contributors to our work who are complementarians and would as a matter of conscience and biblical interpretation limit women's leadership roles.

Holding this line of respectful disagreement as an organization whose very aim is unity is not without its challenges – not least in that every area of the Alliance has women in significant positions of leadership and ministry: directors, board members, council members, contributors as writers, and those in public ministry. I'm also aware that, on the occasions when this topic is discussed, for some – usually men, but not exclusively so – it can be addressed as a "matter of biblical interpretation" and of being true to Scripture. But for some the matter is far more personal. If, as a woman convinced that God has called you to leadership, to preaching, and to Bible teaching, you're exposed to such a discussion, particularly if conducted in an unhelpful manner, it is obvious that you might feel undermined. Your gifting and calling are being questioned. On more than one occasion, it has been necessary for us to address these issues and help the man who has lacked sensitivity or indeed grace to realize the impact of his comments. Indeed, it's amazing how men, in attempting to compliment a woman, can end up undermining her. I sat recently with a group of women leaders and listened with shock to their experiences within the context of church and the wider evangelical community. Very graciously, they told stories of being ignored, patronized, and put down. Here were serious leaders with a catalogue of horror stories going back decades (and in some cases continuing today) of how men had treated them.

Examples include a woman Bible teacher, who, after an amazingly insightful Bible exposition, was told by a senior evangelical leader that, although he didn't believe in women in ministry, what she had done was really good; and women leaders being ignored or left sitting on their own at social gatherings while chairs are filled up at other tables around the room. And comments made which were intended to be humorous but were in fact condescending or downright hurtful.

My personal journey

I spent my first years as a Christian pretty much oblivious to any controversy surrounding women in leadership. Youth With A Mission, with which I worked in Scandinavia, had women in leadership and it never seemed to be up for discussion. Mission agencies seem over the years to have been gender-blind, with women found at every level of responsibility. It was only when the female missionaries came home that the restrictions began to be imposed. It was when I arrived at London Bible College (LBC) – London School of Theology as it is now – that I woke up to the potential problem. As with all areas of controversy, theological colleges became a place where such issues were aired with much passion, perhaps at times not enough knowledge, and certainly a lack of wisdom. I reflect now on how hard it must have been for the women who were part of the college to be exposed to this debating.

Here were women preparing for ministry, sensing that God had called them to it, but being faced with a barrage of arguments questioning the legitimacy of that calling. Within a few years of leaving LBC, Ann and I had made our home in the Pioneer house-church network. Pioneer had been significantly influenced by the Brethren movement and, although many new-church leaders had left the Brethren over the question of the gifts of the Holy Spirit, Brethren theology still held sway over aspects of their understanding of church life. So, as we arrived at Cobham Christian Fellowship, the leadership was definitely male. Eldership within Pioneer as the 1980s progressed was for only one gender. Women were excluded. Women were on occasions given some platform time to speak, but it was the exception rather than the rule. As I look back now I realize I was never completely comfortable with this model of church life. It didn't seem to run true to the whole spectrum of the biblical narrative, although there were New Testament passages that could be quoted (and indeed quite regularly were) to support that position.

This model continued until the late 1980s, when Gerald Coates – the team leader of the Pioneer network – and his emerging team agreed that a biblical review should consider the situation. Roger Forster, a fellow new-church leader who founded the Ichthus Network, had always advocated an egalitarian position. And his theological reflections alongside the views of other theologians won the day and a change of position was agreed.

This was not an overnight revolution. In fact, the impact of that change of position is still working itself out within Pioneer today. The fresh insights from Scripture were brought to various leadership conferences across the network. It was taught as part of Pioneer leadership training programmes. Leadership teams, which were at the time exclusively male, were asked to consider the teaching. From the start it was made clear that this would not be a matter of fellowship. In other words, if leadership teams came to the conclusion that they could not go down this path, Pioneer would respect that decision and no pressure for change would be exerted.

But gradually, incrementally, change began to happen. Women started to join leadership teams and indeed the national Pioneer team. Leadership conferences profiled women speakers and the Pioneer magazine told stories of women taking up positions of responsibility. The story told at the beginning of this chapter was part of this process. By the mid-1990s, a church that I was overseeing became the first to appoint a woman as the senior church leader. This was a breakthrough.

Behind the scenes, however, there was another story to be told. After a few years of married life, I began to sense God pointing His finger at a specific area of my relationship with Ann. As you've read in a previous chapter, for Ann and me, building oneness in our marriage was a challenge which needed significant attention and the support of close friends. As this process continued, I began to sense a niggling feeling as if God were wanting to challenge an aspect of how I related to Ann. I realized that when it came to a disagreement or conflict and I was in danger of losing the argument, there was a biblical weapon that I would on occasion throw into the mix. It would stop a discussion, close down the debate. It was "game, set, and match". It didn't happen all the time, but it was a weapon of last resort. "Wives, submit yourselves to your own husbands as you do to the Lord" (Ephesians 5:22). Of course, it is there in Scripture and it's God's word, but Scripture was never meant to be used that way. And anyway, I failed to recognize the significance of the verse that precedes it – a verse which puts the whole passage into context: "Submit to one another out of reverence for Christ." And, perhaps even more challenging, further down the page: "Husbands, love your wives, just as Christ loved the church and gave himself for her" (verse 25).

As this niggling turned into a conviction, I realized I needed to repent of this way of relating. I didn't want to use Scripture as a weapon; I wanted it to shape me and challenge me, and I wanted it to shape and challenge our marriage. I wanted to recognize that it was God who had brought us together, each with our own God-given strengths, weaknesses, skills, and callings. We had contributions to make, roles to fulfil, but we were a team – called to be "one" within our marriage.

I am so thankful for God's intervention in this area of my life, for not only did it do wonders for our marriage, but I suspect it prepared me for my relationship with Jordan, my daughter.

Jordan is now a married woman with a successful professional career. During her childhood and teenage years, any suspicion of inequality in my treatment of her would, I suspect, have done serious damage to our relationship. With both of our children, rituals developed which reflected their interests and personality types. With Jake, they involved many different kinds of sport, which we would participate in together. With Jordan, although she loved her gymnastics, it was father-and-daughter time – either walking the dog, or having a coffee in the local coffee shop. We would sit there for ages, chatting away, putting the world to rights. It was during one of these chats that we were discussing which church she might connect with when she went to university. I outlined a couple of churches that I knew well and which I thought she might wish to explore. During the course of my description, I happened to mention that one of these churches didn't believe in women in leadership. I can remember to this day the look on her face and the shaking of her head.

"It's very important", she said, "if you join a church, that you read the small print." For Jordan, it was inconceivable that she could consider joining such a church.

More than words: Women in leadership in practice

As we talk about some of the practical aspects of men and women working together, my experience is inevitably drawn primarily to the context of church and Christian organizations. It's good, however, for Christian leaders to stop and reflect on the challenge faced by both male and female members of our churches in responding to life in a world outside the church; a world which, despite legislation, still seems to have in some professions a glass ceiling – for both promotion and equality of pay and conditions. A world where sexist attitudes are still accommodated as part of corporate culture. A world where women still seem to occupy a disproportionately large percentage of the poorest-paid jobs in our society. A world where the opportunity to get into trouble with relationships cannot be avoided as the expectations of the company demand hospitality and shared hotels and travel arrangements. This is a world where the biblical world view is not shared and as a Christian you can appear abnormal. As church leaders, we of course have our own challenges to face. But let's consider how we can support those who are often on the front line of the spiritual battle in their workplace.

Over the years, I have supported three women who have taken on senior leadership roles in Pioneer churches. Their situations are very different but there have been common experiences and lessons learned. Ness Wilson leads Open Heaven Church in Loughborough. What started as a student church twenty years ago, based on and around the campus, is now an all-age church, meeting with two expressions – a gathering for eighteen- to thirty-year-olds and one for children and families. More than 1,300 people have been part of Open Heaven during the last twenty years.

Linda Ward became a Christian as a student and, after connecting with Ealing Christian Fellowship, she was sent for theological and practical training and employed as a schools worker. She went on to merge Ealing Christian Fellowship (ECF) and Bridge Church, Brentford, into Bless Church, becoming the senior leader. This merger required major manoeuvring, including navigating different views of women in leadership in one of the churches, which could have jeopardized the whole project if theological positions had become a sticking point. Linda leads the church of which Ann and I are now members, as well as the West London Leaders Network, which has more than 130 leaders, churches, and ministries meaningfully connecting across the spectrum of theological persuasions.

Jackie Oliver took over the leading of Generation Church in Ewell, Surrey, from her husband Ian. The church had grown and developed in and around their home. Ian had led the church but eventually Jackie joined the leadership team and as it became obvious that it was time for Ian to hand on the leadership, it also became clear that Jackie was the person who should be recognized as the "leadership team's leader" – the senior leader.

While the anointing for leadership was clearly on all three women, practical challenges needed to be faced and overcome. For both Linda and Ness, providing leadership while carrying out the duties of motherhood required careful planning. While both had enormously supportive husbands, the primary responsibility for childcare in the pre-school years fell on them. Diaries needed to be planned well; leadership meetings with children present were sometimes necessary. Working hours had to be flexible and the churches had to be adaptable. Ness recently calculated that, over the last thirteen years, nine babies have been brought to the leadership team meetings. This means that more meetings than not have had a baby present, often being discreetly breastfed while the conversations, discussions, and decisions took place. The process of returning after maternity leave can also prove a challenge for some. Along with the practical aspects can come issues of confidence and even motivation. Ness told me recently, "My reflection is that a gifted woman needs a strong resolve or determination made before children come along that she will 'get back into the game' once time allows."

For Linda and Jackie, taking on the leadership of an existing team brought its own challenges. Bringing about a change in leadership culture is not achieved overnight. In fact, it can take years. In their cases it involved conducting leadership meetings in a way that worked for them, challenging old ways of doing business, refusing to be intimidated by older, more established males. Both Ness and Linda were faced with enormous difficulties in their personal life while continuing to bring leadership to their churches. Serious family illness and death had to be faced and dealt with. For Ness, building a leadership team from among fellow graduates carried its own difficulties, as they came from different church backgrounds and had a variety of views on how churches should be led. At a town-wide church leadership level, the early days were particularly difficult. Who was this young woman with this random group of students? Some leaders were opposed to women in leadership, full stop. Others couldn't get their head around Open Heaven reaching some of the students they had hoped would be joining their congregations. It's a testament to Ness's leadership that she has over the years built strong relationships with leaders across the town, and would be regarded by many as one of the most influential leaders in that town.

In fact, both Linda and Ness have become significant catalysts for unity in the areas in which they live. They have built relationships. They have stood the test of time. And they have proved that their leadership gifting has extended beyond simply their own church.

Church leadership is one of the most challenging of all leadership contexts. All three women have navigated the ups and downs of leadership. They have negotiated new ways of providing leadership. They have gained the backing and loyalty of their male fellow leaders and also of female members of the church, who can at times find it difficult being led by a fellow woman.

As a leader in the church and within wider ministry, I have myself worked in numerous teams alongside women leaders. All kinds of practical lessons have emerged. Openness and honesty have to be paramount. In our mixed leadership teams at the Alliance, we have often asked each other the question: How are we getting on together? It's a great question for teams to ask on a regular basis. In fact, we set ourselves some expectations and review how we're doing against those expectations. Women members have fed back on what it's like being in a team with more men than women. Practical matters have been discussed, such as how we sit in meetings. I have challenged women in teams to try hard not to sit together. How do we travel to and from meetings? What happens at the hotel bar? How do we handle discussion? Do we interrupt? What about confrontation? What about tears? And how do we socialize together?

On the Board of the Evangelical Alliance is an expert in research and polling, who works for a nationally known polling company. She also happens to be a mum with a young child. We wanted her with us for our Board's annual retreat. So the baby came too. If we're serious about women in leadership roles, we have to be flexible. If we're serious about women in leadership roles, husbands need to be willing to stand up and be counted when it comes to childcare.

A vision for the future

Whatever conclusions we come to about the biblical parameters for women and men in leadership and ministry, surely we can all share the aspiration to see all people flourish within their God-given calling? In the churches and ministries I have led, I have been – and indeed continue to be – enriched as men and women together are given the space and respect to make their contributions. I have discovered that men on their own are not enough; as indeed women on their own are not. There is something in our togetherness, in our unity, in our oneness that best reflects the God we serve. "In the image of God he created them, men and women he created them."

We need each other to reflect God adequately to the world. Paul puts it like this in 1 Corinthians 1:11–12: "Nevertheless, in the Lord woman is not independent of man, nor is man independent of woman. For as woman came from man, so also man is born of woman. But everything comes from God."

We were never meant to do it on our own. We are interdependent. We need each other.

Questions

- Whether you are a man or a woman reading this chapter, have you sensed God challenging you on how you relate to the opposite sex?
- Whether you or your church believe in women in leadership, are there steps that you could take to ensure the voice and influence of women is maximized and that any unhelpful behaviour is challenged?
- If you are working in a mixed-gender team, have you ever had an honest conversation about how well you work together?
- As husbands and wives, have you had the conversation recently about how well you are getting on?

Chapter 10

One: Across all ethnic expressions

"Joy is the serious business of heaven."
C. S. Lewis, *Letters to Malcolm*

"So in Christ Jesus, you are all children of God through faith. For all of you who were baptized into Christ have clothed yourself with Christ. There is neither Jew nor Gentile, neither slave nor free, nor is there male and female, for you are all one in Christ Jesus. If you belong to Christ, then you are Abraham's seed, and heirs according to the promise."
Galatians 3:26-29

"It is simply impossible, with any shred of Christian integrity, to go on proclaiming that Jesus by his cross has abolished the old divisions, and created a single humanity of love, while at the same time we are contradicting our message by tolerating racial or social or other barriers with our Christian fellowship."
John Stott, *The Message of Ephesians*

"The early Christians rejoiced when they were deemed worthy to suffer for what they believed. In those days, the church was not merely a thermometer that recorded the ideas and principles of popular opinion; it was a thermostat that transformed the mores of society."
Martin Luther King, Jr, *Letter from a Birmingham Jail*, 16 April 1963

God's challenge

The Evangelical Alliance Council has occasionally been a setting for historic moments in church history. In recent years, the most notable, in my opinion, was the Council meeting that took place on 15 September 2010 at High Leigh Conference Centre just north of London. The Council was made up of eighty men and women, senior leaders from across the whole spectrum of the evangelical world. These were leaders in churches, heads of agencies, and key influencers in areas of business, politics, education, and the media. The Council meets twice a year to hear about, discuss, feed back on, and shape the work of the Alliance, as well as to explore key issues influencing the Christian and indeed the wider world. It was one of my first Council meetings as General Director, and I felt that it was vital, if we were serious about the unity agenda, for the Council to shape our thinking and own the priorities that we as a leadership team sensed God was asking of us.

Having set the scene with a wonderful biblical exposition from Chris Wright, we moved on and began to explore the practical implications. Early in the afternoon, Bishop Wilton Powell from the Church of God of Prophecy and Pastor Agu Irukwu, the senior pastor of Jesus House and UK leader of the Redeemed Christian Church of God (RCCG), came to the platform and addressed the Council, challenging us to push for a unity that was not mono-ethnic. As they spoke, there was a tangible sense in the room that this was a challenge we just could not ignore. Their message to us was simple, yet profound. If we were serious about unity, it had to be a unity that crossed all ethnic barriers and refused to accept ethnic divides. Here was a call for unity in the midst of diversity; a unity for the purpose expressed in the great prayer of Jesus in John 17, "that the world might believe".

As they completed their talks and took their seats, a silence came over the room. We knew that God had spoken to us. As I continued leading the session, I asked myself – and God: "Where do we go from here?" It seemed wrong to move to the next agenda item, simply to press on without recognition of what had taken place in our midst. A hand was raised at the back of the room by Matt Summerfield, the CEO of Urban Saints. He expressed what we were all feeling – that God had spoken to us and that we needed to stop, kneel, pray, and come to a place of repentance for forgetting that the unity we talked about needed to reflect the vibrant ethnic diversity of the UK church.

Let me tell you, such things do not normally happen at the Evangelical Alliance Council. Well, they certainly didn't back then. This September 2010 Council has proved to be a profoundly significant event, as we have committed ourselves to making evangelical unity across all ethnic expressions a priority.

The early church experience

We should not underestimate the theological significance of this issue. The early years of the church were dominated by the apostles and church leaders grappling with both the theological and the pastoral issues associated with their growing realization that the good-news message they had been given was not just for the Jews, but for all people. God was taking them back to the very foundations of the Jewish understanding of their place in the world, and it was about to explode their thinking. If the covenant of Abraham (Genesis 12:1–3) was to be fulfilled, their God was not concerned simply with one small ethnic, religious group. He was the God of all people. As we work our way through the book of Acts, we realize how the Jewish church leadership – those appointed by Jesus as apostles, "the sent-out ones" – struggled with what the Holy Spirit seemed to be doing. You would think they might have realized. Hadn't He made it clear in Matthew 28:19? The Great Commission instructed them to make disciples of all nations; all ethnic groups. Surely that gave them a clear steer. But, somehow, they missed it.

The great breakout that occurred on the day of Pentecost, with 3,000 baptized and added to their number, included both Jews and converts to Judaism. Well, at least everyone was of the same faith, if not the same ethnicity. The signs were all there. Here were people hearing the disciples' words in their own languages. The list is a long one: "Parthians, Medes and Elamites; residents of Mesopotamia, Judea and Cappadocia, Pontus and Asia, Phrygia and Pamphylia, Egypt and the parts of Libya near Cyrene; visitors from Rome (both Jews and converts to Judaism); Cretans and Arabs – we hear them declaring the wonders of God in our own tongues" (Acts 2:9–11).

So the foundations were laid. By the time we get to Acts 6, problems are beginning to emerge. At the start of Acts 6, we hear that when the number of disciples was increasing, the Hellenistic Jews among them complained about the Hebraic Jews because "their widows were being overlooked in the daily distribution of food". These are the challenges of growth, but also of culture and background. By the time we get to Acts 8, we have a revival breaking out in Samaria. This was distinctly dangerous territory for a Jew with an orthodox background. And, perhaps even more shocking, we have Philip witnessing to and baptizing an Ethiopian. Acts 10 becomes a watershed moment as Peter is directed by God via a vision to visit the house of Cornelius, a Roman soldier from the Italian regiment. Peter makes the traditional position clear in his opening remarks to those gathered in Cornelius's house: "You are well aware that it's against our law for a Jew to associate with or visit a Gentile." But Peter has been sent with a divine directive, so he not only enters the house but begins to preach. He hasn't finished, but "[w]hile Peter was still speaking these words, the Holy Spirit came on all who heard the message". It seems as if God is so eager for this breakout to continue that He can't wait for Peter to get to the end of his sermon.

So now we have uncircumcised Roman Gentiles baptized and in some way recognized as part of this church. It's almost out of control. The Holy Spirit is leading the way and the apostles are struggling to keep up. By Acts 13, we have a church established in Antioch with a mixed Jewish and Gentile leadership. They set

Barnabas and Saul apart for the first of their missionary journeys, which will see the gospel taken way beyond its Jewish base, but this will lead to yet further problems.

Were these Gentile converts required to become Jews, taking on board the Jewish laws – particularly those associated with food – and circumcision? Clearly, emotions were running high. The unity of the early church was under significant threat. There were deep theological points to be addressed, but also very practical implications. Peter and Paul have a public falling out, with Paul accusing Peter of double standards: eating with Gentiles one moment and then refusing to do so when guests come down from Jerusalem (Galatians 2:11–13). And we also find groups visiting the new churches with different messages about what was expected in their behaviour, but, more seriously, about what was at the foundation of their faith. So it is in Acts 15 that the great council of Jerusalem is called, with Paul and Barnabas appointed by the church in Antioch to go to the capital to see the apostles and elders and obtain clarity on these key matters.

Thank God for the wisdom and Holy Spirit inspiration given to those who gathered at that council. Much discussion took place. Peter made a contribution, describing the events at Cornelius's house. Paul and Barnabas outlined what "signs and wonders God had done among the Gentiles through them" (Acts 15:12). Eventually James, the brother of Jesus, stood and delivered a judgment. It was agreed that a letter should be sent endorsing the ministry of Barnabas and Paul, and by inference rejecting some of those who had opposed them. They made it clear using the wonderful phrase, "It seemed good to the Holy Spirit and to us" (verse 28). What wonderful insight into the right way to deal with disagreements. The judgment was clear. The Gentiles were not to be burdened with the "custom taught by Moses" (15:1).

It's with all this as a backdrop that the letter to the Galatians is written. There's been conflict in the church. It seems that Paul is writing to a cluster of churches in Galatia. Paul at one point uses very strong language: "You foolish Galatians! Who has bewitched you?" (Galatians 3:1). Some have been led astray by false teaching. Paul takes them back to Abraham and the Genesis 12 covenant: "Understand, then, that those who have faith are children of Abraham. Scripture foresaw that God would justify the Gentiles by faith, and announced the gospel in advance to Abraham: 'All nations will be blessed through you'" (Galatians 3:7–8).

With this as a foundation, Paul takes his argument on to a pivotal moment in the book, which remains a challenge 2,000 years on as we seek to express the life of God in our churches and ministries:

> So in Christ Jesus, you are all children of God through faith, for all of you who were baptized into Christ have clothed yourself with Christ. There is neither Jew nor Gentile, neither slave nor free, nor is there male and female, for you are all one in Christ Jesus. If you belong to Christ, then you are Abraham's seed, and heirs according to the promise.
>
> **(Galatians 3:26–29)**

Paul is making it clear that our faith in Jesus Christ causes us to enter a new family, regardless of ethnicity, religious background, social status, or gender. We are all part of the family. We are clothed in Christ. We are one in Christ. What an amazing truth, but what an incredible challenge.

But do we look like family? Do we behave like family? Do we treat each other like family? Of course, the sad truth is that in so many areas, and particularly in our expressions of church that divide along ethnic lines, we do not. And thus it stands as an offence to the gospel we proclaim.

Our differences are not to do with circumcision, or food, or indeed Old Testament laws and customs. But they include styles of worship and prayer, models of ministry and leadership, theological views on giving and receiving. And, perhaps most importantly of all, we've never taken the time to get to know each other. We have built our churches and indeed our ministries, and there can be a sense that "we don't really need each other".

The church in the UK is primarily made up of what the early church would call Gentiles – non-Jews. But we are Gentiles from an amazing array of ethnic backgrounds. We estimate that between 20 and 25 per cent of the evangelical community in the UK come from an ethnic-minority background. A church I know in central London has more than 100 nationalities within its one congregation. So how does our "family-ness" work out in practice?

Building bridges

During the years leading up to that September 2010 Council, the question of my relationship with those within the migrant church had emerged from time to time. But, I have to confess, it never gained my full attention. That was about to change. Philip Mohabir, a missionary from Guyana who arrived here in 1956, had been a friend for many years. He had a wonderful habit of putting his arm around me, which was always a challenge as I was probably a good foot taller than him. He would say, "My dear brother, how are you?" Philip started an itinerant ministry in Brixton, which included preaching from house to house and in shops, buses, and pubs, before eventually planting churches both inside London and around the UK, as well as in a number of different parts of the world.

It was Philip who in the 1980s started the African and Caribbean Evangelical Alliance (ACEA), which continued until early 2009 and ceased just a few days before I was due to take up my own role at the Evangelical Alliance. Philip was an amazing man of faith and vision – highly respected within the African and Caribbean church but passionate about fostering relationships with indigenous white leaders. He was a genuine bridge-builder. It is perhaps on the foundation of his prophetic prayerful activity that we see the progress we are making today.

Joel Edwards, my predecessor, began his work with the Alliance as a leader of ACEA (1988–92). My relationship with Joel and others in and around the Evangelical Alliance in the 1990s gave me some insight into and appreciation of what was happening, particularly among the Caribbean and African churches. But it was not until the early 2000s that my horizons began to be expanded. I had been asked by the team at Soul Survivor to provide some support and leadership to an enormous mission that was planned for London in 2004. Working on Soul in the City had enabled me to develop a friendship with Dr Jonathan Oloyede. Jonathan was born in the UK but describes himself as "bred in Nigeria" and is the man behind the National Day of Prayer – a regular gathering of prayer and worship at stadia around the country. Jonathan tells a story of attending a Soul in the City celebration at St Paul's Cathedral together with 2,000 young white people. Tim Hughes was leading worship and Jonathan felt the challenge from God: "Strengthen this mission with your gift." Jonathan asked God the obvious question – "How?"; to which he felt a clear response: "Get involved, Jonathan."

Jonathan became part of the Soul in the City leadership team and helped us enormously in so many directions, influencing our programme, literature, and contributions. He opened doors of influence and relationship particularly with the African and Caribbean church. In 2008, when I was involved in chairing the HOPE 08 initiative, we attempted to build on the lessons learned and goodwill engendered by Soul in the City. Eustace Constance, of Street Pastors and Ascension Trust, was a member of our leadership team and attempted to pick up on a nationwide initiative that Jonathan had started in London. While there was much to be thankful for in what was achieved in Soul in the City and HOPE 08, I was still left with a nagging disquiet. We weren't getting it quite right.

I kept recalling a meeting with a number of ethnic-minority leaders. We were sharing vision for the future, plans for the mission. Our hope was that they would get involved. We wanted their faith, their evangelistic zeal, and of course their full churches, to get behind the plans we were making. After about twenty minutes, we stopped and asked for feedback. In a firm, clear, yet grace-filled way, they spelled out their concerns. We – established white church leaders – too often did our planning, set our vision, and then called a meeting and expected them to get involved. This didn't sound like partnership, they said. And it made it difficult for them to significantly influence and shape, or indeed own, the final outcome. It seemed to them that this had been the pattern for years. However much I attempted to plead our innocence, they were of course right. That's not the way a family does business. If we were serious about mission that was truly diverse in culture, style, and ethnicity, people needed to be around the table from the start. There could be no tokenism.

A year of coffee and conversation

As the September 2010 Council came to an end, I knew I couldn't allow what God had challenged us on to be ignored. I had to make a response. So began many months of coffee and conversations around the country. I arranged to meet as many senior leaders from across the migrant churches as I possibly could. These were meetings without agenda. The aim was simply to build relationship, to get to know them, and to understand their hearts, their churches, and their hopes and dreams and frustrations. I was also keen to obtain wise input from them on the next steps we as the Alliance should be taking.

As I travelled from meeting to meeting, I began to realize just how ignorant I was. So much was happening of which I was completely unaware. Enormous conferences attracting thousands of people; books and CDs sold in tens of thousands; international ministries travelling the world. There were also some enormous buildings owned and filled by primarily African and Caribbean leaders. Alongside this was a deep sense of pain that these leaders carried from the past, and some that they were still experiencing. It was important for me to hear this. My friend Israel Olofinjana has recently published a book entitled *Turning the Tables on Mission: Stories of Christians from the Global South in the UK* (Instant Apostle, 2013). In it he tells some of the stories of the migrant missionaries from the global south who are responding to a call to ministry and mission in the UK. There is so much to be thankful for: for the churches planted and the growing number of communities touched and lives changed for the good. But there are also stories of misunderstanding, pain, rejection, and just downright prejudice. Church volunteers threatening to boycott the crèche if it included "black children". Plastic beakers locked up out of fear of contamination. New converts refused baptism because they might be illegal immigrants. Sadly, there are many, many more heartbreaking stories I could list here.

As a white, indigenous church leader, all I could say when confronted with the reality of such incidents in our midst was, "I'm sorry." Not all migrant churches have faced the same level of prejudice, but the fact that some of our brothers and sisters in Christ have stands as an indictment of us as the church here in the UK. But it is also a great challenge for us to hope and pray and work hard to ensure that we see something different in the future.

As my conversations continued, I realized how much I had to learn. But I was also encouraged by the generous welcomes I was receiving. A few of these conversations particularly stand out. It was Pastor Agu Irukwu from Jesus House who set the tone and direction for my year of coffee and conversation with key ethnic-minority church leaders. During an afternoon in his study, we reflected on the Evangelical Alliance Council and established the key people I needed to connect with. It was Pastor Agu who was to become a central building block in our future – a champion for what we believed God was asking of us – and it was he who would introduce me to Revd Yemi Adedeji, who would take on the director's role of the One People Commission.

Bishop Wilton Powell and I followed up the Council with what we now describe as our "Pizza Express Experience". As we shared what we sensed God was asking of us, we realized the common ground and we reflected together on John 17 and found ourselves deeply encouraged. So, as these conversations went on, it was truly encouraging to be approached by Manoj Raithatha, who came with a vision to unite and serve the South Asian churches in the UK. Manoj was from a business background and had tremendous energy and drive. We gladly agreed to provide a home for the work he and the South Asian Forum were pursuing. Manoj commented, "So much has been achieved, from running prayer and training events to launching the eight-week 'Discovering Jesus Through Asian Eyes' course. But, above all, it's the change of mindset, from a 'them and us' culture to 'working as one body'."

One people

As my coffee-and-conversation meetings continued, it became clear that we as the Evangelical Alliance could not simply maintain business as usual. We needed to change. We had already taken some steps towards increasing the diversity of our Council, but that could only be a first step. So it was that on 6 October 2011 a national church leaders' meeting was held at Jesus House in Brent Cross, London, hosted by Pastor Agu.

This meeting agreed that a commission should be established to bring forward recommendations on the future direction of the Evangelical Alliance. The commission was made up of an amazing group of senior leaders: Bishop Eric Brown (National Overseer, New Testament Church of God), Bishop John Francis (Senior Pastor, Ruach Ministries), Dr Tani Omideyi (Senior Minister, Love & Joy Ministries), Bishop Wilton Powell (National Overseer, Church of God of Prophecy), Revd Matt Summerfield (Chief Executive, Urban Saints, and member of the Evangelical Alliance Board), Revd Mike Talbot (Chair of the Alliance Board), Pastor Ade Omooba (Christian Victory Group), Dr Dave Landrum (Director of Advocacy, Evangelical Alliance), Pastor Agu Irukwu (Jesus House), and myself. Others contributed to the final report, including Pastor

Yemi Adedeji, Dr Tayo Adeyemi (New Wine Church), Pastor Kofi Banful (Praise Chapel), Revd Kingsley Appiagyei (Trinity Baptist Church), Lyndon Bowring (CARE), Pastor Omawumi Efueye (House on the Rock), Chrishanthy Sathiyaraj (Bethany Church), Bishop Wayne Malcolm (Christian Life City), Pastor Nims Obunge (Peace Alliance), Hugh Osgood (Cornerstone Christian Centre), Manoj Raithatha (South Asian Forum), Bishop Lee Rayfield (Bishop of Swindon), Pastor David Shosanya (London Baptist Assembly), Roger Sutton (Evangelical Alliance), Apostle Alfred Williams (Christ Faith Tabernacle), and Chine Mbubaegbu (Director of Communications, Evangelical Alliance).

The commission met in late 2011 and produced a wide-ranging report, which was brought to a reconvened national church leaders' meeting. The report was accepted and endorsed by the Board and Council. The report addressed the critical – and I have to admit somewhat disconcerting – question: "How does the Evangelical Alliance need to change in order to reflect, represent, and serve the diversity of the evangelical community across the UK?"

It was clear. We couldn't continue as we were, and practical steps needed to be planned to enable us to move forward. Certain foundations, values, and motivations were clear from the start. First, this was a God movement, a kingdom-of-God agenda. God had been speaking to many of us. He was telling us that this was a time to forge a deeper level of unity. Many of us felt that unity was a God-given prerequisite if we were to see the move of God in this nation that we were asking Him for. Unity wasn't just an optional extra. It was centre stage in His purposes for the church. Second, the commission recognized that relationships were vital. This was a "non-institutional" response, requiring a high level of commitment from leaders, particularly to investing themselves, their time, and their energy in meaningful relationships. Third, the phrase "unity, not uniformity" seemed to sum up our conversations. Our aim was unity in the midst of diversity, and indeed we would seek to celebrate our diversity.

Finally, we recognized that this movement would be challenged, so the mobilization of prayer was essential.

The final report set out specific areas where action was needed, with a long-term commission established to support, advise, and oversee this process. The changes that were needed within the Alliance included: adapting the key messaging coming out of the organization; better representation and influence of the migrant church within the Alliance; the public profile of the Alliance better reflecting the diversity of the church; the advocacy agenda of the Alliance being reviewed in order to reflect issues of concern to ethnic-minority Christians. It was also recommended that others should be invited to join the commission, including Revd Siew-Huat Ong from the Chinese Church in London, and that representatives would be sought from the South American churches, the Korean churches, and indeed other ethnic-minority churches within the UK. John Glass, then the General Superintendent of Elim, was also invited. John would soon take on the chairing of the Evangelical Alliance Council, but also represented a denomination that had many ethnic-minority members and large churches with a great diversity of cultures.

There was, however, one critical decision still to be made. While this was an area I knew was part of my call to the Alliance, I also knew that I desperately needed help to turn these aspirations into reality. This could not simply be a "good idea". It had to be worked out on the ground. I thank God that at this stage Pastor Agu suggested his friend and colleague Revd Yemi Adedeji. Yemi was the right man for the job. He had caught the vision. He knew the UK church scene, as both an Anglican priest and a Pentecostal pastor. In September 2012, he was appointed as the director of what was now called the One People Commission.

Yemi has become a dear friend and a respected colleague within the Evangelical Alliance, helping us to navigate the changes we had committed ourselves to, advising us on key advocacy issues, speaking on our behalf to the media, and challenging us when we failed to recognize our blind spots and cultural assumptions.

I asked Yemi to reflect on the path we have taken together in trying to promote unity while celebrating diversity. Here he tells our story in his own words...

Many people talk, dream, and think of integration across ethnic and church divides but few people are prepared to brace themselves to engage purposefully with strategies that will actually make it happen. One thing that separates Steve Clifford is his humility and authentic desire to cross the bridge and explore the narratives of other ethnic divides without patronizing but with a genuine heart and a desire to build relationships for the purpose of unity that will benefit the wider church.

I remember our many meetings before the inauguration of the One People Commission and my appointment as its director. I still remember a man with a burning desire to learn. As he sat across from me in the study at his house, with his pad and pen at the ready, he would often ask questions on the various concerns of those from different ethnicities and cultures: their fears, their prejudices, and what would be the right method of communicating. We would delve deeper into the dreams and desires of different ethnic leaders, their aspirations, their constituents, their stories, their narratives, and the barriers they constantly encounter. We would spend hours on possible ways of coming alongside them without being patronizing but working together to close the gaps and unite without necessarily wearing the same uniform.

Like a man with a purpose and on a mission, he committed himself to nearly a year's journey of visiting different church leaders across the black and minority ethnic communities. He went beyond just meeting the leaders to creating time to have fellowship with different churches, and would often put himself forward to attend black and minority ethnic church conferences and annual gatherings. He was like a man who had set out on a mission to immerse himself in a diverse cultural context of different church settings and liturgies that were totally alien to his own background, context, and world view. I have no clue how he survived different church expressions across the ethnic divide, but one thing is certain: he demonstrated the fundamental requirement for integration, which is "an authentic relationship and sacrifice". It is against this background that many ethnic church leaders believed, trusted, respected, and absorbed him as a worthwhile and genuine apostle of unity and many have now opened up to relate, connect, and unite for the kingdom with the grace that Steve brings alongside the One People Commission and the Evangelical Alliance.

Steve embodies the unity of which he speaks. He never spoke without reference to Christ's message of unity in John 17. He worked very hard to drive diversity particularly within the leadership team, the Council, the Board, and the general staff at the Evangelical Alliance. He promotes and continuously advances the mission of the One People Commission at every opportunity to demonstrate a prototype of what kingdom unity could look like if we all embraced each other.

My work at the Evangelical Alliance as the director of the OPC is made easy because of the unity that exists between Steve and me at both the planning and the operational stage of every initiative and idea that brings churches to work together. We have since developed values that have shaped our mutual work. These values are rooted in friendship, open relationship, and prayer. It's therefore difficult not to experience each of those values in any of our meetings. We set out to celebrate each other and affirm our distinctive competences while also allowing the other to take centre stage when the opportunity requires.

Today, through the unity that the OPC platform provides, we have seen leaders who had heard of each other but never met become lasting friends, seen them bond and build relationships, and become guest ministers at each other's conferences. Our aim is not to gather leaders for business as usual but to share our pain more deeply, to celebrate our successes together, to pray together for each other, and then to share resources and stories that will take everyone from here to there.

Revd Yemi Adedeki

As I look back on the last six years, as we have explored this area of unity, I realize with deep thankfulness how my life has been enriched. Attending the Redeemed Christian Church of God's congress just outside Lagos, Nigeria, was something I will never forget. I listened together with the one – or was it two, or perhaps even three – million people in this enormous aircraft-hangar structure. It was one kilometre wide and 1.8 km from front to back and yet still not large enough to accommodate the congregation. I listened as Kingsley Appiagyei – a member of the One People Commission and Senior Pastor of Trinity Baptist Church in south London – outlined his call to the UK. He recalled the history of white British missionaries bringing the gospel to his nation of Ghana. Often, these missionaries paid with their lives. They sailed to Africa with their coffins, prepared for what might be just a few days of ministry. In front of this vast crowd, he expressed his gratitude for the seeds of the gospel which had been sown in his nation by these men and women, and of which he and the church in Ghana were the harvest. His call to the UK, he explained, was to bring something of the harvest back for the church in the UK to receive the fruit of its labour.

Connecting with the Korean church in the UK has also been a wonderful privilege. I recently attended a gathering of the Korean Churches Association. The purpose was to welcome the network into membership of the Evangelical Alliance. But, as we met with Korean leaders from across the UK, I was again struck by the richness of the worldwide church of Jesus Christ. We really are a family with an incredible diversity of cultures and styles. Some months before the Korean Churches Association meeting, I had attended an event where I met more than 400 Korean prayer missionaries who had just spent ten days in centres right across the UK, praying for us and our nations. What extraordinary passion I saw in their fervent prayers. How humbling to hear of their thankfulness for the work of Robert Jermain Thomas – a Welsh missionary whom few would have heard of, even in Wales. He is regarded as a hero in Korea and seen by many as the man who brought Christianity to their country and was martyred in the process. It was wonderful to realize we were part of a worldwide church, and that the UK church had a significant contribution to make.

Two of my favourite days of the year take me to the vast ExCel conference centre in East London, where up to 40,000 Christians gather to pray, starting at 8 p.m. and finishing at 6 a.m. the next day. I have not yet made it through the night. The Festival of Life, hosted by the Redeemed Christian Church of God, involves extraordinary worship, prayer, and preaching. Senior politicians, including the then prime minister David Cameron and the former London mayor Boris Johnson, have attended, and are always prayed for. Church leaders from a broad spectrum of the Christian community are invited to participate. This is unity working out in practice, as Chinese, South Asian, South American, Caribbean, and European church leaders are given a platform and invited to speak on the strength of relationships built at the One People Commission.

It's not just the big events that carry significance, however. Perhaps for me the event with the greatest diversity actually took place on *HMS President*, a First World War military boat converted into a floating conference centre and moored on the River Thames. That evening 160 people attended an event that presented the results of research commissioned by the One People Commission on the beliefs and attitudes of young adults within the church. While the research results were fascinating and very significant for the UK church, it was as I looked around that evening that I realized what progress we had made. Here was a room full of young adults and of church and organizational leaders young and old. The ethnic mix was amazing. This was the church in all its diversity; together for a common purpose.

There are so many stories that could be told; so many churches and people I would love to introduce you to. I could not do justice to this chapter, however, without referring to my dear friends Dr Tani and Dr Modupe Omideyi. Tani and Modupe came to the UK to study engineering at Manchester University. But in the autumn of 1980 they were led by God to plant a church in Liverpool. To say that Anfield, their area of choice, was not an easy place for two Nigerians to do ministry in the 1980s is perhaps an understatement.

It was a predominantly white, working-class area, with strong racist elements and a political environment not supportive of Christian mission. Their early years involved enormous sacrifice, including long weekends sleeping on church floors. These two highly educated, talented individuals could have chosen a life of ease, comfort, and wealth, but God called them. So they have dedicated their lives to Anfield. Today, Temple of Praise is a multicultural community of faith occupying a former cinema a few hundred yards from Liverpool FC's stadium. Here is a church with associate ministries committed to proclaiming and demonstrating the good news to their community. They run projects addressing the troubles of the elderly, the disaffected, young people, and those living with poor health, unemployment, or poverty. They are also responding to the needs of asylum-seekers and refugees. They have just opened the first of what could be many free schools.

Building genuinely multicultural churches continues to be a challenge that many aspire to, but Tani and Modupe have, with God's grace, achieved a great deal. Indeed, there is much that others could learn from them. Alongside all this, Tani has become the first ethnic-minority church leader to chair the Board of the Evangelical Alliance in the UK.

The future

As we look to the future, there is still so much ground for us to take. In this, it's important to acknowledge those who have gone before and who indeed continue to work in this area – those already mentioned, but also others such as Dr Hugh Osgood, Free Churches Moderator and a president of Churches Together in England (CTE), Bishop Joe Aldred of CTE, Katei Kirby of the African Caribbean Evangelical Alliance (ACEA), Les Isaac of Street Pastors and Ascension Trust, Pastor Celia Apeagyei-Collins, founder and president of the Rehoboth Foundation, and David Wise, pioneering multicultural church in a Baptist setting. These people have led the way in nurturing relationships, challenging the church, and modelling multicultural ministries. We honour their work and there is so much we can learn from them.

There remain numerous questions to be addressed. Is multicultural church desirable, and, if so, how do we build it? Where will second- and third-generation young adults from migrant families find their spiritual home? As patterns of migration change and indeed some migrants return to nations they had previously regarded as home, how will this affect the UK church? Will indigenous white-led congregations be willing to change in order to reflect the ethnic diversity of so many of our larger cities? And, finally, will indigenous white congregations be willing to be led by ethnic-minority leaders?

In a disjointed and fragmented world, the issues of migration and radicalization have grabbed the attention of government and the media. This might be where we as the church could lead the way, both in our relationships in the Christian community and also beyond that to a society that is desperately struggling to know how to respond. We are called as followers of Jesus, His church, to model a different way; to be a prophetic statement. The apostle Paul exhorts us "to make every effort to keep the unity of the Spirit through the bond of peace. There is one body and one Spirit, just as you were called to one hope" (Ephesians 4:3–4).

As the world builds walls to reinforce racial divides, God calls us to use those bricks to build bridges. I thank God for the migrant church here in the UK. I believe they are a gift to the historically indigenous population. I'm convinced we need each other if we are to see the UK reached with the transforming power of the gospel. This is a time for us to build relationships, to honour each other, to learn lessons from each other, and to be enriched as we celebrate the fact that we are one family.

Questions

- You may be reading this book while living in a community where there is little ethnic diversity. But there could well be groups within your town or village that do not relate well. What would unity across these divides look like?

- Taking down walls and building bridges provides a wonderful picture of reconciliation and relationship-building. What might that look like in your community – inside and outside your church?
- Have you ever visited a church with a predominantly different ethnic culture from your own? If not, then why not try it?
- If you're able to influence these decisions, why not suggest exchanging pulpits with a leader from another church?

Chapter 11

One: Across the generations

"To many young people who grew up in Christian churches,
Christianity seems boring, irrelevant, sidelined from the real
issues people face. It seems shallow."
David Kinnaman and Aly Hawkins, *You Lost Me*

"In the last days, God says, I will pour out my Spirit on all
people. Your sons and daughters will prophesy, your young
men will see visions, your old men will dream dreams. Even on
my servants, both men and women, I will pour out my Spirit in
those days, and they will prophesy."
Acts 2:17–18

As I sat among 10,000 teenagers and young adults in what
is reputed to be the largest marquee available in the UK, the
atmosphere was electric. The band, who were arranged on a stage
way in the distance yet clearly visible because of the enormous
projection screens, started up with a well-known worship song.
Everyone was on their feet and most were jumping up and down. It
was infectious. We were all swept up in it. The evening proceeded
with worship, prayer, interviews, and lots of laughter; and then
came the preaching. Lasting around thirty minutes, it was Bible-
based but seemed to be making a deep connection with those in the
congregation. It included lots of illustrations that made Scripture
seem relevant and accessible. Eventually there was an appeal and
those in the congregation were asked if they would like to take this

opportunity to become a follower of Jesus. This was not one of those easy asks; not simply a quick "Put up your hands" and then put them down. The request was, however, simple: if you wanted to make a response, you were invited to push through the crowds – not an easy process because there were no seats. Those making their commitment needed to come to the front. They needed to make a response with their whole body, making themselves totally visible and vulnerable to their friends. I wondered if anyone was going to be brave enough to respond. And then it started. A few to begin with, but then a flood – hundreds of teenagers and young adults made their way to the front to pray a prayer of commitment. They were then taken to a separate tent for further prayer and advice. As they came forward, the whole marquee was filled with clapping and cheering. It was extraordinary, and I was close to tears. I wondered whether this was what was happening in heaven at such a moment. Hundreds responded that night – and close to 2,000 over the course of the summer. The event was, of course, an evening celebration at Soul Survivor. I would have loved the whole UK church – young and old – to experience it with me.

Over the last few years, I've had the privilege of hanging out with the Soul Survivor team and experiencing first-hand this amazing ministry, during both the summer festivals and the Soul in the City London outreach but also in the week-in, week-out, year-round ministry in local churches, youth leader conferences, publications, and worship ministry. If you had been sitting in that marquee and become caught up with all that God was doing, it would have been easy to come to the conclusion that the UK church was experiencing a revival. There are thousands of young people coming to Christ each summer at Soul Survivor and other similar events. Surely that must be having an impact on the rest of the church...

The truth is, of course, more complex. Some churches – particularly in the large metropolitan centres – are indeed growing churches, packed with young adults, including churches such as Hillsong, Ruach, Life Church, Destiny, Trent Vineyard, Jesus

House, and Holy Trinity Brompton. Recent research suggests[1] that the larger the church, the greater the proportion of the congregation who are under the age of twenty. Over half of those in their twenties going to church attend churches in London, and these tend to be churches with congregations of more than 200.

However, there are thousands of other churches where the attendance of teenagers, young adults, and even young families is the exception to the rule. As part of my role at the Alliance, I'm invited to a wide range of churches and, although these are normally larger, I do on occasion visit a church in a small community. Invariably at these smaller community churches, grey hair is the norm, and the service can at times feel as if it is being conducted in exactly the same way today as it would have been twenty, thirty, even forty years ago. After such visits, I am left wondering whether there will be a church meeting there in ten to fifteen years' time. Clearly, we as a church in the UK have an enormous challenge to respond to. Thank God for all that's going on in children's and youth ministries. My own children benefited greatly from the children's and youth work at Spring Harvest. Year after year, they attended and had profoundly significant spiritual moments of commitment and going deeper with God.

Thank God for the ongoing work of Youth for Christ, Urban Saints, Scripture Union, Soul Survivor, UCCF, 24/7, Prayer Storm, Fusion, Agape, and Navigators. Thank God too for the amazing flagship churches in our metropolitan cities that are seeing young adults coming to Christ and being discipled in the faith. But it can't stop there. If we're serious about seeing the UK reached, we need vibrant expressions of His church touching every community, including towns, villages, and the social housing estates that can so easily be neglected. On the day of Pentecost, the day the church was born, as Peter began to explain to the crowd what on earth was going on, he chose to quote from the prophet Joel: "In the last days, God says, I will pour out my Spirit on all people. Your sons and daughters will prophesy, your young men will see visions, your old men will dream dreams. Even on my servants, both men and women, I will pour out my Spirit in those days, and they will prophesy" (Acts 2:17–18).

In drawing on this prophecy, it seems that Peter is painting a picture of this church which is coming to birth. It's a church within which young and old, sons and daughters will collaborate in order to fulfil the purposes of God. Scripture is not afraid to recognize the distinct contributions made by those of different ages. Young people are commended for their strength, passion, and vision, and older people or elders for their wisdom – and indeed grey hairs are regarded as marks of splendour. If you know me or take time to look at my picture on the cover, you'll not be surprised to know I'm grateful to God for this particular biblical truth...

While different generations will bring their unique contributions to the church, ultimately it's the generations together that best represent the family of God. Being family means that we are not all the same. We won't all listen to the same music, read the same Bible translations on our phone or iPad (or even in a book!), or wear the same kind of clothes, jewellery, or even tattoos. We are different, but we are family.

Homogenous units are great starting points; wonderful mission stations designed to promote healthy growth and life. But we must push through to more than this. In a society that seems to be continually looking to fragment along age divides – distinguishing between "Builders", "Baby Boomers", "Xers", "Millennials", and "Generation Z" – we as a church are called to a oneness that crosses all ages.

As I look back on my early years as a Christian, I recognize the influence of a number of older people who gave me time and offered me their care and wisdom. Pastor Evans, as we knew him, who led the independent Methodist church I found myself attending as a seventeen-year-old new Christian, took me under his wing, invited me to his study, prayed with me, shared his insight into Scripture, and took the risk of giving me opportunities to lead and to speak. An older couple in the church would just invite me back to their home after an evening service. We were so different, but they included me. As I grew up and developed in the faith, Lynn Green, leading Youth With A Mission in the UK, Gerald and Anona Coates, leading Pioneer People, and Roger Forster, theologian and leader of Ichthus, were all mature people who gave me time and insights into life and ministry. I hung around them. I knew I needed something of what they had. I don't remember putting technical terms to it, such as "discipleship" or "mentoring", but through their words and by observing their lives I became a better follower of Jesus. My relationships with them were the keys to my spiritual walk and my growth as a leader in the church.

As I've grown in years and maturity, I've attempted to replicate what I am thankful to have received myself. One of the great delights and privileges of my life has been to meet some amazing people whom I have both learned from and had the opportunity to influence. "Tie Teams", which later became known as "DNA", became an expression of that. It started as a small, informal year-long course, which I and two friends started way back in 1986. The first year, seven young adults joined us for an eleven-month journey of church-based discipleship that focused on evangelism. It was a brilliant year. We had so much fun and laughter, along with challenges, pain, and tears. Deep relationships were built as God was given space to develop not just skills and understanding but character. Since that first year, over a thousand people have participated in a DNA year. Inevitably, more structures have been put in place since those early years, but the principle remains the same: discipleship in the context of church-based relationships.

It's remarkable how often at the end of a meeting someone will breeze up to me and say, "Do you remember me? I did DNA." They are now holding down responsible roles and speak with such affection about the significance of their year of discipleship.

One of those people is Linda Ward, whom I mentioned in Chapter 9. I first met Linda when she was eighteen, a relatively recent convert. She joined a two-week summer mission I was leading. Linda returned home, but quickly rejoined us as a member of one of our discipleship training teams. During the year, she was based in a church on the south coast and involved in a great deal of evangelism and schools work. When Linda returned to her home church at the end of the year, they decided to employ her as an evangelist working particularly in schools. This was a church I worked closely with so it was wonderful to see Linda growing in maturity and responsibility. After a few years, the church decided to plant a church and Linda was identified as a key member of the leadership of that new church. Eventually the original church leader stepped down and it was obvious that Linda was the right person to take on leadership of the new church plant. It's wonderful to reflect back on the young adult who walked through the door to be part of that mission team, a new Christian with little background in the church or indeed the Christian faith, and to see her now leading a significant Pioneer network church in west London – indeed the church of which Ann and I are delighted to be members.

Building tomorrow's church today

What's interesting as I think about those I've had the privilege of influencing over the years is that I recognize how much they have contributed to my life. I'm enriched and challenged in those cross-generational relationships. But there are key contributions I can make to young adults' lives. As relationships develop, I can offer:

- Unconditional love and acceptance
- Encouragement and practical support
- Availability and hospitality
- Honesty and integrity
- Wisdom that is non-judgmental and gives God space to speak and challenge.

The pace of the change that is occurring in the twenty-first-century developed world is even more reason for the older generation to be willing to listen to and learn from younger adults. Understanding and engaging with this new emerging world needs both the wisdom of years and the social media and digital savvy of those who instinctively understand it. We also need to realize that they will often engage with God in a different way and so have fresh insights to bring. One of the great challenges faced by leaders across the country is the question of how we can build a church that is not just for older people. How can we build a church where all generations can feel at home, part of the family?

As part of a response to this question, the Evangelical Alliance commissioned some research in 2015 into the beliefs, habits, and practices of young adults within the church. The aim of *Building Tomorrow's Church Today* was to hear from the millennial generation within our churches, those in the eighteen-to-thirties age range. The findings were fascinating and have provoked significant conversations and indeed changes of behaviour in churches across the country. The questions asked included the form of Christian teaching that millennials found most beneficial. It came as a shock to many pastors that only 40 per cent said sermons/teaching in their own church. In fact, other sources of influence were podcasts, blogs, and social media. The survey also asked questions about how well churches helped young people in a number of different areas in their life. Just 49 per cent said their church helped them to live out their faith in everyday life "a lot".

When it came to how much their church helped them live out their faith at work, one in five (19 per cent) said their church was not really helping them in this, and another 36 per cent said their church was not really helping them have opportunities to find a marriage partner. The research went on to ask about mentoring and we discovered that 30 per cent do not have a mentor or group of friends they can be honest with and accountable to about life and faith. These statistics have to pose enormous challenges for church leaders, particularly when the survey showed that 30 per cent of those surveyed said they experience frequent or indeed continual doubts about their faith. The survey also revealed fascinating insights into these young adults' beliefs. The survey was targeted at Millennials who would in the main be linked to evangelical churches. So, unsurprisingly, 98 per cent believe Jesus rose from the dead, 96 per cent believe Jesus was fully human and fully divine, 95 per cent think that the Bible is the inspired word of God, and 89 per cent feel that Christians should be committed to a church and attend it regularly.

But, when we explored questions of lifestyle and Christian behaviour, some of the historically orthodox biblical views were questioned by a significant percentage. These included views on assisted suicide, abortion, human sexuality including gay lifestyles, and cohabiting. Older and established leaders need to recognize the enormous challenge faced by young adults within our churches. Brought up in the late twentieth/early twenty-first century, they have spent their lives being bombarded by a secular humanist world view that dominates our education system, TV, films, news reports, and social media. The reality is that we are living in an age with a new social orthodoxy that does not recognize a creator or indeed a creator's order for life. As churches, we have to find new ways of engaging with these issues of life. A head-in-the-sand approach will not stand the test of time, and simply quoting a few scriptures and clarifying biblical orthodoxy will not be enough. Our young adults, and indeed those of all ages, desperately need a biblical lifestyle apologetic that will enable them not simply to understand it themselves but to be equipped to engage with their own family, friends, and workmates on these critical issues of life.

If we are serious about building churches that are not just for older people, we have to start giving responsibility and profile to the young adults who are part of our churches. As I look back on my life I'm surprised yet honoured by the risks people took with me: leading international mission teams in my late teens, preaching and teaching in my early twenties, overseeing and planting churches in my thirties. Giving young adults opportunities with support means they will grow in God and they will develop leadership skills. They might not do things the way you would, but we need them to do things differently, don't we?

I know of at least one larger church that, in the light of the *Building Tomorrow's Church Today* research and the feedback they have obtained from young adults in their church, have completely reshaped their public gatherings. It's not been without its pain. Older members of the congregation liked things the way they were and had to be helped to realize that change was necessary if they were to avoid stagnation and if they were to bring forward a new generation of leaders. Speaking as a leader who's now in his sixties and who has been a Christian for over forty years, it's so important that we, mature older members of the church, are prepared to embrace change. Simply keeping things as they are cannot be an option for many churches across the UK. We are living in a fast-changing world and, while the truth of Scripture remains the same, how we express ourselves as church has to be flexible enough to adjust to the changing world that surrounds us.

The challenge of change

Churches that are serious about being a spiritual home that young adults can feel at home in and indeed contribute to need to be willing to change – sometimes radically.

Such change could well include:

- Bringing young adults into the leadership, thus enabling them to influence and shape every aspect of church life
- Publicly profiling young adults so they are leading and speaking in public gatherings
- Allowing young adults to make changes to what might happen when we meet, including:
    * The environment we create
    * The length of the talk
    * The focus of the talk
    * The songs we sing.

- For young adults (although, let's face it, it should be true for all of us), it's not just about Sunday. They want to apply their faith and indeed their reading and teaching from Scripture to every aspect of life and the world around them. Easy, quick-fix answers won't be enough; they'll want to dig deep, ask difficult questions – which we might not have the immediate answer to
- Young adults will push us to build a community that goes beyond a Sunday service and they'll want a community in which others who don't know Christ can be welcomed
- Young adults will want to experiment: Messy Church, youth church, midweek church... they won't always get it right but they will have tried.

What does that mean for those of us who have been around for years? Are we prepared to be mature enough to allow such changes to inconvenience us? Are we prepared for church as we've known it for years to be different, even if that means we might feel a little uncomfortable, even insecure? Are we prepared to let go of some of the things we've held dear for the sake of the greater good? These questions are critical as we embark on change; they need to be considered, discussed, and prayed over. But let's face some facts: for some churches, unless we change, we're finished. Not immediately, but in maybe ten, fifteen, or it could be as many as twenty years. But take a long, hard, honest look at your church: twenty years from now, who will be around? Where will leadership come from? Who will pay the bills? Will there be any children or youth work? Will you be having an impact on the community that surrounds you? It could be that, as you look to the future, you come to the realization that you really have nothing to lose.

"*threads*" is one response that we made at the Evangelical Alliance to support the Millennial generation in a manner that reflected the way these young people engage with the world around them and relate to God. Launched in 2012, it was our attempt to meet a challenge that was being faced by many churches across the country: the problem of the missing generation. In just two decades, the number of twenty-somethings attending church had halved[2] and, according to the English Church Census, only three out of every hundred people in their twenties were attending church. Our own research among our membership base found that while in 1998 25 per cent of our members were aged between eighteen and thirty-four, just ten years later this was down to 3 per cent. Some research had shown that while many young people had gone to church as children, at some point – often during or just after university – they fell away from faith when they began to regard the churches they were attending as shallow, hypocritical, and irrelevant to their daily lives. Many of them still said yes to Jesus, but no thank you to church.

So we created *threads* – a collective of people in their twenties and thirties from all walks of life who meet mainly online (www. threadsuk.com) to wrestle with issues of faith and life, from dating to doubt to eating disorders and divorce, from politics to entertainment, justice, work and finances. If I'm honest, I don't always "get" what the *threads* collective are talking about, the manner in which they are speaking, or the references to popular culture. But I am not the target audience. We realized at the Alliance that if we were truly going to engage with the "missing generation", we had to make faith relevant to their real lives.

threads seems to be hitting a spot, with millions of page views on its website and having won the award for best blog three times at the annual Premier Digital Awards (formerly known as the Christian New Media Awards). On its first anniversary in 2013, one person wrote of the collective,

> The beautiful thing is that we are connecting. Where there once was silence there is now chatter. Where there once was ignorance there is now understanding. *threads* is more than just social media. There is a push and pull found within

this community that means we are stronger as a family in Christ. We are learning and growing. I believe the strategic importance of a community such as *threads* goes far beyond what we can visibly see at this point.

Intergenerational church

One of the things I love about my church is that it's genuinely intergenerational. I love the fact that when we meet, there are babes in arms and grannies and granddads and indeed everything in between. It's messy at times. The babies cry and toddlers run about the building while older people have difficulties with mobility. Communication has to be produced on paper as well as electronically. Younger families struggle to afford accommodation. Students come and go and some stay. Getting the PA system at the right level is a challenge – not too loud but loud enough. But it's worth it. Church weekends are wonderful. The kids get to engage with this wonderful mix of ages. The older and wiser get to cuddle and even feed a baby. Football games are played, cream teas are enjoyed, and we all join in the quiz; and we learn and we worship together. I love the fact that we are all responsible for supporting the parents as they bring up their children and teenagers.

And so we should be, because not only are they part of our church today, but they will be leading our church in the future. The *Talking Jesus* research (September 2015) asked this question of 1,500 practising Christians: What were the two or three main influences on your becoming a Christian? Around 41 per cent identified growing up in a Christian family as a key influence. This was the largest influence by far and has to have a significant effect on our priorities as a church. Our evangelism must begin at home. Seeing the children of church members becoming followers of Jesus and then staying the course to maturity is a responsibility we share with the parents. It's often these church family relationships that open the door to other families to come to Christ. Messy Church has been a wonderful addition to the activities of many churches that have looked to reach out beyond themselves. It provides a space where adults and children can enjoy "doing church" together, exploring the Bible, reflecting on God, playing, and eating together. And all are welcome.

Intergenerational church also has to take seriously the challenge of reaching out to older members of our wider society. While in recent years a great deal of church finances and energies have rightly been expended on reaching out to children and young people, I'm convinced there is an enormous opportunity for the church to reach the elderly. As people live longer and have more free time, the opportunities are endless and relatively simple to organize. Tea-timers, a monthly afternoon of tea, cake, sandwiches, and quizzes, has seen numerous people added to our church and finding Christ. I recently visited an enormous joint church event in south London, Lark in the Park. Alongside activities for teenagers, children, mums, and dads was an afternoon marquee event with the usual tea and cakes but also a singalong, dancing, and bingo, together with a gospel presentation. It was amazing. While age brings all kinds of challenges for the older members of our churches, perhaps it could also be a time of fresh opportunity to work alongside their younger fellow church members in reaching out to a community that can so easily get forgotten, isolated, and lonely.

So let's thank God for every expression of the church. Church in all its multitude of expressions. Church for kids. Church for teenagers. Church for young adults. Church for families. Church for students. Church for the elderly. But let's pray and let's work for expressions of church that bring all together. Where we celebrate family right across the ages.

Questions

- When was the last time you spent some quality time with someone outside your age group and not part of your family? Why not try it?

- Does your church talk about questions of lifestyle and Christian behaviour? If not, how could these conversations be helpfully conducted?
- Does your church feel responsible for supporting the parents of the church in bringing their children to faith and helping them follow Jesus?
- Has your church got a strategy for reaching out to the older members of your wider community?
- Is your church/are you willing to change?

Chapter 12

One: When we disagree

"I tell you that if two of you on earth agree about anything they ask for, it will be done for them by my Father in heaven. For where two or three gather in my name, there am I with them."
Matthew 18:19–20

"Warn a divisive person once, and then warn them a second time. After that, have nothing to do with them."
Titus 3:10

"Whenever equally biblical Christians who are equally anxious to understand the reading of scripture and to submit to its authority reach different conclusions, we should deduce that evidently scripture is not crystal clear on this matter and therefore we can afford to give one another liberty. You can also hope – through prayer, study and discussion – to grow in understanding and so in our agreement."
John Stott, *Evangelical Truth: A Personal Plea for Unity, Integrity and Faithfulness*

1966 was not only the year England won the World Cup (we need to keep reminding ourselves of that), but was also the year in which two of the most senior evangelical leaders in the UK, Revd John Stott and Dr Martyn Lloyd-Jones, had a major disagreement at an Evangelical Alliance assembly. The background to the bust-up, which took place in October of that year, was evangelical uncertainty over how to respond to the formation of the World Council of Churches (WCC) in 1948, and its growing influence. The ecumenical movement, as it was known, had as its ideal the reuniting of Christendom, bringing together churches and denominations with the strapline "One church for one world". The inaugural conference of the WCC in Amsterdam had brought together 351 delegates representing 147 branches of the Christian church.

Right from the start, views on the significance of the event differed greatly. An American Methodist bishop described it as the most significant event of the twentieth century, marking "the beginning of the end of all inter-denominational animosities", while Dr Donald Barnhouse believed "that such an organisation will be remembered as the beginning of a Babylonish thing which is pictured not as the bride of Christ but as the great whore of the book of Revelation".[1] The list of those who initially agreed to its formation was notable for a number of significant absentees, including the Roman Catholic Church, the Southern Baptists, and a large number of smaller evangelical groups. However, during the 1950s and early 1960s, the ecumenical movement gained impetus and in 1966, just a month before the evangelical assembly on the subject of unity, the British Council of Churches – an offshoot of the WCC – set a date (spring 1980) for the achievement of church reunion. This was not the greatest preparation for the Evangelical Alliance assembly and caused even more tension and anxiety – particularly as some Anglican evangelicals were calling for open dialogue with members of the WCC, while others were very concerned.

It was agreed that both views on the nature of the ecumenical movement should be heard at the assembly, as it explored the larger question of the nature of unity. Evangelicals on both sides of the debate were in agreement that the ecumenical movement was dominated by theological liberalism, but they disagreed on what to do about it. For some, like Dr Lloyd-Jones, evangelicals in mixed denominations, such as John Stott in the Church of England and evangelical Methodists or Presbyterians, for example, were being significantly compromised by the fact that their churches were members of an "unsound" body such as the WCC and the British Council of Churches. Dr Lloyd-Jones, of Westminster Chapel, London, was invited to explain the views of those who were against any form of association with the ecumenical movement at a public rally on the evening before the assembly began. Lloyd-Jones went further than expected. In a powerful presentation, he proclaimed:

> Unity, while it is spiritual, must be visible. Our Lord said, 'That the world might know' – the world might know that they are one. It is something that is to be visible as well as spiritual. So I say that we should consider this matter because the New Testament compels us to consider the church and the unity of the church... We as evangelical Christians have been less interested in the question of church unity than anyone else... Everybody seems to be talking about church unity except evangelicals... [With] our knowledge and understanding of scripture, we of all people ought to be the first to preach the vital necessity of church unity.[2]

Lloyd-Jones continued in what was interpreted by many as a call to evangelicals as individuals and in churches to come out of doctrinally mixed denominations and come together as a fellowship or association of evangelical churches:

> Surely the Holy Spirit will only bless his own Word; and if those of us who believe it would only come together, stand together as churches constantly together, working together, doing everything together, bearing witness together, I believe we will then have the right to expect the Spirit of God to come upon us in mighty revival and reawakening.[3]

As Dr Lloyd-Jones took his seat, Revd John Stott from All Souls, Langham Place, a leading Church of England evangelical who was chairing the meeting, brought the evening to a sensational end by indicating that he wished to disassociate himself publicly from what had just been said. "Scripture", Stott said, "is against him. The remnant was within the church not outside it. I hope no one will act precipitately." Stott was arguing from Old Testament history.[4] "However corrupt or heretical Israel had become, there were always some faithful believers (the remnant) who maintained the true faith and who God honoured even as they remained part of Israel."[5]

Stott and Lloyd-Jones had two very different views of the church, which surfaced when the issue of unity was explored, and thus they came to very different conclusions as to the way forward. Although the assembly continued with other discussions, it was agreed at the end that there was not a significant appetite for what Lloyd-Jones was advocating in an organized or structural way. One immediate consequence was significant tension between Anglican evangelicals and their non-conformist friends, and even within the predominantly evangelical denominations such as Baptists, where being part of a mixed denomination was beginning, at least for some, to be seen as a hindrance to effective church life.

Reflecting on the debate and its outcome, David Hilborn notes,

> For Stott, a theologically tainted denomination like the Church of England remained part of the one true church of Jesus Christ, despite its taintedness. As long as there were evangelicals who remained faithful to the authentic (evangelical clergy) gospel within it. For Lloyd-Jones there was a point of taintedness beyond which evangelicals had to 'come out and be separate', and realign with authentic believers from other streams…

It could be argued that Stott's position has since been vindicated. The growth of Holy Trinity Brompton and Alpha, the proliferation of evangelical bishops, three evangelical Archbishops of Canterbury – Donald Coggan, George Carey, and Justin Welby – and Stott's own global influence could all be cited as reasons why he was right.

Lloyd-Jones' supporters, however, might suggest that the Church of England has continued to decline in number while "pure" and more independent evangelical streams such as Newfrontiers and the newly revitalized Fellowship of Independent Evangelical Churches have grown.

These two twentieth-century evangelical giants, whose influence extended way beyond the UK, had managed to disagree so publicly that the consequences would live on for generations to come. Differing views on the institutional ecumenical movement would continue within evangelicalism for a number of years, but perhaps as it became obvious that the goal of "church reunion" by spring 1980 was not going to be achieved, the significance of the WCC and indeed the fear of the movement began to wane.

A number of evangelical churches that had previously kept their distance from the British Council of Churches were now drawn into the new structure of Churches Together in England nationally and locally – and indeed began to associate freely with it during the late 1990s and early 2000s. (These included networks such as Ichthus, Pioneer, Elim, Assemblies of God, New Testament Church of God, New Testament Church of Prophecy, and Redeemed Christian Church of God.)

By way of a postscript to the 1966 conflict, Timothy Dudley-Smith in his biography of John Stott (*John Stott: A Global Ministry*, IVP, 2001) recalls a meeting on 19 December 1978 between Dr Lloyd-Jones and John Stott at Lloyd-Jones' London home. Stott noted that "he could not have been more affable and welcoming. We sat in his roomy ground-floor study where he does his writing and Mrs Lloyd-Jones brought us coffee and chocolate biscuits". Among other things, Dudley-Smith records their conversation regarding the 1966 assembly and Lloyd-Jones' outspoken criticism of evangelical Anglicans. Stott expressed his concerns over Lloyd-Jones' presuppositions about evangelical Anglicans and his seeking to clarify whether Stott could ever imagine leaving the Church of England. Stott recalled that, on three separate occasions during the conversation, Lloyd-Jones expressed his desire that the two could work together. "I wish we could be together, you and I (said Lloyd-Jones). We belong together. Together we could make a terrific impact on the church and the country." Stott replied, "But, Dr Lloyd-Jones, we are together – theologically, though not structurally."

Dr Lloyd-Jones died in 1981 and Stott wrote by way of appreciation that "the Doctor... [was] at heart a man of love and peace... a spiritual father to many of us".

More recent disagreements

Evangelicals within "mixed" denominations face ongoing challenges. This is most publicly obvious within the Church of England and the wider Anglican Communion, which has a large influential evangelical wing (as noted above), yet exists alongside fellow members of the Church with very different theological starting points. The same would be true of evangelicals within Methodism, the United Reformed Church, and to a lesser degree the Baptists, as the evangelicals within the Baptist family could comprise as much as 90 per cent of the whole, with a large percentage being members of the Evangelical Alliance. For evangelicals within the Church of England, the debate on the role of ordained women within the Church has placed them on either side of the divide, with many arguing passionately for women in all roles in ministry, but a significant percentage of (in the main) conservative evangelicals having grave concerns and arguing that Scripture precludes women priests and bishops. The final agreement on the recognition of women bishops was ably negotiated in no small part owing to the mediation skills of David Porter, the current chief of staff and strategy at Lambeth Palace, and the ex-chair of the Evangelical Alliance Board. In my conversations with people on both sides of the disagreement, I have learned that the final solution left them with elements of dissatisfaction, but both sides have felt able to live with the compromises and the Anglican Church remains together.

The issue of human sexuality has, however, taken the Church of England to a new level of disagreement. Debates and conversations have been held, reports produced, and powerful lobby groups are currently at work; all of this being conducted in front of mainstream media that are reporting almost weekly on every nuance of the process. The issue is made even more complex as the Anglican community is not simply restricted to England or indeed the UK, but is to be found around the world, with strong voices to be heard on both sides of the theological divide, including from North America and Africa. As I write, the possible outcomes are still in the balance. This is undoubtedly a time to pray for Justin Welby, John Sentamu, and Paul Butler – the three most senior bishops of the Church of England, each of whom is evangelical in his theology. Unlike the issue of the ordination of women, with a few exceptions evangelicals within the Church are united in holding a historically orthodox biblical view on the subject. (It's worth recognizing that there is a small, but potentially influential, group called "Affirming Evangelicals" who continue to identify as evangelicals but who favour same-sex blessings and in some cases gay marriage.) Although the pastoral outworkings of the orthodox position might vary, there is a high level of theological agreement. Time will tell as to the outcome of this matter and whether the Anglican Communion will be able to hold together across the world and indeed in England. What we can be certain of, however, is that things are not going to stay the same, and evangelical leaders and members must prepare themselves for challenging years ahead.

For some Anglican evangelicals this could be "the last straw", and they may feel unable to continue to identify membership with a church that has moved so far away from orthodoxy. Some will establish links with the Anglican Communion in other parts of the world; some could choose to leave the church completely. For others, their premise is a strong desire to stay. The concept of the faithful "remnant" remains, and they possess a deep sense of loyalty to the institution that has been their spiritual home. For them, the national church provides a missionary opportunity both internally and to the wider society. The Church of England, as a truly national church, has a presence in every community and, as the established church, is able to influence government and civic institutions. The Church of Scotland has recently faced this issue as it has significantly changed its position on human sexuality, much to the disappointment of evangelicals within the Church. The result, which is still being worked out, has meant a number of evangelical leaders and churches choosing to leave the denomination, thereby facing the consequence of forfeiting church buildings, pension funds, and employment. Other evangelicals have chosen to stay. The tension between evangelicals over the question of staying or leaving has been painful and has not always been expressed in a Christlike manner.

The Lloyd-Jones and Stott debate continues, fifty years on. The missional opportunities within a mixed denomination such as the Church of England are without question, but the complexities of living and working in, and offering allegiance to, an institution with such a variety of theological views and priorities continues to raise questions. Could this energy be better spent if focused in other directions? Lloyd-Jones argued "Leave". To him, it was not worth the effort and believers would be tainted in the process, while Stott argued in favour of remaining. To him, God was still at work in Anglicanism.

What do we mean by unity?

As I look back on my years in Christian leadership, I've come to the conclusion that we use the word "unity" in a number of different ways. It is in some ways a reflection of our interpretation of Scripture, our theological persuasions, our ecclesiology (view of the church), our personality type, our ministry focus, and our gifting. I've observed unity used in at least five different ways – each of which carries biblical validity, and which some of us will feel particularly drawn to or in some cases cautious about. (Chapter 4 has explored some of the biblical foundations for these expressions of unity.)

Spiritual unity

Few, if any, would disagree that there is a unity which comes out of our shared life in Christ and our participation in the family of God. Paul exhorts the church in Ephesus to "make every effort to keep the unity of the Spirit through the bond of peace. There is one body and one Spirit, just as you were called to one hope when you were called" (Ephesians 4:3–4).

This spiritual union is invisible; it reflects our spiritual family ties. We have been born into a new family. We have the privilege of praying, "Our Father in heaven." Such unity means that, when we meet as fellow members of the family, we find a recognition at the core of our being. We begin to see each other as brothers and sisters in Christ. So we find ourselves, despite differences in age, culture, ethnicity, and even ecclesiastical or theological backgrounds, able to pray together. It is this spiritual unity which is the building block of our local expressions of church. We are not like a social club, a political party, or a sports team. It's far deeper than that. We share fellowship with Father, Son, and Holy Spirit.

Such invisible spiritual unity is not without its challenges, particularly when we come together from different parts of the church and indeed where there are significant areas of disagreement. Of course, none of us has access to the "Lamb's book of life". Only God ultimately knows who is part of the family, and He isn't at this stage letting us in on the secret. So, as a normal practice, as I relate to those who claim the name of Christ within the mainstream orthodox tradition of Christianity, I operate on the assumption of spiritual unity, shared membership of the same family, which will at the very least enable me to find ways of having fellowship and praying together. It is in this context that I have discovered that even with those with whom I might have significant theological differences, there is much that we can find agreement on as we pray and worship together.

Relational unity

Spiritual unity provides a wonderful starting point for other expressions of unity. Relational unity emerges out of spiritual unity. It puts flesh on the bones of our theological concepts. We begin to build friendships together. It's amazing to reflect on how much time Jesus devoted in His three years of ministry to building relationships with those He chose to be with Him. It seems for Jesus that there were the close friends, Peter, James, and John, and then there were the twelve, the seventy, and indeed the 120. Jesus invested relationally in all of these people and almost certainly more – He appeared to more than 500 after His resurrection.

It's true for most of us. Our relationships exist at different levels, but they are still important. They should be invested in and affirmed; relationships require time and energy. They have to be built, and then maintained. I'm grateful to God for the relationships I have with those around me. Some are deeply significant and have shaped my life and ministry. Others are more superficial and less intense, but they are still friendships, they are relationships, and can at times be profoundly significant. For us as an Evangelical Alliance team, one of our values is that we are relational. As a leadership team, we are not just doing a job; we are friends called to serve God together. This is reflected in how we meet. We eat together at my house, we share life experiences with each other, and we pray together. In my role across the evangelical community, I'm seeking to nurture and develop relationships – that means family updates, meals, coffees and teas as we meet together, as well as shared business and looking for collaboration.

Missional unity

Some of the amazing stories that are emerging (as explored in Chapter 8), in towns and cities across the country, are these "unity movements". The emergence of these movements has a common theme: Christian leaders meeting together, praying together, eating together, building relationships and trust; and out of these relationships long-term commitments are emerging to do mission together. All over the country it's becoming the norm to do the kinds of missional initiatives we have become familiar with (foodbanks, Street Pastors, debt counselling services, etc.) together, rather than simply as one individual church. Missionary unity can be most challenging for the Christian community when it comes to shared evangelistic initiatives, and so it is that in some cities, following open and honest respectful conversations, church leaders have agreed that, when it comes to gospel proclamation, differing views on what the gospel actually is make it more sensible for such initiatives to be run separately or by clusters of churches that share a common view of the gospel.

Confessional unity

As is the case with a number of Paul's letters, the theme of unity is central to the book of Philippians. He is writing to a church that is clearly facing problems in this area. In Philippians 1:27 Paul challenges the members both on their behaviour and on their theology: "Whatever happens, conduct yourselves in a manner worthy of the gospel of Christ. Then, whether I come and see you or only hear about you in my absence, I will know that you stand firm in the one Spirit, striving together as one for the faith of the gospel." Paul seems to be challenging the church in Philippi to recognize its unity – spiritually, relationally, and missionally, and also with regard to being "as one for the faith of the gospel". For evangelicals particularly, finding a unity around our confessional essentials has been important over the years. From the Evangelical Alliance's conception, a statement of faith has attempted to affirm the common ground of our evangelical tradition. It is important to note that while Paul is calling for unity, it is not unity at any price, which would deny fundamental truth. Nor, however, is it a unity that separates us from anyone who fails to agree on every area of detailed biblical interpretation. Sadly, over the years, the evangelical family has found numerous ways to disagree and fragment over what should certainly be regarded as non-essentials or of secondary importance. This disunity has at times been a major hindrance to our evangelistic work.

Institutional unity

It seems an inevitable expression of human coexistence that we form institutions for which we provide structures, rules, names, and brand identity, and to which we offer our allegiance and which in the long term take on a life of their own and fight for their existence. There is nothing intrinsically wrong with institutional unity, whether to a denomination, a network, a Churches Together group, or an Evangelical Alliance, but, for all of us, ensuring that the institution continues to serve the purpose for which it came into existence and, indeed more importantly, work for the advancement of God's kingdom today requires us to keep asking ourselves searching questions. We must never exist as a church, organization, alliance, or council simply to maintain that existence.

Sadly, in my observations of the Christian community, too many institutions have kept going when they really should have closed down, finished well, and handed on the building, finance, or resources to others who could have used them more effectively. I have to confess that institutional unity is the expression of unity that least excites me and in which I see the most danger. Institutionalism is an attitude of mind that sucks life, faith, and creativity out of people and indeed organizations. God save us from institutionalism in whatever context He has called us into. It's certainly true that the younger generation who are taking on roles of influence in the church today have less loyalty to the institutions to which they are currently aligned and are far more likely to either move on or close them down.

Hope for the future

Over the last fifty years, since 1966 and the Lloyd-Jones–Stott public disagreement, there have been a number of significant areas of conflict, pain, and separation within the evangelical community. However, I detect what I trust to be early indicators of hope as we look to the future. For some time, unity has been developing at a local level. Initiatives such as HOPE, Gather (bringing local unity movements together), Redeeming Our Communities, Soul in the City, Message 2000, and Gweini in Wales have all seen unity expressed in wonderfully missional ways.

The challenge has, however, seemed far greater as we have considered the national scene. Yet even here there is reason to be hopeful. Stemming from a series of conversations between Lyndon Bowring (Executive Chair of CARE – Christian Action Research & Education), David Coffey (former president of the Baptist World Alliance), and myself, later joined by Nola Leach (CEO of CARE), four friends who had known each other for years, a series of informal private meetings began to draw together leaders representing the various "tribes" within evangelicalism. The object of these meetings was to explore evangelical unity at a national level. The gatherings took place in a variety of settings, from small (eight to twelve people around a meal table or half a dozen sitting in a lounge) to eventually a couple of twenty-four-hour gatherings in a private hotel for a larger group. Those invited covered a wide cross section of the evangelical world – men and women from different theological, ecclesiastical, and ethnic backgrounds. After opportunities to build relationships, the conversation would turn to areas of disagreement. The list was long, and in some cases revived painful memories. It included a number of historical decisions that had been made and practical steps that organizations had taken. The emergence in the student world of Fusion, working on campuses across the country alongside UCCF. The decision of Spring Harvest and Word Alive to go their separate ways. The migrant church failing to be welcomed in the UK by the white indigenous church and more recently having been excluded from early-stage planning for missionary activities. New churches such as my own and our attitude towards the historical Pentecostal churches. Alongside these were theological disagreements and how they had been handled. The charismatic/ non-charismatic divide needed attention, as did the fallout from the atonement debate provoked by Steve Chalke's book *The Lost Message of Jesus* (Zondervan, 2003). The insensitivity with which the debate on the role of women in the church had been conducted, and the ongoing issues concerning human sexuality.

As the meetings progressed, it became clear that relationships were being nurtured and trust was being built – a culture was emerging of respectful hearing of each other in a non-defensive manner, and a great deal of common ground was established as we affirmed the desire to proclaim the good news. However, alongside all that, there was a recognition of the church's responsibility to engage in social action. The two twenty-four-hour meetings at the hotel included some powerful moments of honest disclosure, confession, repentance, prayer, shared worship, and breaking bread together.

While there's still ground to be taken and relationships to be nurtured, there are also significant reasons to be hopeful. On the second of our twenty-four-hour days in Winchester, the gathering divided into groups of six or seven and conducted an exercise in evangelical doctrine and practice, exploring what matters were considered to be of primary importance and what were secondary. The sheets from the various groups were then displayed on the wall. The common ground between the groups was amazing. From the breadth of the evangelical community, there was so much agreement on what was of primary importance, the issues we could unite around. These were those primary Christian truths relating to the person and work of Christ as defined in the great ancient creeds – together with the wonderful historical Reformation and evangelical emphasis on the authority of Scripture, the atoning death of Christ, the justification of sinners by grace alone through faith in Christ, the work of the Holy Spirit, and the return of Christ, which are part of the present-day evangelical community wherever it is expressed.

But evangelical unity is not just about theology – it is equally seen in a commitment to action, service, evangelism, social engagement, preaching, and teaching. Of course, a joint commitment to these primary truths and activities leaves evangelicals with plenty of freedom to explore secondary issues without fear of being excluded or rejected, even though there might be disagreements on them. The list produced by the groups in Winchester stated – although not every individual would agree with them – that secondary issues included the nature of baptism, women in leadership, styles of worship, church government, views of hell, Israel, evolution, eschatology, war and pacifism, the nature of election, charismatic gifts, gender roles, forms of leadership, and money.

(As I look back on these conversations, the issue on which we struggled most over how best to categorize it was the biblical view of human sexuality. All of us would recognize the final authority of Scripture in determining our ethical decisions, but for most of us the ethics of sexual behaviour did not sit comfortably as a primary truth, although the practical implications are of primary concern for both the church and indeed society as a whole.)

One of the first fruits of these evangelical gatherings beyond simply the building of relationships, understanding, and mutual respect has been the desire to express that unity. As I write, plans are being made that in 2017 the church will acknowledge the 500th anniversary of the Reformation, through an affirmation of our evangelical unity. So it is that in most of the festivals, events, and conferences that will take place during 2017 a shared act will take place focusing on John 17's prayer of Jesus. We will make some declarations of our unity in Christ. We will pray prayers and engage in some symbolic acts, recognizing our oneness in Christ. In his book *All One in Christ Jesus*, published in 2009 as part of the Keswick Foundation Series and to highlight the theme of that year's convention, David Coffey made the following comment by way of an introduction:

We are not meeting together in the way we should. We are not talking together in the way that we should. We are not addressing the things which divide us. We are not seeking with urgency the fresh consensus on the essentials of the evangelical faith which could contribute to a deeper expression of our unity. And above all, we are not one in mind, in the single area where evangelicals have traditionally excelled. We are not united in God's mission.

I conclude this chapter by honouring my dear friends David Coffey, Lyndon Bowring, and Nola Leach, who have sought under God to provide an answer at least in part to the great challenge David outlined back in 2009.

Questions

- Are there any relationships you have that have been damaged by disagreement? Should you take the first step and suggest getting together?
- Have you ever, either alone or with friends (or perhaps in your small group), listed and considered the primary truths of the Christian faith?
- Can you think of some meaningful way in which your church could celebrate and affirm your oneness in Christ over the coming year?

Chapter 13

One: When unity fails

"The way of separation is to pursue truth at the expense of unity. The way of compromise is to pursue unity at the expense of truth. The way of comprehensiveness is to pursue truth and unity simultaneously, that is, to pursue the kind of unity commended by Christ and his apostles namely unity in truth."

John Stott, *The Living Church*

"I don't want to spend the next ten years of my life talking about human sexuality." This is a comment I made to a friend in 2009 as I prepared to take on my current role at the Evangelical Alliance. I had seen what my predecessor Joel Edwards had endured, and I knew there were other matters that were just as – if not more – important, to which I wanted to give my attention. Well, I had pretty much managed to avoid the subject until January 2013 when a well-known Christian magazine published an article by my friend Steve Chalke in which he challenged the historically orthodox biblical interpretation of issues relating to human sexuality.

Conflict is never pleasant. Like most, I prefer to avoid it. In fact, Scripture exhorts us, "If it is possible, as far as it depends on you, live at peace with one another" (Romans 12:18). I'm definitely a live-at-peace-with-one-another kind of person. Conflict is hard enough even when we face it in the context of family, friends, neighbours, or workmates. It's stressful and emotionally draining. Conflict escalates when it affects the wider group. We have already explored the issue of conflict in the local church and the long-term impact it can have, particularly if not handled well.

It's amazing how much time Paul spends addressing the subject of conflict and disagreement in the early church. A whole book (1 Corinthians) is devoted almost entirely to this matter. But what happens when it plays out at a national level? What happens when the conflict is carried out not just in a private meeting and the exchange of emails and letters? How does it work out when it feels as if the whole world is watching? Or at least a significant part of the Christian world. How can we handle conflict well when it's being reported on by the BBC, national newspapers, and a torrent of social media comment?

Let's face it, the Christian community hasn't always handled conflict well. The Evangelical Alliance itself has had its fair share of mishandled conflicts over the years. My public disagreement with my friend Steve Chalke and the Alliance's questions over our own relationship with Oasis – the organization he founded – had the potential to become one of those high-profile disasters. While going through this conflict, I did at times wonder whether in years to come books would be written and case studies produced identifying what happened in 2013 and 2014 as a great example of how not to handle conflict.

One of the things I love about Scripture is that it wasn't written by spin doctors. Leafing through the pages of the Bible, we get the good with the bad, the "Praise the Lord" alongside the "Oh dear". It's strangely encouraging to read in Galatians 2 of the conflict between two senior apostles, pillars of the early church. Peter has arrived in Antioch, where Paul is and where God is clearly at work. Gentiles are coming to Christ in large numbers. Peter is enjoying the fellowship, happily eating with all members of the church – Jews and Gentiles all mixed together. That is until a deputation from Jerusalem arrives, sent by James. Suddenly we are told in Galatians 2:12 that Peter begins to adjust his behaviour, separates himself from the Gentiles, and stops eating with them. Peter is not alone.

Barnabas – Paul's travelling companion – and some other Jews join Peter in the same act of separation. Paul's not going to stand for it and challenges Peter. "When Cephas [Peter] came to Antioch, I opposed him to his face, because he stood condemned" (2:11)… "when I saw that they were not acting in line with the truth of the gospel, I said to Cephas in front of them all…" (2:14). A very public conflict.

Paul called it what it was: "hypocrisy" (verse 13). He knew Peter could not be allowed to get away with it. This could have been the thin end of a very large wedge, and Peter was in danger of dividing the church. Two separate meal tables could lead to two separate churches, two Lord's suppers, two apostolic church-planting movements. Peter had come under pressure as these delegates from Jerusalem arrived. He had forgotten the revelation he received from God following his encounter with Cornelius, when the Holy Spirit fell on a whole Gentile household.

Somehow, the fact that he had defended that revelation and rehearsed the story in Acts 15 before the council of Jerusalem was put to one side. Paul needed to confront Peter and Barnabas and the other Jews, and it couldn't just be done privately. Their hypocrisy had been publicly revealed and it needed to be publicly challenged.

As I have explored evangelical history in the UK and beyond, I have seen that relationships between evangelical leaders have fluctuated greatly. When I came into post in 2009, I was of the view that on the ground in towns and cities across the UK there was a lot to be thankful for. We had just completed an amazing year of mission, HOPE 08, and I had seen first-hand the collaboration between churches from right across the evangelical spectrum and beyond. It seemed that, when it came to fun days, foodbanks, Street Pastors, Passion plays, and Easter exhibitions, differences in theology and ecclesiology were of secondary importance.

Although some churches found shared gospel proclamation difficult, the picture in the main was of local unity wherever possible and respect when conscience required some degree of separation.

The national scene, however, seemed more complex. I was aware of a number of historical issues which seemed to remain a source of some pain and disagreement. So it was that I spent the first eighteen months of my time at the Alliance visiting evangelical leaders from the many different "tribes' of the evangelical community. We took time to eat and drink together, shared personal family stories, and rehearsed some of the areas of conflict. As a card-carrying charismatic from a new-church network, I knew that some conservative evangelicals had raised their eyebrows at my appointment. What was the Evangelical Alliance coming to, they thought? How on earth could someone from this background represent the breadth of the evangelical constituency? After all, weren't these new-church leaders weak on theology and simply interested in experience?

I look back on those meetings with real thankfulness as we shared and prayed together. We discovered so much common ground. Some of the historical pain was discussed. But there was also the opportunity for us to laugh as I related how my new-church-leader friends quizzed me on what it was really like working alongside the dour conservative evangelicals. As we talked, some agreed to join or contribute to our Council, and we agreed that steps needed to be taken to deal with some of the outstanding historical concerns. (That's another story, explored in Chapter 12.)

Staring conflict in the face

At the end of 2012 and into early 2013, the Christian community was pretty much united across ecclesiastical and theological divides on the issue of the government's proposed redefinition of marriage. With a few exceptions, most churches were in agreement that a biblical view of marriage involved a committed loving relationship for life between a man and a woman. David Cameron's government was proposing to bring forward legislation to make it possible for those of the same sex to marry. Although it would not be forced upon the faith communities, provision would be made for those who chose to participate in this newly-defined form of marriage to do so in churches that approved of the change. The Evangelical Alliance had positioned itself at the heart of this debate, as part of the Coalition for Marriage. Working with three other national organizations, we were aiming not only to win the argument but to see the legislation defeated. It was during this time that I heard from a number of friends that an article by Steve Chalke was being planned for the February edition of a well-known Christian magazine, which would be available mid-January. The article would challenge how the church has related to gay people and question the historically orthodox biblical view of same-sex relationships and marriage. While this article would not argue for a redefinition of marriage, it did make it clear that Steve had conducted a dedication and blessing service following the civil partnership of two gay Christians. The article would eventually argue that

> [the] outworking of the Church's historical rejection of faithful gay relationships is our failure to provide homosexual people with any model of how to cope with their sexuality, except for those who have the gift of, or capacity for, celibacy. In this way we have left people vulnerable and isolated. When we refuse to make room for gay people to live in loving, stable relationships, we consign them to lives of loneliness, secrecy, fear, and even of deceit. It's one thing to be critical of a promiscuous lifestyle – but shouldn't the Church consider nurturing positive models for permanent and monogamous homosexual relationships?[1]

The timing was difficult, and the deadline for the publication was imminent. I immediately made contact with the magazine's editors, making the request that they, together with Steve and Oasis, consider delaying the article until after the Coalition for Marriage campaign and the parliamentary vote. The decision came back that publication would go ahead as planned. In early January, I met with Steve and Joy Madeiros, CEO of Oasis Group. It was a good, warm meeting. After discussing Steve's change of mind on this subject and my conviction that his interpretation of Scripture was not sustainable, we went on to discuss how we would handle this disagreement well.

Steve and I go back years. We have worked together on a number of projects and we had sat on the Spring Harvest Board together. We also had a regular, small Christmas celebration that we both attended with our wives. Steve was a friend, and we both knew the publication of this article would result in headlines. It was important to agree how we would handle the conflict. We wanted to speak well of each other, believe the best of each other, pick up the phone and talk to each other if things escalated.

On 15 January, the article was published and a longer piece was made available via the Oasis website. We were right. The response was enormous. Some were delighted that a high-profile evangelical leader had been prepared to argue publicly for a fresh interpretation of the biblical teaching on same-sex relationships. Others were shocked. Steve was one of the highest-profile evangelical leaders of his generation. Wonderfully entrepreneurial, he had developed Oasis into a flagship of social enterprise. He had preached at some of the UK's largest conferences and festivals. He had appeared on radio and TV as a spokesperson for the Christian faith. Steve had, however, already undermined his credibility as an evangelical leader at least in some circles. His book *The Lost Message of Jesus*, published in 2003, had challenged one of the classic evangelical views of the atonement (penal substitution). Considering this historic disagreement less than a decade earlier, some did not view Steve's repositioning on homosexuality as a great surprise.

At our offices, the phone began to ring and the emails started to arrive, as did the requests for interviews. We knew we had to respond; getting the tone as well as the content right was critical. How we responded would put down a marker for the ongoing debate. Below are the two pieces – a statement and a more detailed biblical reflection – that we published on our website within hours of the magazine being released:

The Bible & Homosexuality: A response to Steve Chalke

Statement from Steve Clifford, General Director, Evangelical Alliance:

Steve Chalke is a friend of mine. We go back many years. I am convinced that when the history of the Church in the UK is written, Steve's contribution over the last 25 years will be recognized as profoundly significant. So with this as a backdrop I am writing my response to Steve's article. While I understand and respect Steve's pastoral motivations, I believe the conclusions he has come to on same-sex relationships are wrong.

It is with both sadness and disappointment that I reflect on how Steve has not only distanced himself from the vast majority of the evangelical community here in the UK, but indeed from the Church across the world and 2,000 years of biblical interpretation.

Steve has raised issues that touch on deep areas of human identity. At a Soul Survivor seminar last summer, a Baptist minister who lives with same-sex attraction introduced his talk to a marquee full of young people by indicating that he would love to find a theology in the Bible which would support a sexually active gay life. But, he said, "I've come to the conclusion that it is not there and I don't want to live in rebellion to the one that I love." This pastor is just one of tens of thousands of Christians who have come to the conclusion that sex was designed by God to be expressed within a committed relationship for life between a man and a woman – we call this marriage – and have chosen to live a celibate life.

Steve Chalke's challenge to historic biblical interpretation is in danger of undermining such courageous lifestyle decisions. Last year, the Evangelical Alliance produced a resource for leaders entitled *Biblical and Pastoral Responses to*

Homosexuality – put together by a commission of eight and peer-reviewed by 40. I trust this resource reflects a considered, gracious, and mature response. It follows on from the highly respected *Faith, Hope and Homosexuality* book produced some 14 years ago, combining a clear and succinct statement of biblical teaching on marriage and sexuality. It expressed regret for the Church's past and present failure in relation to the lesbian and gay community. Realistically and honestly, it engages with real-life scenarios to help Christians, and especially pastors and others in Christian ministry, discern how we can speak and live the truth in love.

Generations of Christians have faced the challenge of making the gospel relevant within their cultural settings. The danger we all face, and I fear Steve has succumbed to, is that we produce "a god" in our own likeness or in the likeness of the culture in which we find ourselves.

[Note: in my subsequent conversations with Steve, he challenged me on my reference to God without a capital, as if He were just another "god". I accepted that observation and have apologized for creating that impression.]

Steve's approach to biblical interpretation allows for a god in the likeness of twenty-first-century Western European mindsets. His call for "Christlike inclusion" is not radical enough in its inclusiveness. We all come to the gospel in our brokenness, with an attachment to things, self-centredness, addictions, fears and pride. We all need a saviour in every area of our lives, including our sexuality. We all live with pain. The radical inclusiveness of the gospel means we are all welcomed. In a wonderful grace-filled process we find repentance and forgiveness and Christ commits Himself through the work of the Holy Spirit to bring transformation to our lives – a lifelong process.

This is the radical inclusiveness I believe the gospel offers to all of us. God doesn't leave us on our own, He promises to work in us, to bring us to our ultimate goal, which is His likeness.

Inevitably, Steve's article will open again the conversation on human sexuality. But as we have this discussion let's remember that Jesus requires us to disagree without being disagreeable. We must listen honestly and carefully to one another, being courteous and generous. In 1846, our Evangelical Relationships Commitment was created to guide us in our relationships with other Christians – especially those we disagree with.

Not radical enough – a biblical reflection, February 2013

The philosopher Dallas Willard writes: "The aim of God in history is the creation of an all-inclusive community of loving persons, with Himself included in that community as its prime sustainer and most glorious inhabitant."

The vision that Willard sets out is compelling and speaks into the crux of Steve Chalke's recent article. Steve is someone whom I respect enormously, but I think he is wrong. This is due, in part, to an insufficiently radical view of inclusion. The two big questions we must consider are these: *what did Jesus' vision of inclusion look like in the first century? And what does Jesus' vision of inclusion look like in 2013?* In answering these questions, we need to deploy the tools of exegesis (what *did* it mean?) and hermeneutics (what *does* it mean?). In other words, our task is to consider what the teaching and praxis of Jesus looked like to His contemporaries and to the earliest recipients of the gospels, and how to apply Jesus' teaching and praxis to the challenges of our contemporary world.

The kingdom of God: The invitation, the life, the central claim

In the first century, Jesus declared that: "The kingdom of God has come near. Repent and believe the good news!" (Mark 1:15). In proclaiming this good news, Jesus was announcing that God was doing something radically new and He was inviting people to be part of it.

In essence, Jesus was inviting people to embrace what Tom Wright describes as an "utterly risky way" of being human. It was the way of turning the other cheek and going the second mile, the way of losing your life to gain it. Crucially, this life was not to be lived in isolation but in community – a community of celebration which brings jubilee or freedom, a community of love of God and love of neighbour within which all, including the most disreputable, are welcome. A community into which no one is forced and from which anyone can walk away (as the rich young man did). A community of infinite mutual forgiveness in which right living comes from repentance and faith in God and His power as seen in Jesus' ministry, and a community which is led, and lives, by the Spirit of God, not by violence, coercion or persecution. The earliest members of this community, disciples of Jesus, were characterized by their exclusive profession that "Jesus the Messiah is Lord" (Romans 10:9).

The radically inclusive nature of Jesus' invitation

In response to Jesus' kingdom invitation, the gospel writers note how all sorts of people, especially those on the margins of society, responded positively: tax collectors, soldiers, zealots, prostitutes, the poor and the wealthy. This is vividly described in the parable of the banquet (Luke 14:15–24). Where religious leaders drew lines around people to say whether they were in or out, Jesus destroyed them. Indeed,

Jesus' appeal was widely commented on by those in positions of power and authority. In his gospel, Luke notes how the Pharisees and teachers of the law complained, "This man welcomes sinners, and eats with them" (15:2).

The transforming power of the kingdom

Inclusion into Jesus' community resulted in the transformation of people's lives. Tax collectors were to stop collecting any more than they were required to, soldiers were to stop extorting money and accusing people falsely, zealots were to stop using violence, prostitutes were to stop providing sexual services to others in return for payment and attitudes to money were to change. Anyone with two shirts was to share with those with none, and anyone with food was to do the same. It really was that radical. Inclusion into Jesus' community without an experience of, and response to, God's transformative power was simply not an option. Of course, not everyone was able to accept this sort of inclusion. It was too difficult for some. In response to Jesus telling a rich young man to "go, sell everything you have and give to the poor... Then come, follow me", Mark describes how "the man's face fell" and "he went away sad, because he had great wealth" (Mark 10:21–22).

The challenge of Jesus – everybody welcome

So the community grounded in the exclusive claims of Jesus is both radically inclusive and radically transformative. And this takes us to our contemporary context. So how can the contemporary Church embody the Christlike, inclusive and transformative community described in the New Testament and offer meaning to our complex, hurting and misunderstood world?

First, we are called as Jesus' disciples to invite and welcome everyone into His community, regardless of their gender, ethnicity, sexual orientation and class. The categories that divided people in previous generations and cultures are blown apart by Jesus. In the words of the apostle Paul: "There is neither Jew nor Gentile, neither slave nor free, nor is there male and female, for you are all one in Christ Jesus" (Galatians 3:28).

Subject to God's transforming power

Second, the community of Jesus is called to embrace a radically "risky way" of being human. We can't be part of God's inclusive community without subjecting ourselves to the transforming power of His Spirit. We can't be residents of the kingdom without being subjects of the king. Inclusion into Jesus' community will affect every aspect of our human existence – our self-understanding, relationships, work, and approaches to sex, money and power. In all of these areas and plenty of others too, we are to take Jesus into the whole of our lives. Willard states that: "The greatest challenge the Church faces today is to be authentic disciples of Jesus. And by that I mean they're learning from Him how to live their life, as He would live their life if He were they." This is massively challenging but we should not be discouraged. John Newton, the hymn writer and former slave trader, once said: "I am not what I ought to be, I am not what I want to be, I am not what I hope to be in another world; but still I am not what I once used to be, and by the grace of God I am what I am."

So, how are we to apply this thinking in the evangelical community and to the challenge that Steve Chalke presents us with?

Centred on Jesus

In the first place, our principal focus needs to be on Jesus and living our life as He would live it if He were us. We need to resist the temptation of making God in our own image, and allow Him to remake us in His. The Evangelical Alliance invites prospective members to sign a statement of faith that centres on Jesus as the source of our identity. It is precisely on the basis of our understanding of Jesus' uniqueness and our commitment to everything He is that we seek to be radically Christlike.

Supporting each other

Within the context of our movement, we are working to support one another in working out how to apply Jesus' teaching to the challenges of the 21st century. We don't pretend that this is easy, but we won't duck the difficult issues either, including questions about gay relationships. We recently produced a resource for church leaders looking at biblical and pastoral responses to homosexuality which we believe reflects an authentic, mainstream New Testament response to homosexuality in general and sexually active same-sex partnerships in particular.

Creating space for grace

We don't confuse our statement of faith with our work on contemporary issues. Our commitment to applying Jesus' teaching in our 21st-century context means we won't avoid difficult issues and we will respect those who take a different view. We believe we can – in fact Jesus commands us to – disagree without being disagreeable. So, we must listen carefully to one another, being courteous and generous, seeking in all things to acquire the mind of Christ. The Evangelical Relationships Commitment stands alongside the Basis of Faith as a commitment we make to each other.

Going forward

Try as I might (and believe me I have tried), I can only see that Scripture places sexual union in one unique context: a committed relationship for life between a man and a woman – that which we call marriage. Steve's interpretation and application of Scripture is, I think, wrong, as he fails to recognize the radical call to discipleship within our sexuality, whether married or unmarried or gay. Like the rich young ruler of Mark 10, some will regard this as a hard teaching and will walk away sad. The challenge for the Christian community is to support one another as we seek to follow Jesus in contemporary culture – with all the challenges, conflicts and pain that can involve. That is, after all, what it means to be a radically inclusive and transformative community. That is what it means to be the body of Christ.

Sadly, the next weeks and months became filled up with the Oasis/Steve Chalke issue. There were so many interviews, both mainstream and Christian; there were articles written, emails sent, letters received, and phone calls made. As a leadership team and Board, we were determined to handle this well. We wanted to be respectful of both Steve and Oasis but at the same time recognize the disagreement and its serious nature. We made it clear from the start that Steve's relationship with the Evangelical Alliance as an individual member was a matter of his personal conscience, which we did not police. If he could with a clear conscience sign our statement of faith and make his annual donation, he would remain a member, alongside tens of thousands of others. But the relationship between Oasis and the Alliance was in question, as the bar was set higher for organizational membership. Both churches and organizations are expected to maintain good relationships with fellow members. Conversations had already started between Mike Talbot, the chair of the Evangelical Alliance Board, and John Whiter, the chair of Oasis. But these gained momentum when we received an official complaint from a well-respected and long-established member organization.

By the summer of 2013, the situation was becoming clearer. John and Mike were meeting, emails were being exchanged, and the Oasis Board made it clear that Oasis as an organization had "no corporate view on this issue" other than a desire for an open discussion to take place. While this position was a helpful clarification, the difficulty crystallized around public perception. While "no corporate view" was the official position, it was felt by many across the evangelical world that a "campaign" was being conducted to challenge the historically orthodox view on human sexuality. Steve Chalke as the high-profile founder of Oasis was regularly writing, speaking, and responding to interviews on this subject. The Oasis website was populated with resources designed to support that position, with no balancing material from a different viewpoint.

So it was that at the September 2013 Council of the Evangelical Alliance, after much prayer and debate, a request was made to the Oasis Board. First, that Oasis issue a public statement unequivocally declaring that Oasis had no corporate view on this issue, and that they place that fact on their website. Second, that the website, in addition to its existing material, should include resources equally profiling the traditional Christian view, or the Oasis Board should remove from their website the material relating to human sexuality so that it could appear on a site outside their control.

By December 2013, the issue was coming to a conclusion. The Oasis Board had met and indicated that they were willing for their website to include an introductory video message from Steve Chalke explaining that Oasis was a diverse organization, including people with a wide range of opinions on all sorts of issues (perhaps not as strong or clear as we were hoping for, but a step in the right direction). But they were not prepared to either remove material or include material that would provide a balanced overview of the subject.

After the anniversary of the *Christianity* article, the Board and then the Council of the Evangelical Alliance met, with both sides agonizing over the next step. The Board initially agreed not to seek Oasis's withdrawal but subsequently passed a unanimous motion seeking the Alliance Council's guidance. Following a very open debate involving approximately seventy leading evangelicals who make up the Council, a significant majority voted in favour of Oasis's withdrawal. Mike Talbot was commissioned to formally contact John Whiter and inform Oasis of the decision. Mike's letter to John reflected the pain and sadness of many who had walked this journey of conflict.

Mike wrote to John in the warmest terms, and with "a heavy heart", requesting that Oasis implement the offer to withdraw from membership. (Mike had gained the impression from John that, should no agreement be found, John hoped his Board would choose to withdraw from membership.) Mike went on to say, "Alongside the deep sadness that accompanied the Council's decision was also a recognition that although there are differences of understanding between Oasis and the Alliance at present, nevertheless we value the friendship we have."

Mike's letter reflected the atmosphere in which the high-profile conflict was conducted, although in the end the Oasis Board were unwilling to withdraw from membership and the Alliance was forced in May 2014 to discontinue Oasis's membership. In the end, the conflict with Oasis moved beyond the subject of human sexuality. The issue that resulted eventually in Oasis Trust's removal from membership became one of relationship and of how that relationship is worked out in the context of the Alliance's diverse evangelical community, and what could be legitimately expected of that community. Oasis were unwilling to comply with a request made by the Board and Council of the Alliance. The Board and Council concluded that membership of the Alliance should require a willingness to respect and respond positively to such a request. In the end, with sadness and pain, Oasis were removed from membership.

The lessons learned

The Oasis/Steve Chalke conflict was protracted and painful for all concerned. But I believe both sides came out of the process well. There were some on both sides of the debate who would have liked more fireworks, but it seems to me, looking back on the events, that we managed to disagree and indeed to separate in a Christlike way. However, there are always lessons to learn. Family business is best conducted respectfully and privately but, in an age of mass communication, privacy is not always possible. Inevitably, the Oasis conflict hit the headlines, but in all of our public and private conversations about both Steve and the organization, we attempted to speak well of them and all they had achieved. Steve and I have held on to our relationship through the conflict – an occasional coffee, a few phone calls, and bumping into each other in various social settings. It's not been without its tensions. Steve disagrees with the decision the Alliance made and there has been the occasional need to clarify things that were said. But I continue to respect Steve and indeed all that he and Oasis have achieved not just in the UK but around the world.

Drawing the chairs of our respective Boards, Mike and John, into the conflict proved to be really helpful, as it prevented it from becoming over-personalized. The problem could be clarified and worked through and, although in the end a parting of ways became necessary, we were able to do this with mutual respect. In the end, this conflict took sixteen months to run its course. At the time, it seemed to last for ever. The need for various boards and councils to have their say inevitably extended the time, but, with matters as serious as this, not rushing to speedy conclusions has got to be a sound approach. It provides an opportunity for the body of Christ to speak and for the corporate wisdom of the elders to be heard.

How Christians conduct themselves on social media was certainly highlighted throughout this conflict. It's amazing what people seem willing to say on Twitter or Facebook that you couldn't imagine them saying face to face. A few years ago, we worked with a small group of social media users to come up with Ten Commandments for using social media. This needs to be revisited. We need to challenge each other over the use of social media.

The conflict also raised a question in many people's minds as to the role of the Christian media and their responsibility for reporting on and profiling particular issues. I have discussed it at some length with my friends in the media and I am still unsure. I'm left wondering how the conflict between Peter and Paul might have been reported in a twenty-first-century setting and whether that would have enhanced the integration of Jews and Gentiles or whether it would have set it back. Clearly, Christian journalists have a job to do but they are also part of a family. Sometimes families get into a mess and just need some time and space to sort things out away from the public gaze.

Conflict with God

The Oasis conflict was not the first and I'm sure will not be the last I will face while at the Evangelical Alliance. It has, however, been the most high-profile.

All this talk of conflict brings me back to that "live at peace with everyone" scripture. I've come to realize that it can affect my relationship with God.

It was a few years ago now, but I remember the scene well. It was during the Christmas break, and Ann and I were having a lazy morning. I was lying in bed reading my Bible, and I found myself in an honest moment with God as I told Him there were some bits of the Bible that I found really hard to take.

I should explain: we were right in the middle of the debate on the redefinition of marriage. The issue of human sexuality was a focus of many interviews, conversations, and articles. As I lay in bed I was remembering a conversation with a dear friend who had shared with us the fact that he lived with same-sex attraction, but had now decided he wished to explore an intimate relationship. It had been a tough conversation, as we were friends and still are. I was grateful that he felt able to trust us with his story, his struggles, and indeed the conclusion he had come to. But my love for my friend, my reading of Scripture, and my understanding of how the church had interpreted that Scripture for almost 2,000 years, meant that I couldn't just celebrate with him and say, "It's OK; it doesn't matter", or "I'm sure God wouldn't mind". I really wish I could have celebrated with our friend. I wish the Bible was less clear – at least from my reading of it – on some of these issues. It would be so much simpler if the Bible's views of marriage were not exclusively heterosexual.

But as I lay in bed that morning, it wasn't just the issues of human sexuality that bothered me – some of those Old Testament stories of God at work, His holiness, and His judgments can be hard to take. There are bits of the Bible, in both Old and New Testament, which cut across my sensitivities, brought up as I was in a Western European education system and bombarded as I am by a secular humanist agenda. I'm attracted to the God so supremely revealed in Jesus; the God whom the apostle John sums up with three words, "God is love". But it seems there is more to God than my twenty-first-century preferences. There is more than the parts of the Bible that I choose to underline, or the stories I regularly read and preach from.

As I lay there thinking, I was overcome with a deep sense of my own arrogance. I realized I was in danger of wanting to put God into a neat box and wanting to make Him acceptable to my sensitivities. Maybe my God of love was more of a Hollywood God than Yahweh, the God revealed in Scripture. It was a profound moment. I found myself asking for forgiveness and thanking God for the Bible, in which and through which, with the aid of the Holy Spirit, He has chosen to reveal Himself in all His magnificent fullness.

I have reflected on that morning over the last few years, and have realized how every generation of Christians has faced the challenge of how to contextualize the gospel for its own generation. What stories, metaphors, images, and historical truths will best connect and make accessible this wonderfully loving, sovereign, and eternal God. The challenge however, for each of us, is how to contextualize without compromising or sanitizing the God of Scripture and, indeed, the God revealed in Jesus.

I'm reminded of Romans chapter 12, where the apostle Paul makes it clear to his readers where the will of God is to be found: "Do not conform to the pattern of this world, but be transformed by the renewing of your mind." How easy it is, with so many strong messages bombarding us day in and day out, to find ourselves "conforming". The dominant world views that fill our daily diet of TV, social media, film, and newspaper are so persuasive that it makes me want to "conform".

My prayer is that I will see things more clearly and there will be a transformation of my mind so that I will better know His will and understand His ways and not find myself in conflict with God, even if at times I am with some of His people.

Chapter 14

One: United in action

"So when I speak of mission, I am speaking of all that God is doing in His great purpose for the whole of creation and all that He calls us to do in co-operation with that purpose."
Chris Wright, *The Mission of God's People*

"Without true Christians loving one another, Christ says, the world cannot be expected to listen, even when we give proper answers... [so] after we have done our best to communicate to a lost world, still we must never forget that the final apologetic which Jesus Christ gives is the observable love of true Christians for true Christians. As with the Early Church so with us, people should say above all 'Behold, how they love one another'."
Francis Schaeffer, *The Mark of a Christian*

"In every chorus of human voices, the harmony depends on the 'key-note' being rightly struck... That note I am now appointed to give, and it is LOVE."
John Angell James, 1–3 October 1845, at the Conference on Christian Union held at the Medical School in Liverpool

"I want you to know how hard I am contending for you and for those at Laodicea, and for all who have not met me personally. My goal is that they may be encouraged in heart and united in love."
Colossians 2: 1–2

The three-month period between accepting and taking up the role of General Director of the Evangelical Alliance was something of a whirlwind. There was so much to be sorted out and not a lot of time to make sure that I extricated myself well from the things I was at that time involved with. I also realized I desperately needed time to prepare for this new job that was coming my way at some speed. So it was that Ann and I cleared our diaries as far as was practically possible to allow for a month of prayer and preparation. It was during that time that we rented a cottage for two weeks in North Yorkshire. It was great to be away from the everyday stuff of life and to make room for God to speak to us.

Taking on this new role had been very much a joint decision. Ann and I had over the years been involved in lots of leadership and ministry roles together and I knew that this post at the Alliance was not one I wanted to take on without her 100 per cent support, right there beside me in it. We spent that time away praying, reading, walking, and talking. We had a flipchart and covered the walls of our large lounge with pages of notes. I still at times refer to them. It was during this time that I began to realize the spiritual significance of the foundations on which the Alliance was built. It was as I read about the organization's history that I sensed I was discovering the DNA of a profoundly significant movement of God.

Its long history (we celebrated 170 years of the Alliance in 2016) was not without its high and low periods, and included events and actions which perhaps now, with the gift of hindsight, we might wish had not taken place. But, nevertheless, as I read the Alliance's history it felt as if I was tracking God at work, and in this role would be serving the church not only in the UK but across the world.

It was particularly as I read of the events surrounding the 1846 great assembly, and the preparation for that event, that I began to realize there were important lessons for us to learn and perhaps spiritual territory for us to explore.

Organizations need to be able to answer a set of simple questions about themselves. Why do we exist? What are we called to do? Where are our values to be found? How are we going to achieve what we feel we're called to do? So often it is as an organization explores its early days, the motivations that resulted in its formation, the key agendas which occupied the time and attention of its founders, that a clear direction begins to emerge for its future. In this chapter we will take some time to explore this history, as it provides us not only with key insights into the journey that we as an Alliance are on, but will, I trust, encourage us to see how God is at work in His church across the UK.

The early days

In 1843, an entirely speculative conference was planned by a keen group of Christians who wanted to know whether fellow evangelicals were also sensing that God was calling them to work towards Christian unity. They booked a large hall in London by faith, placed adverts in the newspapers, and invited friends. They received requests for 11,000 tickets for a venue that would hold 3,000. This incredible response gave the organizers the encouragement they needed and so planning began to establish a formal Evangelical Alliance.

This new call to unity had inherited and developed the pan-evangelical spirit of the Wesleyan/Whitefield revival of the previous century. What was encouraging was the fact that both Anglicans and non-conformist evangelicals were at the heart of this planning process. Non-conformists still encountered significant discrimination within British society and were resentful of evangelical Anglicans' unwillingness to address this. This left some Anglicans fearful of the growing interest among some non-conformists in the possibility of the dis-establishment of the Church of England. Along with this, both Anglicans and non-conformists were concerned by the growth of Tractarianism within the Church of England – a high-church expression of faith from which a number would eventually join the Roman Catholic Church.

A number of preparatory meetings were held. The handwritten minutes of one of these meetings, which took place on Tuesday

23 March 1845, reports on the Revd A. Cox, who proposed the following motion:

> The great object of the Evangelical Alliance be to aid in the manifesting as far as practicable, the unity which exists among the true disciples of Christ, to promote their union by fraternal and devotional intercourse, to discourage all envying, strifes and divisions, to impress on Christians a deeper sense of the great duty of obeying our Lord's command to "love one another" and to seek the full accomplishment of His prayer – that they may all be one, as thou Father art in me and I in thee, that they may also be in us, that the world may believe that thou has sent me...

The motion was carried.

In October 1845, a large gathering met at the Medical Hall in Liverpool, with delegates from twenty different denominations present. John Angell James – a non-conformist clergyman and writer – was asked to chair the meeting. His opening remarks set the context:

> In every chorus of human voices, the harmony depends on the "key-note" being rightly struck... That note I am now appointed to give, and it is LOVE.

Writing in *One Body in Christ*, Ian Randall and David Hilborn comment, "The bulk of those attending the Liverpool conference were evangelicals with pan-denominational sympathies, who wished for a new body which would act as a positive force for unity, rather than being known for its opposition to the beliefs of others."

Such helpful challenges, revealing from the beginning the pre-eminence of love and the desire for a positive approach to unity, rather than a focus on what we disagree about. So it was that in 1846 the inaugural conference of the Evangelical Alliance was held in London from 19 August to 1 September. The setting was the Freemasons' Hall in Great Queen Street, London. A surprising choice of venue, you might think, with the signs of the zodiac decorating the walls! It appears the hall was a popular London meeting place, and carried no spiritual significance for those early evangelical leaders. In the century that followed, evangelicals would come to a clear view on the theological and ethical problems with Freemasonry and such a choice would be unthinkable today.

Around 900 delegates attended the assembly, with 84 per cent coming from Britain, 8 per cent from the US, and 7 per cent from mainland Europe and the rest of the world. It is humbling to realize the commitment of those travelling thousands of miles to be present at what they must have perceived as an historic event, especially when one considers that they did not have the ease of modern travel. For some, the journey would have taken weeks and incurred significant costs.

Our archives at the Alliance provide us with detailed records of what took place during the fourteen-day conference. Within two days, there was a unanimous agreement to proceed "to form a confederation under the name of the Evangelical Alliance". So the hard work began. The assembly had representatives from nine major English and Welsh denominations, six Scottish denominations, and three Irish denominations, plus members representing ten denominations in America and members from five countries across continental Europe. With such a large group from such diverse backgrounds, it must be regarded as almost miraculous that a joint basis of belief was agreed. Hard work was needed on issues such as baptism, the sacraments, and hell. But it seems that there was a strong desire to come to a place of mutual agreement and understanding. It took them from the third to the end of the fifth day before Edward Bickersteth could present the Basis of Faith to the assembly. In his presentation, he stressed that although the doctrines in the statement might keep some people out of the Alliance, this was not to be taken as suggesting that they were outside the church (an important clarification for years to come).

There is no doubt that the "right of private judgment" set out in the Basis of Faith helped in this process. In *One Body in Christ*, Ian Randall and David Hilborn comment that:

> the right of private judgment in Protestant thinking meant that there was room for fresh interpretation of scripture and thus it followed that no basis of faith was ultimately binding.

Over the years, the Evangelical Alliance Basis of Faith has had minor adjustments made in order to help modern readers in their clarity of understanding (Appendix 1 has the latest, amended version agreed by the Council in 2005).

The Basis of Faith has over the years provided a helpful touchstone in affirming the distinctly evangelical faith that we profess. It has proved sufficiently broad to include the spectrum of those who would identify with the word "evangelical". Other statements of faith are available within the evangelical community, and adopted by denominations or organizations. These make specific mention of areas of doctrine or practice that they regard as critical to their church or ministry. The list often includes very particular understandings of, say, the end times, the nature of hell, the work of the Holy Spirit, and believers' baptism. It would seem to me that the Alliance's statement has served us well as a streamlined statement that was designed not to exclude but to include the broad evangelical family.

The final days of the conference were devoted to the discussion of a series of propositions urging practical co-operation among evangelicals. The intention of the final agreement, known as the "Practical Resolutions", was to have in place agreed best practices for how evangelicals would disagree with each other agreeably and how they would relate to each other on a day-to-day basis. As I look back on the last 170-plus years of evangelical history in the UK and indeed across the world, I do wish more attention had been given to these Practical Resolutions. A great deal of time and energy has been exerted in debating the Basis of Faith and its implications for biblical understanding. However, I would argue that not enough attention has at times been given to how we get on with each other – particularly when we have different views on a particular issue.

As with the Basis of Faith, the Practical Resolutions, renamed the "Evangelical Relationships Commitment" (reproduced below), have been reworked to aid understanding in a twenty-first-century context, but the essence remains the same.

Evangelical Relationships Commitment

The Evangelical Relationships Commitment is a modern rewording of the eight Practical Resolutions originally agreed at the 1846 Assembly that launched the Evangelical Alliance. They were written to guide members in their relationships with other Christians.

Affirmations

1. We welcome as Christian brothers and sisters all who experience the grace of new birth, bringing them to that fear and knowledge of God which is expressed in a life of obedience to His word.

2. We recognize our Christian duty of trust and mutual encouragement to all who serve Christ as Lord, not least to those who conscientiously prefer not to be identified with the same churches, alliances, or councils as ourselves.

3. We respect the diversity of culture, experience and doctrinal understanding that God grants to His people, and acknowledge that some differences over issues not essential to salvation may well remain until the end of time.

Actions

4. We urge all Christians to pray as Christ prayed, that we may be one in the Father and the Son, and so by the Spirit promote personal relationships of love, peace and fellowship within the Body of Christ, His universal church.

5. We encourage all Christians earnestly to contend for biblical truth, since only as we are open to learn from others and yield fuller obedience to the truth will we be drawn closer to Christ and to each other.

6. We call on each other, when speaking or writing of those issues of faith or practice that divide us, to acknowledge our own failings and the possibility that we ourselves may be mistaken, avoiding personal hostility and abuse, and speaking the truth in love and gentleness.

7. We owe it to each other, in making public comment on the alleged statements of our fellow Christians, first to confer directly with them and to establish what was actually intended. Then to commend what we can, to weigh the proportional significance of what we perceive to be in error, and to put a charitable construction on what is doubtful, expressing all with courtesy, humility and graciousness.

8. We rejoice in the spread of the Gospel across the world and urge all Christians to commit themselves to this task, avoiding unnecessary competition and co-operating, wherever possible, in the completion of Christ's kingdom of peace, justice and holiness, to the glory of the one God – Father, Son and Holy Spirit.

How challenging these commitments are in an age of mass communication and social media. What I love about these resolutions is that they are very practical in nature. I love the way they spell out what is required for unity to be realized in the day-to-day issues of life. This is love worked out in practice. The Basis of Faith and the Evangelical Relationships Commitment stand alongside each other as two of the requirements we make of churches and organizations coming into the Evangelical Alliance, and indeed part of the process of being accepted into membership involves ensuring that they are of good relational standing with other churches or organizations in their geographical area or field of ministry.

Revd M. Vernet (one of the French delegates, who was simultaneously translated into English), commented during the assembly discussions:

> I do not say to love one another, because we do that already, but to unite ourselves together by love. We have been too much occupied with our own affairs, and have aided and assisted each other too little... But the time is come when it is necessary that, in loving him who is love, we should love one another, and walk together.

There was, however, one subject which very nearly derailed the assembly and was the source of a great deal of tension. It was the ownership of slaves by evangelicals, a practice that was common in southern states of America and which the British wished to exclude from any form of membership. Revd Edward Fraser from the Methodist Church of Jamaica, described in the original minutes as "a man of colour", addressed the assembly thus:

> Your kindness must be attributed to that feeling, which is known to dwell in the bosom of British Christians, towards that race of men from whom I came... I shall be quite content, if a more vigorous Christianity is impelled through the world, assured that it will eventually put a stop to that man-destroying, soul and body-destroying, slave trade, as well as effect the conversion of Africa.

British Christians had been at the forefront of the anti-slavery movement, of which William Wilberforce was the champion in parliament. Right from the start it was clear that this Alliance could not simply be confined to the spiritual realms; it had deep concerns about how faith was worked out within society as a whole. While none of the American delegates were slave owners, they had slave owners in their congregations, and the matter was far less clear-cut to them than it was to the British.

The comment was made by William Patton and several American delegates that they had not come to join an anti-slavery society. A sub-committee was formed to deal with this matter. An agreement was reached and then lost again. The Americans appeared to hate being told what they should or shouldn't do by the Brits. So it was that the idea of an international Alliance, which had been the original intention, was dropped.

A British suggestion was adopted that a set of loosely linked international organizations could operate with a degree of independence in some areas. This was seen as the only workable solution. It meant that the British evangelicals would not be drawn into fellowship with slave owners and that each Alliance body could rightly say that it was not responsible for the actions taken in another region. Rather than one organization, a loose network of autonomous national and regional Alliances was set up.

I have to confess that as I read the account of the debate surrounding slave ownership, I was proud of the stance taken by our British evangelical forebears. At a conference devoted to Christian unity, there was for them a matter which was of even greater importance. They were willing to jeopardize the assembly and in the end forfeit their aspirations for a worldwide Evangelical Alliance because of this crucial issue.

For every organization, there are moments when it has to say, "We cannot step over that line." Or times when the behaviour of an individual, church, or organization has taken them to a place in which we as an organization can no longer remain in a close working relationship with them. Over the years, as an Evangelical Alliance, we have on occasions had to withdraw membership from churches and organizations. Certainly in my time, it has been done with a great deal of pain and sadness.

The early years of the Alliance's existence saw membership grow quickly, with 5,000 listed by 1850. The first edition of the monthly magazine *Evangelical Christendom* was published in 1847, and it would continue for 107 years. In September 1855, one of the Alliance's earliest religious liberty campaigns started. A letter was sent to the Sultan of Turkey appealing for the removal of the death penalty for Muslim apostates. Messages were also sent to Queen Victoria, Franklin Pierce (US president from 1853–57), Napoleon III, and Emperor Franz Joseph I of Austria to request their support. The campaign proved successful and was the first of many such initiatives. Mostly this meant focusing on issues relating to religious liberty and operating alongside politicians, particularly those in the Foreign Office, to petition governments around the world on freedom of worship and witness. Throughout the 1850s, 60s, and 70s, the Alliance participated successfully in a number of high-profile campaigns in Turkey, Russia, Italy, and Spain. One example from 1863 involved Earl Russell, the Foreign Secretary, instructing the British ambassador to Persia to appeal on behalf of Nestorian Christians who were being persecuted by local Muslims. As a result, the Shah of Persia donated money to have destroyed churches rebuilt and the local Muslim leader was sacked.

Alliance representatives also embarked on personal visits to heads of state and experienced many exciting journeys across Europe. One example from 1879 involved a deputation travelling from London to Vienna to present an appeal to the Austro-Hungarian Emperor on behalf of persecuted Christians in Bohemia. They arrived in Vienna only to find that he was at his Hungarian palace. So they got back in their horse-drawn carriages and travelled on for a few more days to Budapest. They eventually managed to secure agreement that meetings for worship and Bible study in Bohemia would be permitted. Other journeys included meeting the King of Prussia in Cologne in 1855 and the Queen of Spain in Madrid in 1863.

It's interesting to reflect that, right from the start, the Alliance was concerned about issues of justice and religious liberty, and not simply for evangelical Christians. Today, the Alliance has a Religious Liberty Commission, which unites with three key Christian organizations working in the field of the persecuted church. Together, we speak with one voice, call the UK church to prayer, and continue the international religious liberty work of the Alliance's founders.

Prayer was also a priority. It was agreed at the 1846 conference that the Alliance should organize a week of prayer each year, to take place in the first week of January. Support for this idea grew, and by 1860 the Universal Week of Prayer was established, with themed prayer books being sent out to contacts all over the world. This went on for more than 100 years until the newly formed European Evangelical Alliance took over its organization, and still runs it today.

Evangelism was also given a high profile from the very beginning. In the 1850s, interdenominational evangelistic meetings sponsored by the Evangelical Alliance were held on Sunday evenings in central London. Many outreach events were also organized in support of the 1859 Ulster Revival, and when Dwight L. Moody, the great American evangelist, visited the UK in 1873–75 along with the singer Ira Sankey, the Alliance was an active vocal supporter of their meetings.

This focus on evangelism would continue through the years, including Alliance representatives giving help to the leaders of the Welsh Revival in 1904–5, and playing a major part in the planning and organization of the Billy Graham campaign at Harringay in 1954 and subsequent missions in the 1960s and 80s. The current focus on evangelism follows this rich vein of Evangelical Alliance commitment. Our Great Commission website[1] provides an amazing resource for the UK church as it signposts resources and provides encouragement and support for all expressions of evangelism. Right from its birth, the Alliance has been clear that the unity it seeks is not a unity for unity's sake. It has to be for a purpose. There is a world to be reached with the good news of Jesus and a society to be transformed for the common good.

Lows as well as highs

The 170-plus years of the Alliance's existence have not been without their lows, and on occasions greater attention should have been paid to our "Practical Resolutions". In the late 1860s a founder member of the Alliance, Thomas Rawson Birks, a respected evangelical leader, was forced to resign from the Alliance following the publication of his book *The Victory of Divine Goodness*, because of his departure from the traditional view of hell and the afterlife. The argument that followed resulted in fifteen members of the Council resigning.

The question of the great preacher, writer, and church leader Charles Spurgeon's views on baptismal regeneration resulted in his resignation from the Alliance, again in the 1860s. On Sunday 5 June 1864, Spurgeon preached at his home church, the Metropolitan Tabernacle, on Mark 16:15–16. During the sermon, he explained that baptism without faith would not save anyone, and strongly criticized the teaching of the Church of England and the baptismal service as it appeared in the *Book of Common Prayer*. Most controversially, he questioned the integrity of Anglican ministers – many of whom were fellow members of the Alliance – in this matter.

Spurgeon would eventually return to membership at a later date, and played a significant role as the Alliance responded to the advance of liberal theology and the biblical interpretation known as higher criticism. In 1888, Spurgeon was invited by the Evangelical Alliance to speak at Mildmay Conference Hall and Exeter Hall on these themes.

> Spurgeon was to take a strong stand against an influential, academic approach to scripture which was emerging from mainland Europe. His fear was that this approach undermined the authority of scripture and was making inroads to the British church, and of most concern to him, the Baptist Union of which he was a member and would

at one stage leave. Spurgeon maintained that the Baptist Union were susceptible to heretical influences because they did not have a clear doctrinal basis, in this he encouraged the denomination to learn from the Evangelical Alliance who were able to define exclusively who were part of the fellowship.[2]

In 1905, the Alliance was taken to the High Court by Percy Field, who had been sacked as General Secretary. In the 1950s, despite the amazing impact of the Billy Graham visits in 1954 and 1955, the Alliance nearly went bankrupt. The cost of the "crusades" had not been well budgeted for. In the 1960s, the public disagreement between John Stott and Martyn Lloyd-Jones at a conference organized by the Alliance resulted in loss of membership and the danger of permanent damage to evangelical unity. (This is covered in greater detail in Chapter 12.)

It is the hallmark of high-quality leaders and long-standing effective ministries and churches that they have developed resilience, which enables them to stand the test of time; facing low points, working through the issues, resolving the conflicts, and coming through to the other side. I am grateful to those who over the last 170 years have been willing to face the challenge of leadership in the Alliance. I'm convinced that the church in the UK needs an Evangelical Alliance. But were it not for this rich history involving times of great highs and lows, we would never have had one, and we would never be able to start one today.

Some highs from more recent years

But what of some more recent highs?

Tearfund

In the 1960s, coverage of the global refugee crisis associated with the Biafran war in Nigeria sparked a generous outpouring of compassion by Christians across the UK, with many people sending in donations to the Evangelical Alliance. In response, a fund was established to distribute the gifts to evangelical agencies caring for refugees around the world. As money continued to come in through the 1960s, George Hoffman, a former curate, was employed to help develop the work of the fund. On 29 May 1968, George Hoffman and others met for the first time as The Evangelical Alliance Relief Fund – the original plan had been to call it EAR Fund, but fortunately at the last moment the name was changed and Tearfund was formed.

In the years since 1968, Tearfund has continued to work with some of the most vulnerable and needy communities around the world, always compelled in its work by a commitment to reach the very poorest with God's love. Today, it is one of the UK's top ten emergency relief agencies, with a highly respected and effective model of relief and development, delivered primarily through the local church.

Home for Good

In 2011, a desperate shortage of foster carers and adoptive parents inspired a group of Christian leaders who were also foster carers or had adopted children to challenge the UK church to begin to meet the needs of so many children across the nations. The group was spearheaded by Krish Kandiah, who at the time was Executive Director: Churches in Mission at the Evangelical Alliance and himself passionate about this issue as an adoptive parent and foster carer. After hard work throughout 2012 to develop a strategy, the Home for Good campaign was launched in 2013 as a joint initiative between the Evangelical Alliance, Care for the Family, and the Churches' Child Protection Advisory Service (CCPAS). The campaign was so successful that, in September 2014, Home for Good became a charity in its own right, working to further inspire, encourage, and equip the UK church to provide homes for children in need. In the same way that Tearfund was conceived and born out of the Alliance nearly fifty years ago, we pray that it will go from strength to strength – not for its own sake, but for the sake of those children desperately in need of homes for good.

Biblefresh

You could have been forgiven for thinking that these burly bikers had taken a wrong turning as they rode into the big top at Spring Harvest, Skegness, in April 2011. But they were in fact members of the Christian Motorcyclists' Association, who helped us to launch the UK's first set of Viral Bibles. Over the following twelve months 200 limited-edition Viral Bibles, published by Hodder, were given away at major Christian festivals and events. Each person who received a Viral Bible was asked to underline the verses that were most meaningful to them before passing the same copy on to another person, who would then continue the process.

This was just one of the projects that formed part of our Biblefresh campaign in 2011, which, in the year when the whole world was celebrating the 400th anniversary of the King James Version, aimed to reignite people's love of the Bible. The campaign was kick-started by the Evangelical Alliance and inspired by the Bible Society's research, which showed that Christians – including leaders – were increasingly struggling to understand lesser-known passages or read the Bible regularly, and were unfamiliar with difficult texts. Starting in early 2010, the Biblefresh campaign involved a large movement of 120 churches, agencies, colleges, and festivals. Charged with the task of rekindling people's passion for the Bible, the campaign provided practical steps for churches on reading, training, translation, and experience. The range of projects run by each Biblefresh organization was wide and varied. During the year, Viral Bible Projects and a Get a Grip tour of talks helped people to experience the Bible in new and creative ways. Four hundred Biblefresh theological college courses ran around the UK and 8,000 Biblefresh handbooks were sold. Biblefresh helped bring Scripture to life and engage those who might never have picked up a Bible before.

One People Commission and South Asian Forum

After the One People Commission was established in 2011, following the formation of South Asian Forum in 2010, the impact on the life and work of the Alliance has been profound and their story is told in some detail in Chapter 10.

Alliance in the Celtic nations

There was a recognition in the 1980s and 90s that if the UK Alliance was to be truly representative of the whole of the UK, it needed to have expressions within the Celtic nations. In 1987, a Northern Ireland office was opened, in 1989 a Welsh, and in 1992 a Scottish. Each is a unique expression of the Evangelical Alliance within the Celtic nations.

Gather

In 2010, we began to see a national network of unity movements being formed – a gathering of those who believe that when churches and leaders set aside their differences and start to form friendships, pray together, and undertake mission initiatives for the sake of their local areas, God commands the blessing. What would happen if Christian leaders of unity movements formed friendships across the UK from city to city, town to town, and began to pray and do mission work together for the sake of the UK? This was the question we asked when we launched Gather, led by Roger Sutton. Through Gather, we are prayerfully building a movement and not an organization that encourages and supports unity movements in growing and developing their prayer, friendships, and missionary activities. (You can read more about Gather in Chapter 8.)

Advocacy and people

The public voice of the Alliance to the media and to government has been a central part of our work. We are committed to representing evangelicals and work with Christian organizations to speak up and ensure that the church is valued and understood by the rest of society. We also seek to advocate for the poor and the marginalized, the modern-day orphans and widows.

Our mission team, our *threads* work among young adults, and our new centre in King's Cross, London, are all indications of God, life, and blessing in recent years. But, beyond the campaigns and the great initiatives, it's important to recognize the people – those who under God have made all this possible. The recent history of the Evangelical Alliance cannot fail to recognize the enormous contribution made by its former General Secretary Clive Calver, who led the organization between 1983 and 1997. The interview panel that appointed Clive took what many regarded as a significant risk (they probably felt they did when they appointed me, too!). Clive was leading British Youth for Christ (later renamed Youth for Christ) and was a young and relatively inexperienced leader, particularly when it came to church matters. The Alliance was in need of fresh life and leadership and, without doubt, Clive was the right man for the job. The wonderful synergy that was found between the Evangelical Alliance and the newly emerging Spring Harvest was a marriage made in heaven and it allowed the Alliance to gain profile and new members in a way that it had not experienced since its conception in 1846. It was Clive's work in the media and with government that raised the advocacy profile of the Alliance – an aspect of our work which our members greatly appreciate. Under Clive, the organization grew in income, and staff size increased dramatically.

Within ten years, the Alliance that had emerged was hardly recognizable from what Clive had inherited. It was Clive who recruited Joel Edwards, initially to lead what was at the time known as the African and Caribbean Evangelical Alliance. Joel then became part of the main leadership team, and, when Clive moved on to lead the American aid agency World Relief, Joel was appointed as his successor and for eleven years (1997–2008) led the organization, building on the foundations laid by Clive but bringing his own way of doing things, particularly as he developed the public voice. Joel became a regular contributor to the media, speaking with passion and conviction on a wide range of issues.

But it's not all about history. We need to include the people of today. I look across the organization and I am in awe at the amazing people God has brought together to serve the church in the UK. These are people who work for the Alliance not simply to pay the bills but because of a deep conviction of God's calling – some truly talented people far better at what they do than I could ever be: young leaders alongside older; men and women; those from a wide variety of ethnic backgrounds. It's also important to acknowledge the role of our Board and Council, who represent the diversity of the evangelical tradition and ensure that we keep on track with what God is asking of us.

The future

I trust that, as you read this chapter, you are encouraged by a rich history of unity at work, even if painfully at times. But what of the future? What will the coming years hold? How will we serve the church across the UK? I'm convinced that the future is to be found within the historic DNA. It must be unity with a missionary imperative. It must be John 17 worked out in the day-to-day stuff of life. God save us from becoming just another institution with an institutional mindset, which fights for its continued existence at all costs, but has lost the life of the Spirit. The vision for God's kingdom and a commitment to vibrant, passionate relationships that express the heartbeat of God formed the pioneering, risk-taking spirit that brought the Alliance together in 1846, and it is only that same spirit that will maintain it for generations to come.

Questions

- As you explore your organization or church's history, are there keys (perhaps in its core DNA) that speak to your present?
- As you consider your organization or church, can you answer the following questions clearly:
    - * Why do you exist?
    - * What do you do?
    - * Where are your values to be found?

Are you as an individual, church, or organization a member of the Evangelical Alliance? If not, we would love you to consider joining: www.eauk.org/join

Chapter 15

One: For the One

They call it the immovable ladder. And it's been there for at least three centuries.

It's in the Church of the Holy Sepulchre in Jerusalem, the site which tradition says is the location of Jesus' crucifixion, burial, and resurrection. Visitors who turn their attention to the main façade will notice below an upper-storey window what has become perhaps the most infamous ladder in the world. This ladder is one of the most extraordinary symbols of disunity in the church of Jesus Christ. No one is exactly sure how the ladder got there, although some suggest it was probably left by a mason doing some restoration work in the early eighteenth century. But the question that really matters is not so much how it got there but why it's still there. It no longer serves any useful purpose. Yet it remains immovable because the six religious groups that manage the site cannot agree on what should be done with the ladder or indeed who owns it. The strongest claimant appears to be the Armenian Apostolic Church, who own the ledge upon which the ladder sits. The others who bear responsibility as custodians of the building are the Greek Orthodox, Roman Catholic, Coptic, Ethiopian, and Syriac Orthodox Churches.

Arguments, and indeed on occasions violent clashes, are not uncommon in and around the church. In 2008, a video hit the internet of a fist fight between Armenian and Greek monks in this ongoing dispute, centred on a small section of the roof. At all times one Coptic monk is to be found seated on a chair placed on a certain spot in order to maintain their ongoing claim to that part of the property. On one particularly hot day, a monk moved his chair 20 centimetres so he could get some shade. This small act was regarded as a violation of agreements between the churches and as an act of provocation, and it resulted in a fight following which eleven people ended up in hospital. I know it sounds like a joke, and it would be if it weren't so tragic.

How did it come to this almost 2,000 years since Jesus prayed for His disciples in that upper room? How have we got it so wrong? Surely Jesus wasn't just hoping for a spiritual unity, an invisible oneness as part of our inclusion in the family of God. How was the world going to know that Jesus really is in us?[1] Is the global church being obedient to the command of Jesus to "love one another as I have loved you"?

Loving each other can't mean having 300 years of conflict over the repair of an ancient monument, or indeed a fist fight over the ownership of a section of a roof. This can't be what Jesus had in mind. Certainly, it isn't the kind of church I want to identify with. It causes a corporate "shaking of the head" both outside the church and inside it. At best, this is the working of a dysfunctional family; at worst, it's reminiscent of a criminal gang.

Sadly, having been a leader in the Christian community for over thirty years, I've observed a number of such "shaking one's head" moments; some already referred to in this book. Buildings sold off in prime locations simply because one denomination doesn't have a viable congregation to occupy it – sold to the highest bidder and lost to the family for ever. Churches competing with each other to purchase a property, thereby allowing the owner (often a multinational business) to squeeze the price upwards – resulting in a loss of resources to the family of God. Struggling and declining churches both locally and nationally thinking that merging in their mutual weakness will create a strong and vibrant new church. And, let's face it, those of us who call ourselves evangelical are wonderfully entrepreneurial, but do we really need so many small and sometimes struggling ministries, both at home and abroad, duplicating administration, infrastructure, and resources? I thank God for all the church-planting that has taken place in recent years, but it hasn't always been strategic. Sadly, church-planting in some of the tough places, such as the social housing estates, hasn't been so popular, while at times, particularly in our large metropolitan areas, it can feel like the battle of the denominational or network brands. Church-planting can't be about simply drawing a congregation from the increasingly mobile existing church community. Tim Keller helpfully challenged a recent church leaders' gathering with the reflection, "Why do we call it progress, when one church grows at the expense of others? In the human body, we would call such a process cancer" (Tim Keller, Movement Day event in New York, October 2016). If church-planting is to contribute strategically to the life and health of the church as a whole, surely the primary focus should be on seeing those who are far from Jesus coming into a relationship with Him.

When I became a follower of Jesus, I thought I'd signed up to something larger than this. What captivated me was a big vision, bigger than my church, bigger than any organization, denomination, or ministry. I signed up to seek His kingdom first and I agreed that I was willing to take up my cross and follow the one who through His life, death, and resurrection inaugurated this kingdom. I've grown to realize that this kingdom challenges everything; it challenges every empire – including church empires. It challenges every tribe – including my denomination, my network, and indeed the Evangelical Alliance. It challenges every power base and institution, because ultimately the day will come when every knee will bow. I gave my allegiance to a king whose mission has permanence and who invites me to join His mission for the world. Chris Wright challenges us on this: "We ask, 'Where does God fit into the story of my life?' when the real question is: Where does my little life fit into this great story of God's mission?"[2]

So, what of our structures, organizations, and institutions, to which we have committed so much time, energy, prayer, and resources? Do we walk away from them? Do we abandon them? God forbid. Of course we need them locally, nationally, and internationally. But they are only a means to an end, not an end in themselves. They are simply the scaffolding designed to support the living building that will emerge. It is a church that Jesus has committed Himself to building. But we have the privilege of working with Him on this amazing project. It is a building made up of people like you and me in all our struggles, pains, and even sin, whom Jesus is in the process of refining, making into His likeness. We have come to know Him and love Him and we are desperate for others who live in the communities that surround us to come into that relationship as well. So these structures have value only to the extent that they serve the bigger vision – the advancement of God's purposes, the building of His church, the coming of His kingdom. While committing ourselves to them, we hold them lightly, and when they begin to take on a life of their own, when they begin to suck life out of us – demanding our worship and fighting for their existence at the expense of all others – we prayerfully seek to redeem them, redirect them, or as a last resort kill them off before they kill us.

As we explored in Chapter 8, we are living at a time when new structures are emerging. We're using the language of unity movements. These movements are finding their identity not in a theology or a particular ecclesiastical movement but on the basis of a passion to see transformation physically, socially, and spiritually in geographical locations – usually a town, a city, or a region. These unity movements bear all the hallmarks of a God movement and they are emerging not just across the UK but in many different parts of the world. Within these movements, relationships are seen as critical, and flexible structures emerge out of time spent praying, eating, and enjoying activities together. These are leaders who love the place God has called them to and feel a God-given responsibility for its welfare. These movements are not restricted to church leaders, but include Christian leaders from across the area – leaders in so many spheres: business, arts and entertainment, social and healthcare services, education, politics, and leisure. Transformation of our communities requires the church in all its fullness to make its contribution, working in collaboration, recognizing the unique and diverse gifting God has given His people. The old structures and institutions must make space for these emerging structures, while these new structures must make it a priority to ensure that they embrace the church in all its rich diversity. Their unity must be one that crosses all divides, whether of gender, class, age, or ethnicity.

The psalmist puts it like this: "How good and pleasant it is when God's people live together in unity! ... For there the Lord bestows his blessing, even life for evermore" (Psalm 133). And so we conclude by asking the question "Why unity?" And the answer is first and foremost because it's pleasing to God. We are "one" for the sake of the one true God; God who is one yet is revealed as three – Father, Son, and Holy Spirit. The Godhead challenges and models relationship to us and calls us to an intimacy within the family of God. Our Father in heaven, like an earthly father, desires His family to live together in harmony. There's a blessing from the Father bestowed to the children as we live together in unity – indeed, as we manifest the unity already won for us on the cross. But the blessing is not just for us; we are blessed that others might benefit from that blessing. It's a blessing that tangibly manifests the love God has for the world He created. In a strange and mysterious way, it seems as if the reality of who Jesus is is made known as we, His followers, demonstrate the love and unity of the family to the world – thus making visible the invisible through the love we have for each other.

Appendix 1

Evangelical Alliance Basis of Faith

All our members agree that the below statements are true.

We believe in...

- The one true God who lives eternally in three persons – the Father, the Son and the Holy Spirit.
- The love, grace and sovereignty of God in creating, sustaining, ruling, redeeming and judging the world.
- The divine inspiration and supreme authority of the Old and New Testament Scriptures, which are the written Word of God – fully trustworthy for faith and conduct.
- The dignity of all people, made male and female in God's image to love, be holy and care for creation, yet corrupted by sin, which incurs divine wrath and judgment.
- The incarnation of God's eternal Son, the Lord Jesus Christ – born of the virgin Mary; truly divine and truly human, yet without sin.
- The atoning sacrifice of Christ on the cross: dying in our place, paying the price of sin and defeating evil, so reconciling us with God.
- The bodily resurrection of Christ, the first fruits of our resurrection; His ascension to the Father, and His reign and mediation as the only Saviour of the world.
- The justification of sinners solely by the grace of God through faith in Christ.
- The ministry of God the Holy Spirit, who leads us to

repentance, unites us with Christ through new birth, empowers our discipleship and enables our witness.

- The Church, the body of Christ both local and universal, the priesthood of all believers – given life by the Spirit and endowed with the Spirit's gifts to worship God and proclaim the gospel, promoting justice and love.
- The personal and visible return of Jesus Christ to fulfil the purposes of God, who will raise all people to judgment, bring eternal life to the redeemed and eternal condemnation to the lost, and establish a new heaven and new earth.

Appendix 2

What is an evangelical? By David Hilborn, Principal of St John's College, Nottingham, chair of the Evangelical Alliance Theological Commission

Evangelicals often appeal to the derivation of their name from the Greek New Testament word for the gospel or good news of Jesus Christ. On their own account, they are gospel people, committed to simple New Testament Christianity and the central tenets of apostolic faith, rather than to later ecclesiastical accretions. As such, they seek to maintain and present the authentic teaching once for all entrusted to the saints (Jude 3). As the leading Anglican evangelical John Stott points out, this means that evangelicalism is neither a recent innovation nor a deviation from Christian orthodoxy.[1]

Although evangelicals sometimes see these emphases embodied in the ministries of the radical Oxford preacher and Bible translator John Wycliffe (c.1330–84), the prophetic Czech church leader Jan Hus (1372–1415), and other pre-sixteenth-century pioneers such as Peter Waldo and Girolamo Savonarola, the shape of evangelicalism as we know it today was formed more decisively by the Protestant Reformation. Led by Martin Luther in Germany, John Calvin in Geneva, and Ulrich Zwingli in Zurich, Protestantism was driven by the rediscovery of core gospel truths which were seen as having been neglected by the medieval Catholic Church. These truths were summarized in three *solas*. The first of these was *Sola Scriptura* – By Scripture alone. This entailed the conviction that God's objective truth was supremely revealed through His Word in the Old and New Testaments, and that the Bible must always take precedence over reason, tradition, ecclesiastical authority, and individual experience. The second was *Sola Gratia* – By grace alone. This was the conviction that God takes the initiative in salvation and the outworking of His plan for the world. It held that we know the truth first and foremost not because we deduce it rationally from observation of nature, but because the God of truth has revealed it to us. In fact, without this divine initiative in grace, we are powerless and lost. The third pillar of the Reformation was *Sola Fide* – By faith alone. This emphasized that although God takes the initiative in salvation, He nevertheless elicits our response and includes us intellectually, emotionally, and physically in the outworking of His purposes. Hence our being saved by grace through faith. Luther, Calvin, and Zwingli differed on finer points of theology, and on the ways in which these Reformation principles should be worked out in relation to church and state. All of them in turn diverged from more radical reforming groups such as the Anabaptists in this area. Even so, it is with the Reformation that we see the term "evangelical" first deployed in relation to a specific party or world view within Christianity. Early on, it tended to describe the Lutheran strand of Reformation thought and practice, but by the mid-seventeenth century it was being more widely applied to a range of Protestant convictions.

While the great Reformation *solas* define the theological foundations of evangelicalism, its specific social and historical character did not decisively mesh together until the 1730s, when an American Calvinist, Jonathan Edwards, and two Church of England clergymen, George Whitefield and John Wesley, developed a revivalist application of Reformation principles through itinerant preaching, evangelism, and a deepened emphasis on conversion or new birth, assurance of faith, and personal holiness. In particular, these revivalists stressed that assurance of salvation was the normative pattern of Christian experience, and that this could be given to an individual in a moment. Such assurance gave evangelicals the freedom and the inner dynamic for their now-familiar activism in preaching the gospel and engaging in good works.

Against this historical and theological background, the following five points, adapted from key studies of the movement by David Bebbington and Alister McGrath, represent a workable summary of evangelical characteristics:

> Biblicism – Through the Scriptures of the Old and New Testaments, the God who is objectively there has revealed universal and eternal truth to humankind in such a way that all can grasp it.
>
> Christocentrism – God's eternal Word became human in the historical man Jesus of Nazareth, who definitively reveals God to humanity.
>
> Crucicentrism – The good news of God's revelation in Christ is seen supremely in the cross, where atonement was made for people of every race, tribe, and tongue.
>
> Conversionism – The truth of the eternal gospel must be appropriated in personal faith, which comes through repentance – that is, a discernible reorientation of the sinner's mind and heart towards God.
>
> Activism – Gospel truth must be demonstrated in evangelism and social service.[2]

Although they are still conflated by some academics and many journalists, an important distinction needs to be drawn between the terms "evangelical" and "fundamentalist". Fundamentalism is now often used to refer to any type of dogmatic (and often backward-looking) thought, usually in religion. However, it originated with a series of Christian theological papers, "The Fundamentals", published in America between 1910 and 1915. Although these papers were written by a group of evangelicals concerned to restate their defining beliefs, by no means all of them would qualify now for the label "fundamentalist". After the Second World War, a division between relatively progressive and conservative American evangelicals on issues such as biblical criticism, ecumenism, and social engagement became evident in North America, and gradually the term "fundamentalism" was reserved for the latter group. More recently, distinctions between the two constituencies have also emerged in such matters as young earth creationism, the state of Israel and its role in biblical prophecy, and the role of women in church leadership. Where evangelicals tend to agree to disagree on such things, fundamentalists are more monolithically conservative in their approach to them.

Revd Dr David Hilborn
Principal of St John's College, Nottingham
Chair of the Evangelical Alliance Theological Commission

Notes

Chapter 3
One: The heartbeat of God

1. Michael Cassidy, *The Church Jesus Prayed For*, pp. 49–50.

Chapter 4
One: The invisible made visible

1. Quoted in Michael Cassidy, *The Church Jesus Prayed For*.
2. Cyprian, Bishop of Carthage, *On the Unity of the Church*, c. AD 250.
3. Jürgen Moltmann, *The Church in the Power of the Spirit: A Contribution to Messianic Ecclesiology* (Harper & Row, 1977), p. 64.
4. Chris Wright, *The Mission of God's People* (Zondervan, 2010, p. 46).

Chapter 7
One: In the local church

1. *The New International Dictionary of New Testament Theology* (Zondervan, 1975).
2. David Coffey, *All One in Christ Jesus*.
1. *Building Tomorrow's Church Today*, Evangelical Alliance, October 2015: http://www.eauk.org/church/research-and-statistics/building-tomorrows-church-today.cfm
2. N. T. Wright, "For Everyone" series, *Acts* (SPCK Publishing, 2012).

Chapter 9
One: Men and women

1. Elaine Storkey, *Scars Across Humanity* (SPCK, 2015).
2. Interview with Elaine Storkey in *idea magazine*, November 2015: http://www.eauk.org/idea/scars-across-humanity-the-scourge-of-global-violence-against-women.cfm
3. *Ending Domestic Abuse, A Church Pack by Restored*: http://restoredrelationships.org/resources/info/51/
4. Evangelical Alliance report, "How's the Family?", 2012: http://www.eauk.org/church/resources/snapshot/hows-the-family.cfm

Chapter 11
One: Across the Generations

1. The special English Church Census editions in September 2006 and November 2006.
2. Peter Brierley, *Pulling Out of the Nosedive* (Christian Research, 2006).

Chapter 12
One: When we disagree

1. Gilbert Kirby, "Evangelical Alliance Broadsheet", Winter 1959.
2. Transcript from Dr Martyn Lloyd-Jones' address at the national assembly of evangelicals, Westminster Central Hall, 18 October 1966.
3. Same transcript.
4. D. Murray on Dr Martyn Lloyd-Jones.
5. David Hilborn – personal communication.

Chapter 13
One: When unity fails

1. Steve Chalke, "The Bible and Homosexuality, Part 1", *Christianity* magazine, February 2013, http://www.premierchristianity.com/Featured-Topics/Homosexuality/The-Bible-and-Homosexuality-Part-One

Chapter 14
One: United in action

1. www.greatcommission.co.uk
2. Mike Nicholls, *C. H. Spurgeon: The Pastor Evangelist* (Baptist Union of Great Britain, 1992).

Chapter 15
One: For the One

1. John 17:23.
2. Chris Wright, *The Mission of God's People*, p. 553.

Appendix 2
What is an evangelical?

1. David Bebbington, *Evangelicalism in Modern Britain: A History from the 1730s to the 1980s* (London: Unwin Hyman, 1989), pp. 4–8.
2. Alister McGrath, *Evangelicalism and the Future of Christianity* (London: Hodder & Stoughton, 1995).